D1213313

ENTITIES AND INDIVIDUATION

Studies in Ontology and Language
In Honour of Neil Wilson

Université d'Ottawa
BIBLIOTHÈQUES

LIBRARIES
University of Ottawa

Edited by
Donald Stewart

Problems in Contemporary Philosophy
Volume 13

The Edwin Mellen Press
Lewiston/Lampeter/Queenston

9000002627

Library of Congress Cataloging-in-Publication Data

Entities and individuation : studies in ontology and language : in honour of
Neil Wilson / edited by D. Stewart.
    p. cm. — (Problems in contemporary philosophy ; 13)
    "Originally the papers were part of a conference at the University of
Guelph sponsored by the Guelph McMaster Doctoral Programme in
Philosophy in honour of Professor Wilson"—Introd.
    Includes bibliographies and index.
    ISBN 0-88946-341-7
    1. Philosophy—Congresses. 2. Wilson, Neil L.—Congresses. I. Wilson,
Neil L. II. Stewart, D. (Donald) III. Guelph McMaster Doctoral Programme
in Philosophy. IV. Series: Problems in contemporary philosophy ; v. 13.
B20.E57   1989   88-26644
110-dc19   CIP

This is volume 13 in the continuing series
Problems in Contemporary Philosophy
Volume 13 ISBN 0-88946-341-7
PCP Series ISBN 0-88946-325-5

B
20
·E57
1989

A CIP catalog record for this book
is available from the British Library.

© 1989 The Edwin Mellen Press. All rights reserved.

For information contact **The Edwin Mellen Press**

Box 450
Lewiston, New York
U.S.A. 14092

Box 67
Queenston, Ontario
CANADA L0S 1L0

Mellen House
Lampeter, Dyfed, Wales
UNITED KINGDOM SA48 7DY

Printed in the United States of America

Contents

Introduction

The present volume is a collection of papers by an international group of scholars who admired the work of Professor Neil Wilson, late of McMaster University. Originally, the papers were part of a Conference at the University of Guelph sponsored by the Guelph McMaster Doctoral Programme in Philosophy in honour of Professor Wilson who was one of its founding members and its Director for many years.

Neil Wilson came to McMaster in 1969 after a distinguished career at Duke University in North Carolina. He was one of the first and one of the best of a generation of Canadian philosophers to contribute significantly to the development of the relatively new field of semantic analysis that emerged after the War in the United States from the fusion of Logic, Pragmatism and Ontology. At a time when most philosophy in Canada was historical in character, Neil stood out for his direct contribution to contemporary issues. Though this contribution was wide ranging, he was best known for his influential paper, "Substances Without Substrata" where he developed his now famous Principle of Charity.

Many of the papers in this volume take their initial inspiration from this seminal work. David Bell, for example, takes his title, "What Would The World Be Like If...?", from Wilson's paper, and looks at some interesting cases where the answer to this question is "Exactly the same". Thus, for him, Wittgenstein's solipsism turns out to be a realism and Husserl's epistemology of intentional objects turns out to be exactly the same as our world of facts. What changes is not the world but the way we describe it.

Robert Binkley, in a paper which would have pleased Neil enormously, because it is both insightful and funny, applies Wilson's principle to the realm of contemporary action theory. He argues that we cannot individuate events as spatiotemporal particulars as, for example, Myles Brand has attempted to do. Evan Simpson, on the other hand, applies the principle to sensation in order to "deconstruct" it. For Simpson, so long as we are willing to take a suitably wide view of concepts, then there is "nothing 'raw' in the perception of the qualities of things". Further, the presence of concepts in all sensation ensures that they may be described without any subjective remainder. This means that we all experience the same sensations, a position Michael Stack finds himself not uncomfortable with in his paper "Rationality and Realism". The main thrust of the paper is to contrast rational realism of the sort espoused by Wilson with scientific realism. The difference, for Stack, is that scientific realism has change built into it while rational realism claims to yield *The Truth*. Stack rejects this concept of truth in favour of scientific realism and, along the way, manages a couple of shots across bows of such old philosophical stand-bys as consistency, precision and clarity.

John Heintz's paper, "Individuals", contrasts a Quinean space-time view in which individuals are "stages" with a Wilsonian view in which individuals are substances. Though Heintz judges that Wilson's axioms for individuating objects are not completely adequate he maintains that Wilson had defined the project correctly by insisting that individuation can only be grasped in terms of languages as a whole. The question, for Heintz as for Wilson, is — which language, space time, substance or some other, is fundamental? Only when that question is answered satisfactorily can we know what individuals are.

Hector-Neri Castaneda takes on a different problem, one that first raised its head with Parmenides: what are we to do with perfectly respectable non-existent objects such as Don Quijote? Castaneda does not bar us from thinking such non-existent objects as Parmenides did. Far from it; for him the question is how we are to construct a semantics which allows us to quantify over the Don Quijotes of our world, rather than exclude them as "Russell's Robust Sense of Reality" did. This task he sees as the prolegomenon to what he calls Guise Theory.

As a balance to Castaneda's inclusion of the unreal in formal semantics, we may, perhaps, prescribe Elmer Spragues's "Ontic Antics Diagnosed" which deals with the existence of those peculiarly philosophical objects which "fade away to nothing" when examined closely. Sprague would cure us of theories about such objects as Russell's sense data and Davidson's mental and physical events by urging us to rely more fully on "the normal forms of discourse."

Romane Clark approaches the question of existence quite differently. He eschews any and all antecedent metaphysical positions in order to see what the copula contributes to predication. He emerges with the view that the copula cannot be dispensed with as a mere expression of mood. Rather, it serves both to specify concepts under which objects of reference are subsumed in predication and to indicate its mode of combination with those objects.

This discussion of the nature of existence is capped by Nicholas Griffin's paper on why Russell was virtually forced into saying that "E!a" was meaningless by his early theory of judgement. Griffin gives us Russell's later theory of judgements as well.

Finally, we have Francois Lepage's paper "Intensional Logic And The Pragmatics of Belief". Lepage proposes a new strategy for dealing with statements of belief which he calls pragmatic and applies this strategy to Kripke's conundrum of how one can believe both that London is not pretty and that *Londres est jolie.*

Many of these papers were written by Neil's friends, his colleagues and his former students, both at McMaster and at Duke. Many other of his friends and former students, and they are now scattered from New Zealand to Canada, were unfortunately unable either to contribute papers to the conference or to attend. I would like to thank all of them, as well as the contributors to the volume, for their good wishes and for the kind help I have received in organizing this project. Finally, I would like to extend my sincere appreciation to Mrs. Judy Martin and to Mrs. Theresa Spotton who have carried the brunt of the work in preparing the manuscript for publication and to the Social Sciences and Humanities Research Council of Canada for its financial assistance and its support.

Donald Stewart

Remembering Neil L. Wilson

John E. Thomas

It hardly seems possible that twenty-eight years have passed since I first met Neil Wilson while a graduate student at Duke University.

Neil had just arrived from Bishops University and dropped in to visit us at the shacks that went by the name of "university housing." Bo and Lynn Clark, Bob Binkley and Hector Castaneda will testify how imperfectly these structures participated in the ideal form of "human dwelling."

When Neil dropped by we offered him a glass of Kool Aid which he accepted graciously with his characteristic "Christopher Plummer" smirk. I should add, because of my religious background, I was forty-two before I found out it wasn't a sin to take a drink. Unfortunately for Neil the timing was all wrong, his visit antedated my emancipation. But, as I said, that was twenty-eight years ago. Back then no amount of reflection on McTaggart's A and B series could have clued us in to how quickly the river of time would carry us way past the half-way mark between *The Blue Lagoon* and *On Golden Pond*.

Indeed as Neil battled with health problems during the last few years of his life one sensed he had come to grips with his own finitude. John, he would say, "Don't let anybody fool you. Old age isn't what it's cracked up to be."

Over the years Neil and I argued over a wide range of philosophical problems from the Barcan formula and the sempiternity hypothesis to the ontological implications of the "backward E."

He would quote with approval Russell's observation:

The process of sound philosophizing ... consists mainly in passing from those obvious, vague, ambiguous things that we feel quite sure of, to something precise, clear and definite ... involved in the vague thing we start from.

All of which I heartily endorsed except when in one of my philistine moods I would insist that he had lengthened the cords of his logical apparatus beyond the strength of the stakes of natural language. On these days I would twit him with Sparshott's observation:

> "May be the proper aim of philosophy is to discover what philosophy is, so that we can stop thinking about it without feeling that we may be missing something."

At which point he would shoo me out of his office, admonishing me for voicing such heresy.

In many ways Neil Wilson was a highly complex person. He was a rare blend of high intelligence and dry wit. He loved to see people come but he also loved to see them go. In the corridors of University Hall he could be heard complaining about the lack of social life in our department. The following week he could withdraw into himself in a roomful of people.

Unlike most of his McMaster colleagues, however, Neil's office door was always open — conveying a message of accessibility to both colleagues and students alike.

Those of us who were privileged to sample Neil's cooking still savour his spiced roast of beef. Neil's parties were memorable. We fondly recall the utter and child-like delight he took in his battery-operated bow tie. One flick of the switch and the bulbs in the bow tie would light up his impish grin.

We were chatting one day about one of the great loves in Neil's life — his dog Sheba. Sheba was getting along in years and Neil was looking ahead to the inevitable parting. Trying to be helpful I said, "when that happens Neil you must get another dog right away". "No," he said, "I couldn't do that." "Why not?" I asked. "Because," he replied, "the dog will outlive me and that wouldn't be fair to the dog."

We are paying ample tribute to the serious aspects of Neil's philosophical thought in the papers delivered at this conference. I thought it might be fitting to concentrate in this tribute tonight on some of the lighter moments in Neil's writings.

In this regard, I must confess, I feel a certain sympathy for Edwards' sentiment:

> "I have tried in my time to be a philosopher; but I don't know how, cheerfulness always kept breaking in."

Unlike Edwards, however, Neil can lay just claim to being a philosopher, but that did not prevent cheerfulness from breaking in. Listen to this from "Events, Facts and Identity Conditions":

> Suppose it is a fact that John kisses Mary at 11:59 p.m. on Tuesday. It is also a fact that she neglects her Lavoris and John never subsequently kisses her and in fact had not previously kissed her. So we have the uniqueness condition satisfied and can speak of the kissing of Mary by John (which is, of course, identical with the kissing of John at 11:59 on Tuesday). In my view the time is of the essence of the event, because the time is of the essence of the proposition, and *a fortiori,* of the fact. Had this great burst of romantic fervour found expression at 11:58 a different proposition would be true, hence a different event would have occurred. If you disagree with me on this, that's fine, because then you will have to agree with me on the crucial point I am about to make.
> It is tempting to suppose that John kissed Mary on the porch. He didn't, he kissed her on the lips. The crude suggestion that John kissed Mary on the porch must, in my view, be regimented to: There is a time *t* such that John kissed Mary at *t* and John was on the porch at *t* (they don't tell us where Mary was; she may, for all we know, have been hanging by her heels from an upstairs window.)

Now these highly theoretical observations have practical application. I always had difficulty with the old song "I wonder whose kissing her now." Until I read Neil's paper I hadn't realized that "now" is not a one-place predicate term ranging over a *favoured region of her anatomy* but an egocentric term analyzable into "*t* subscript."

Some of Neil's most cheerful comments may be found in his missive entitled "The Writing of a Dissertation." He warns

> The greatest difficulty facing the dissertation writer is that of divesting himself of the Pneumatological Illusion. Every doctoral candidate, deep down, thinks his stuff is directly inspired by the Holy Spirit. There are three consequences of this syndrome:
>
> 1) Anyone else's failure to understand is philistinism
>
> 2) failure to agree is blasphemy
>
> 3) however many sentences are added in later drafts, not one divine sentence will be dropped.

The next bit of advice runs:

> Always remember: People will sweat over Plato and Aristotle; they will not sweat over you and me. It's up to you to do the work. It's up to you to sell your stuff, to cast it in a form in which the message is easily accessible. *You must communicate.*

Or again:

> If there is a disagreement between you and your supervisor, you should *at least* take into account his point of view.... Occasionally, however, the following sequence of events occurs. The supervisor spends an hour [to make a point]. Finally the candidate sees the light and agrees that a change will have to be made. The supervisor congratulates himself on actually having earned his salary that day. But, lo and behold! *The same damned crap appears unchanged in the next draft.* Don't do that.

Finally,

> The fault with most dissertations is that they are boring (and repetitious and long winded). The fact that the authors themselves can read them without lapsing into catatonia testifies to the prevalence of the pneumatological illusion. If your thesis bores *even you*, well, cheer up.

Neil's readers came to look for his breathtakingly swift refutations and summations like:

> Now Hume's thesis won't do as it stands. If Hume were right there could be no such thing as confusing causation with correlation. But there is such a fallacy. Hence Hume was wrong.

Or again:

> It is true that Hume is not saying quite what I want him to say. One senses that the mind-body problem is intruding itself and the whole passage is redolent of philosophical psychology .... But *the thing is* that Hume decides to raise his arm and professes to be surprised that his arm actually rises. I submit that this astonishment is intellectual and spurious. He can't be surprised. If his arm hadn't risen then that *would* have been surprising.

One could go on. Let me conclude with an epistolary gem from "The Two Main Problems of Philosophy."

> People who know more about Kierkegaard than I do ... tell me that the major thrust of his attack on essentialism is to point out that the trouble with Hegel's system is that he left himself out of it. The present sketch of a philosophical system is relentlessly essentialistic and is, I daresay, much more open to the charge than Hegel's philosophy. In order to supplement it I shall pose a question ....

> "What would the world be like if I, N.L. Wilson did not exist but all of my effects outside of me existed? Now *you* may answer this question as you please. For my part I submit that this is a quite different world and a much poorer one to boot."

Neil, we concur in this judgment. Without you this would not only have been a different world, it would have been a much poorer world to boot.

What Would The World Be Like, If ...?

David Bell

1. Introduction

In his paper "Substances without Substrata", Neil Wilson poses what he calls "a simple little problem".[1] We are asked to say what the world would be like if Julius Caesar had all the properties of Mark Antony and Mark Antony had all the properties of Julius Caesar — given, that is, that the properties of being called 'Julius Caesar' and of being called 'Mark Antony' are to be included among the properties in question. Wilson's answer is: "Clearly, the world would look exactly the same under our supposition. ... Our attempt to describe a distinct possible world has just produced the same old world all over again".

Now this answer, as it stands, seems to be incorrect. If we take certain uncontroversial facts of Roman history as simply given, then Julius Caesar actually possesses the following properties: he conquered Gaul, was murdered on the Ides of March, 44 B.C., was called "Julius Caesar", and so on. In the counter-factual situation we are asked to envisage, however, he, that is *Julius Caesar,* never conquered Gaul, was not murdered but committed suicide, and was indeed called "Mark Antony". This hardly seems to be the same old world all over again. To be specific: a world in which Julius Caesar is murdered in 44 B.C. is just *different* from one in which he commits suicide in 31 B.C. That someone else (Mark Antony) has, so to speak, picked up all the properties shed by Caesar does not in any way make these two worlds converge again. On the contrary, this presents us with still further points at which they differ; for while in the actual world Antony committed suicide in 31 B.C., in the counter-factual situation he is murdered in 44 B.C., and so on.

There is a strong temptation, however, to feel that it is specifically the exchange of names between Caesar and Antony which somehow makes the actual and the counterfactual situations coincide. For, one might suppose, in the counterfactual situation it will surely be a man called "Julius Caesar" who is murdered on the Ides of March, who conquers Gaul, and so on. And isn't this, as Wilson claims, just the same old world all over again? Kripke writes about a similar temptation: "When I say that a designator is rigid, and designates the same thing in all possible worlds, I mean that, as used in *our* language, it stands for that thing, when *we* talk about counterfactual situations. I don't mean, of course, that there mightn't be counterfactual situations in which the other possible worlds people actually spoke a different language".[2] Now as Wilson originally sets up his "simple little problem" there is an important element of indeterminacy. He writes "I am assuming that the properties of being called 'Julius Caesar' and of being called 'Mark Antony' are to be included among the properties in question". What is left indeterminate, however, is precisely *by whom* they are to be thus called. In other words, are we being asked to envisage and to describe in *our* (unmodified) language a situation which obtained some two thousand years ago? Or are we being asked to describe a situation in which, in addition to certain changes in historical fact, there are also changes in the language *we* use to describe them — so that, in particular, the reference of the names "Julius Caesar" and "Mark Antony" are no longer as they normally are? I have suggested that Wilson is wrong to think that the first alternative leaves the world as it is; there are signs however that it is the second alternative that he has in mind. He says for instance: "We are considering a class of sentences in English which constitute the true state-description, that is, which correctly describes the actual world. Next we consider the state-description which would be obtained from the first by uniform replacement of the word 'Julius Caesar' by the word 'Mark Antony' and [*vice versa]*".

Now this is puzzling. In the state-description to which we would actually subscribe (*SD1*), there would appear the following sentences:

1. Julius Caesar conquered Gaul.

2. Julius Caesar was murdered in 44 B.C.

3. Julius Caesar is called "Julius Caesar".

4. Mark Antony committed suicide in 31 B.C.

5. Mark Antony is called "Mark Antony".

If we now substitute the one name for the other, as Wilson suggests, we obtain the following state-descriptions (*SD2*):

1* Mark Antony conquered Gaul.

2* Mark Antony was murdered in 44 B.C.

3* Mark Antony is called "Julius Caesar".

4* Julius Caesar committed suicide in 31 B.C.

5* Julius Caesar is called "Mark Antony".

In what sense can it be said that *SD2* "adequately describes the actual world"? Well, *SD2* is *ex-hypothesi* not a state-description to which *we* would subscribe: so we presumably need to imagine a counterfactual situation in which there are people for whom *SD2* would be a correct description. Assuming that such people have the same rules for conjunction as we do, then they will presumably say, for example, "Mark Antony conquered Gaul, and Mark Antony is called 'Julius Caesar'".

We seem to have got our wires crossed. If, in the counterfactual situation, Antony *is called* "Julius Caesar", then one would expect 1* to read "Julius Caesar conquered Gaul". But then why do we find that they actually *say* that it was Mark Antony who did this? If on the other hand they believe that the conqueror of Gaul was indeed Mark Antony (i.e. the person they call by that name) then what on earth do they mean when they say that Antony is called "Julius Caesar"?[3] It looks as though *SD2* is unconstruable. And the reason seems to be that while sentences 1*, 2*, and 4* belong to the language spoken in the counter-factual situation, sentences 3* and 5* belong to our language. We have mixed up what would be said *in* the possible state of affairs with what should be said *of* it.

We can rectify this situation if we allow (albeit against our better judgement) that the two names may also be intersubstituted within contexts of direct quotation. In that case we obtain *SD3*:

1' Mark Antony conquered Gaul.

2' Mark Antony was murdered in 44 B.C.

3' Mark Antony is called "Mark Antony".

4' Julius Caesar committed suicide in 31 B.C.

5'   Julius Caesar is called "Julius Caesar".

Unlike *SD2*, this state-description is internally coherent. But if, as Wilson suggests, it is intended to correspond to the situation in which (as *we* would say) Caesar has all the properties of Antony and *vice versa*, then for the reasons already given, it describes a possible world quite different from the actual one.[4]

Perhaps we can try a different approach. On a number of occasions Wilson asks "What would the world be like if such-and-such were the case?" and then answers that "The world would look exactly as it does". The shift here from how the world would *be* to how it would *look* is significant. Let us imagine two journeys into the past. On the first journey we visit Rome as it actually was, say, on the Ides of March 44 B.C. In the Forum a throng of citizens has gathered round a corpse. This was Caesar, we're told, the conqueror of Gaul. Just then the crowd is addressed by a stocky figure, who begins: "Friends, Romans, countrymen, lend me your ears ...". In general, then, the journey goes very much as we would have predicted — and tends to confirm the accuracy of Shakespeare's version of these events.

On the second journey, however, we visit a quite different situation: one in which Caesar and Antony have exchanged all their properties. So it is now in fact Mark Antony's corpse which lies in the Forum; and it is Caesar who delivers his eulogy. But what do we find? We find that, as before, everyone says that it is Julius Caesar, the conqueror of Gaul, whose corpse lies here — and indeed, as far as we can tell, this person does possess all and only the properties of the actual Julius Caesar. Just then someone — Mark Antony, we're told — addresses the crowd: "Friends, Romans, countrymen ..."; and so on. In other words the two situations are, in every respect, indistinguishable. Notice, however, that *we* would describe this latter situation, from the outside, so to speak, in terms of *SD3*;[5] those *in* the situation, on the other hand, would subscribe to *SD1*, the very state-description which for us too describes the actual world.

If I am right, then it would seem that Wilson is in effect exercised by the possibility that distinct different worlds can be described by one and the same state-description. But he takes himself to be addressing the converse situation, namely one in which a number of different state-descriptions are equally true of one and the same world — a world which is, indeed, the actual world. This, at any rate, is the state of affairs with which so-called Bridgman questions seem to confront us. "I propose the term Bridgman question", Wilson writes, "to apply to any question beginning 'What would the world be like if ...?' where the answer is 'Exactly the same as it is'." He then goes on to remark that "the question originally posed about Caesar and Antony does not concern just an isolated puzzle, but rather is an example of a general technique which might be expected to take us quite a long way in quite an interesting direction". Now although I don't think that the puzzle about Caesar and Antony is of the right sort, I do believe that Wilson's general puzzle is an interesting one, and that it does provide us with an interesting "general technique". I shall spend the rest of this paper exploring these suggestions.

For a number of reasons the name 'Bridgman question' is inappropriate;[6] instead, therefore, I shall prefer to talk about *fact-preserving questions*. To repeat: a fact-preserving question is any question of the form "What would the world be like if such-and-such were the case?", where the antecedent is apparently counter-factual, but to which the correct answer is: "The world would be as it is". One of the earliest examples of a fact-preserving question I have been able to find is Leibniz's: he asks, in effect, what the world would be like if every right-left spatial relation in it were instantaneously and simultaneously reversed. He answers: "... these two conditions, the one as things are, the other supposed the other way round, would not differ from one another ... in truth the one would be just the same as the other, as they are absolutely indiscernible".[7]

Now there are two lessons which, I think, we can learn from our consideration of the Caesar and Antony exchange: the first is the need to bear in mind the question *by whom* a given description or language is being used; and the second is the importance of distinguishing clearly the issue of how the world is (or would be) from the issue of how the world looks (or would seem to be). With respect to this latter point, however, it may well seem that Leibniz's example is objectionable; for surely, it might be said, although the ordinary and the reversed worlds would indeed be indistinguishable, that is, they would *look* the same, they would nevertheless *be* different. And just this was the conclusion we reached in the case of the Caesar-Antony exchange. In the earlier case, however, we imagined certain specific individuals to be other than they are. We rigidly designate those individuals and then suppose that they change some or all of their properties. In Leibniz's example, in contrast, we are not dealing with rigidly designated objects, but with what, for the moment, we might call vaguely "relational phenomena". And no matter how one defines "right" and "left", that definition will still determine the same results in the mirror universe as it does in the actual one. The supposition that in one *a* is *really* to the left of *b*, whereas in the other *a* merely looks (but in fact *isn't*) to the left of *b*, is simply empty.

Now, quite generally, if there is a question to which we possess the correct answer, then we are *ipso facto* in a position to make the corresponding true assertion. Of course, as philosophers possessed of a robust sense of reality have reminded us, merely because some bizarre hypothesis just happens to fit the facts, that as yet gives us no reason to believe that the hypothesis is true. Russell, for example, asked what the world would be like if it had been created by God, *ex nihilo*, a mere five minutes ago — yet created in such a way as to contain all the apparent evidence of a more distant historical past which it does in fact contain, including all our apparent memories. That the world would be as it is, he insisted, provides no reason to believe that the hypothesis is true. And this is surely right; it would be madness to believe that we actually inhabit a universe which is just five minutes old, say, and which flips in and out of its mirror image every few seconds. But this merely shows that the true assertion which corresponds to a genuinely fact-preserving question is not the straightforward assertion of its antecedent. The form of assertion which *is* justified can perhaps best be expressed in this way: The world, that is the actual world, can be redescribed without loss or remainder by employing such-and-such principles of description. So, as I suggested earlier, we are not here concerned with descriptions of other possible worlds, but rather with other possible descriptions of this, the actual world. I shall call these *fact-preserving redescriptions*.

In view of what is to follow, it is I think worth emphasizing one point here. The assertion which corresponds to a fact-preserving question is a genuine assertion: it makes an intelligible, non-trivial claim which posseses a determinate truth-value — it is true just in case the world can be thus redescribed, otherwise it is false. Moreover, the redescription itself will be just as true, or false, as its more familiar counterpart; for a good translation merely maps true sentences onto true, and false onto false. Indeed this is all that I mean by calling such a redescription "fact-preserving". Another way of putting this would be to say that I am concerned with alternative ways of talking which possess the same expressive power: anything that can be said in the one can be said in the other.

In what ways then can the invention and investigation of such alternatives be claimed to be "a general technique which might be expected to take us quite a long way in quite an interesting direction"? I shall try to answer this question by showing how the technique can be used to make sense of two philosophical doctrines; and in order to put the technique through its paces, so to speak, I have intentionally chosen two of the most elusive, esoteric, and implausible theories that I know. The first is Wittgenstein's solipsism in the *Tractatus*; the second is Husserl's account of the phenomenological reduction in *Ideas* and elsewhere.

2. Wittgenstein's Solipsism

There are a number of different forms which solipsism has, or might have, taken — sceptical, methodological, epistemological, and so on — but I shall be concerned here only with metaphysical solipsism in its most austere guise. And this, I take it, is the doctrine that *I am the world*, that the world and I are in the strictest sense one and the same. I shall not defend the attribution to Wittgenstein of this doctrine, except to remark that if "I am my world" (5.63),[8] and if "The world is *my* world" (5.62, 5.641), then it follows by the transitivity of identity that *I am the world*.[9] And similarly, if "The world and life are one" (5.621), then it follows that I am life; which explains why Wittgenstein could conclude that "... at death the world does not alter, but comes to an end". (6.431). Wittgenstein's *Notebooks* further confirm his commitment to the view that "... what the solipsist *means* is quite correct" (5.62); for among his notes are many that are incompatible with any other metaphysic. Perhaps the strongest is his exclamation: "What has history to do with me? Mine is the first and only world!" (2.9.1916).

If we take such remarks as these at face value (and I think we should) then we seem to be presented with a most bizarre and outrageous metaphysical theory. This adverse impression can be tempered somewhat if we lay down, in advance, three conditions which any acceptable metaphysical solipsism must meet. First, it must not be empirically false. It follows, therefore, that any solipsistic doctrine which asserts or implies, say, that the present population of the world numbers exactly one; or that whenever I talk I talk only to myself; or that, contrary to popular belief, it was in fact I who wrote *King Lear,* composed *The Goldberg Variations,* and proved the incompleteness of Peano arithmetic — any such theory will be straightforwardly false, and can be immediately dismissed as such. In other words I shall henceforth take it as an unconditional requirement on the acceptability of any solipsistic theory that it be fact-preserving.

The second requirement is that solipsism be internally consistent. And from this it immediately follows that, for the solipsist, the world can contain as a proper part no entity designated by such expressions as "I", "myself", "my ego" and the like; for if the world contained me as a proper part it could not be identical with me. So, if we are to avoid both empirical falsity and internal incoherence, we must deny that such expressions as "I", "myself" and the like, as they occur in the solipsist's theory, refer to that empirically encounterable, spatio-temporal, physical thing called David Bell. For in *that* sense I, David Bell, am certainly a part, a proper part, but a very small part indeed, of reality as a whole. In the present context, then, the relevant conception of the self is rather that of the subject of experience, the bearer of subjectivity, what Wittgenstein called *"Das denkende, vorstellende Subjekt"* (*5.631*). And that such a self is not one item amongst others is a necessary condition of the possibility of a coherent solipsism.

The third requirement is unproblematic: it is that solipsism should be philosophically interesting. A theory which successfully avoided empirical falsity and internal inconsistency, but which remained ultimately a mere idle conundrum or curiosity would therewith remain philosophically inadequate and unacceptable. Solipsism may be bizarre; but if it can be shown to be consistent, compatible with the facts, and philosophically interesting, then it surely deserves our concern.

Initially, perhaps the best way to provide a motive for the solipsist's claim that "I am the world" is, negatively, to establish what is being denied by it. And here I can do no better than quote a passage from William James which vividly and delightfully captures some widespread intuitions about subjectivity and objectivity, about the self and the world:

> The human race as a whole largely agrees as to what it shall notice and name, and what not. And among the noticed parts we select in much the same way, for accentuation and preference, or subordination and dislike. There is, however, one entirely extraordinary case in which no two men are ever known to choose alike. One great splitting of the whole universe into two halves is made by each of us; and for each of us almost all the interest attaches to one of the halves; but we all draw the line of division between them in a different place. When I say that we all call the two halves by the same names, and that those names are '*me*' and '*not-me*' it will at once be seen what I mean. The altogether unique kind of interest which each human feels in those parts of creation which he calls *me* or *mine* may be a moral riddle, but it is a fundamental psychological fact ... The neighbor's *me* falls together with all the rest of things in one foreign mass, against which his own *me* stands out in startling relief.[10]

Now phenomenologically this just seems wrong; at least I can honestly report that *my* world isn't in the least bit like *that*. The universe I inhabit, while it manifests virtually endless variety, simply isn't split into two radically different halves. And my own *"me"* does not stand out "in startling relief". Wittgenstein expressed both these points tersely: "All experience is world, and does not need the subject" (9.11.1916).

We might amplify his thought as follows. Metaphysical solipsism is the doctrine that I am the world, or in Jamesian terms that the *"me"* and the *"not-me"*, far from representing one great splitting of the whole universe, are in fact indistinguishable. Now as an identity statement, the claim that "I am the world" can be read, so to speak, in either direction. Read from left to right, it identifies the world in its entirety with me; and this is traditionally how solipsism has always been construed: it is the doctrine, we are told, that only I exist. The insight which underlies the solipsism of the *Tractatus,* however, is that the statement of identity can be read, as it were, from right to left. In which case (to put it for the moment more picturesquely than precisely) it is me that disappears, leaving behind precisely — the world. As Wittgenstein writes: "Here it can be seen that solipsism, when its implications are followed out strictly, coincides with pure realism. The self of solipsism shrinks to a point without extension, and there remains only the reality coordinated with it". (5.64).

If, in Wittgenstein's phrase, "all experience is world, and does not need the subject", then as he himself observed, "what the solipsist wants is not a notation in which the ego has monopoly, but one in which the ego vanishes".[11] Just such a notation as this has been presented by Wittgenstein,[12] in his parable of the oriental despot. We are asked to imagine an oriental state whose despotic ruler is a solipsist and who imposes on his subjects his own preferred, solipsistic way of talking. For the despot, who is the centre of this language, there is no need to — indeed there is no possibility of — identifying anything as the bearer, or owner, or subject of any states of consciousness of which he is aware. Accordingly he expels from his language any terms which might be taken to refer to such a bearer or owner, and which have no other function. When he is in pain he says: "There is pain". When he has a thought he says: "It thinks", and here the pronoun is to be understood as in "it is raining", or "it is snowing".[13] The less philosophically fortunate subjects of this state, on the other hand, are to adopt a quite different way of talking. When one of them is in pain (or is thinking) the others say: "So-and-so is behaving as the Centre does when there is pain (or when it thinks)". The subjects can, of course, use the first person pronoun: one of them might call out "I behave as the Centre does when there is pain!" — when for example he hits his thumb with a hammer.

The subjects of this despotic state can (as *we* would say) refer to their own states of consciousness, to one another's states of consciousness, and to the states of consciousness of the despot at the centre. And conversely (though again as *we* would say) the despot can refer to his own states of consciousness, and also to those of his subjects. Thus, for example, the despot ascribes experiences to others by saying "So-and-so is behaving as the Centre does when there is pain". That the Centre refers to himself externally, so to speak, *as* the Centre, reflects the fact that his knowledge of his own body and its states is on all fours with his knowledge of another's body and its states. For the solipsist, in other words, far from its being the case that "his own *me* stands out in startling relief", it is rather, as Wittgenstein wrote in the *Tractatus* that

> If I wrote a book called *The World as I found it*, I should have to include a report on my body, and should have to say which parts were subordinate to my will, and which were not, etc., this being a method of isolating the subject, or rather of showing that in an important sense there is no subject; for it alone could *not* be mentioned in that book. (5.631).

There are a number of points to be noted about life in the solipsist's state. First of all, anyone can be the centre of the solipsistic language. There are no particular characteristics possessed by the despot in virtue of which he is uniquely or even comparatively well suited for that role: anyone would do. Secondly there need be no difference between the attitude or the behaviour of these people and our own, when it comes to such things as emotions, sensations, feelings and the like. They are not automata, and they do not conceive of, or respond to one another as automata. When one of them cries out "I behave as the Centre does when there is pain", others typically sympathise, fetch doctors, administer analgesics, and so on. In short, everything would be as it is; what we have here is merely an alternative way of talking which is fact-preserving in that anything *we* can say can be translated into solipsist-ese.

But in exactly what sense would a language of the kind we are envisaging be *solipsistic*? Well, clearly, it would be solipsistic only for the person at the centre, and fully to appreciate the difference between our normal way of talking and the new one we must put ourselves in that position. If I am the centre, what do I find? I find that *the world* contains suffering and joy, thoughts, sensations, perceptions, and the like. Some of these will be contingently related to a body called "the Centre", but then, equally, some will be related contingently to ambient temperature, say, or time of day. In addition to thoughts, feelings, sensations and the like, which are events in the world, there will also be football matches, hurricanes, and eclipses of the sun. And these too are events in the world. *None* of these occurrences involves any identification of, or ascription to, a bearer or owner. In this new way of talking a hurricane is just as much, or as little, *"mine"* as is a headache. From this point of view we can, I think, begin to get some leverage on the claim that "I am the world". This slogan is an expression of the fact that from within the solipsistic frame of reference there is no possibility of distinguishing what is *mine* from what is *not-mine*; indeed, the very notion of ownership proves otiose, for "all experience is world, and does not need the subject". And so it can make no difference whether I call everything "reality" or "myself". These two terms fail to mark any distinction *within* the world. At best they can correspond merely to two different aspects of the world as a whole.

I am suggesting, then, that there is a solipsistic redescription which is both fact-preserving and internally coherent. In the *Philosophical Investigations* Wittgenstein writes: "If I were to reserve the word 'pain' solely for what I had hitherto called 'my pain', and others 'L.W.'s pain', I should do other people no injustice, so long as a notation were provided in which the loss of the word 'pain' in other connections were somehow supplied.... But what should I gain from this new kind of account? Nothing. But, after all, neither does the solipsist *want* any practical advantage when he advances his view!" (Sect. 403). If an alternative, solipsistic notation has no practical advantages, then why should we bother with it? Does it, we need to ask, have any *philosophical* interest? I can only gesture towards an answer to this question here. But in so doing I hope to allay, at least partially, the doubts some may have as to the viability of solipsism. For surely, it will be thought, solipsism must contravene the requirements laid down by Wittgenstein in the so-called private language argument. Isn't the private language argument precisely a *refutation of* solipsism?[14]

We can begin by asking: What sort of philosopher might we expect to find as the centre of a solipsistic language? One thing is clear, he will hardly need to be reminded that in general so-called "inner processes" stand in need of outward criteria (cf. Sect. 580). The existence of such criteria is built into the very grammar of his language; for he conjugates the verb *to ache,* for example, as follows:

> It aches
> You behave as the Centre does when it aches
> He behaves as the Centre does when it aches
> ... and so on.

Nor will the solipsistic centre need to be reminded that, in the first person case, no criteria of personal identity are involved in the ascription of "inner" states. As Wittgenstein says in the *Investigations:* "When I say I am in 'pain', I do not point to a person who is in pain, since in a certain sense I have no idea *who* is. ... What am I getting at? At the fact that there is a great variety of criteria for personal *'identity'*. Now which of them determines my saying that '*I*' am in pain? None". (Sect. 404). And again, the solipsistic centre is likely to find the very notion of a private, essentially subjective, incommunicable experience deeply unattractive. For his language functions, perspicuously, by relating forms of behaviour of others, to forms of behaviour of the Centre, and ultimately relating these to unowned events in the world. And finally, the solipsist will have no grounds for asserting such philosophically suspect theses as those which we express by saying, e.g., "Only I can really know when I am in pain"; or "I can only imagine another's pain on the model of my own"; or "I know what the word 'pain' means only from my own case"; and so on.[15] I am suggesting, in short, that the solipsist will have interesting things to say about the distinction between subjectivity and objectivity; about the nature of the self; about self-knowledge, self-identity, and the ownership of mental states; about the asymmetry between first and third person psychological sentences; about the language which we use to describe our "inner" life; and much else besides. But crucial to this enterprise is the possibility of a fact-preserving, yet solipsistic, redescription of the actual world.

3. The Phenomological Reduction

The phenomenological reduction, or epoché,[16] is an immensely complicated affair. Husserl himself remained dissatisfied with his numerous attempts at introducing and explaining it; and I certainly don't intend to touch on all its ramifications here. I shall merely try to throw some light on some aspects of it. In particular I shall be concerned with a problem that Eugen Fink is reported to have raised: "... Fink spoke of the phenomenological investigator's *peculiar* difficulty with language due to the fact that ontological positing is taken up into the very essence of the terms of everyday life, so that every description involves verbal hypostatization".[17]

The peculiar difficulty seems to be the following. Phenomenology is intended by Husserl to be a *descriptive* science, and as such its results will presumably comprise judgements which are expressed in meaningful, declarative language — though we can leave open for the moment the question whether that language will be a natural or an artificial one. But this requirement seems flatly incompatible with the method of phenomenological reduction, the aim of which is precisely the suspension of judgement, the avoidance of all reference to, or belief concerning any object in the world whatsoever. According to Husserl, in performing the epoché "we put out of action the general positing which belongs to the natural attitude; we bracket everything which that positing encompasses with respect to being; [and this includes] thus the whole natural world".[18] The reduction in essence just *is* this suspending, bracketing, inhibiting, turning off, neutralizing, or putting out of action of all our beliefs, judgements, and presuppositions concerning the actual world. And as Husserl rightly remarks: "As a consequence, all psychological experience is also put out of action".[19] In other words, all judgements concerning ourselves, our minds, our states of consciousness and the like must also be suspended in the epoché. The method of reduction is emphatically not a device which cuts us off from one part of the natural world (from the material world, say), merely to direct us to a different part of that world (for example, to psychological or subjective states and events): it is the suspension of all judgements concerning the natural world *in its entirety*.[20]

Now one's initial reaction at this point is likely to be puzzlement: surely such a procedure, if rigorously carried out, will simply leave us with nothing to say, with no judgements whatsoever that we can legitimately make. And yet, paradoxically, Husserl time and again maintains that in the phenomenological reduction "nothing is lost", that in a certain sense "everything remains as of old".[21] It seems as though, on the one hand, the reduction should prevent us from saying anything, but that, on the other hand, it doesn't stop us from saying anything. For "we can even go on calmly speaking in the way we must as natural human beings; for *as phenomenologists* we are not supposed to stop being natural human beings, or positing ourselves as such, when we speak".[22]

This paradoxical impression is communicated particularly strongly in the well-known passage where Husserl contemplates and describes the apple tree in his garden, first in the natural attitude, and then as a post-reduction phenomenologist, so to speak. The two descriptions turn out to be, *verbatim,* the same; for the thing described is, in both cases "attractive", "an apple tree", "in the garden", "blossoming", and so on.[23] As Husserl himself says: "so to speak, everything remains as of old ... the tree has not lost the least nuance of the moments, qualities, and characteristics with which it was appearing" (i.e., to us in the natural attitude).

So what is the difference? How, if at all, does the description we give in the natural attitude differ from that which we give after the reduction? This, in all its obscurity, is what Husserl says:

> It is clear that these descriptive statements [i.e. post-reduction ones], even though they may sound like statements about actuality, have undergone a *radical* modification of sense; similarly, the described itself, even though it is given as "precisely the same", is yet something radically different by virtue, so to speak, of an inverse change of signs. "In" the reduced perception ... we find the perceived as perceived, to be expressed as "material thing", "plant", "tree", "blossoming", and so forth. Obviously the *inverted commas* are significant in that they express that change in sign, the correspondingly radical significational modification of the words.[24]

So the terms in which we couch our description of the material object, and those we use to describe the intentional object, or *noema,* are identical — except for the inverted commas. And yet these self-same signs express, respectively, a radically

different sense. Moreover, after the reduction this sense must be devoid of ontological commitment: there must be no reference to items in the natural world —
no reference, for example, to apple trees and their properties. Fortunately there is,
I believe, a model to hand which can make some sense of this.

Those familiar with Frege's writings[25] will find talk of "suspension of judgements"; the possession by an expression of a sense without, therewith, the possession of its normal reference; the possibility that homophonic expressions may be
systematically ambiguous, sometimes referring to an object in the world, say, and
at other times referring to a sense — they will find such talk reassuringly compre-
hensible. Frege's earliest work, the *Begriffsschrift,* in fact begins with a distinction between a mental act of judgement, and a mental act which, while it has the
same conceptual content as the judgement, does not involve any "recognition or
non-recognition of the truth of this [conceptual content]".[26] And he suggests that
in ordinary language (though not in the concept-script) a judgement is expressed
by a free standing sentence in the indicative mood, whereas when the judgement
is suspended we might "qualify the expression with the words 'the circumstance
that' or 'the proposition that'".[27] It was some twelve years later, with the introduction of the distinction between an expression's sense and its reference, that Frege
was able to give a precise account of what this move consists in. In "On Sense
and Reference", for example, he writes: "... in every judgement, no matter how
trivial, the step from the level of thoughts [i.e., senses] to the level of reference
(the objective) has already been taken".[28] But why, he asks, do we want every
proper name to have not only a sense, but also a reference? "Why is the thought
not enough for us? Because, and to the extent that we are concerned with its
truth-value".[29] But if we are *not* concerned with its truth-value, if our aim is
precisely to *suspend* judgement, if we wish to refrain from all reference to 'the
objective', then the procedure is still, as it was in the *Begriffsschrift,* to prefix our
expressions with an intensional functor. "In order to speak of the sense of an
expression *'A',* one may simply use the phrase 'the sense of the expression *'A'.* In
reported speech one talks about the sense, e.g., of another person's remarks. It is
quite clear that in this way of speaking *words do not have their customary reference, but designate what is usually their sense"*.[30] I shall abbreviate the phrase
"the sense of the expression *'A'"* thus: δ: *A*. Unlike the *Begriffsschrift* suggestions, the intensional functor "δ" applies both to sentential and subsentential
expressions; but in both cases it maps an expression onto its normal sense. Very
briefly, then, the sentence

1. Margaret Thatcher loves Ronald Reagan

is to be understood as expressing a judgement which has as its content a thought (i.e., a sense), and this is determined by the senses of the component expression. The singular terms possess references which, in this case, are material objects in the natural world. The sentence as whole has a truth-value. On the other hand, however,

2. δ: Margaret Thatcher loves Ronald Reagan

is non-assertoric, cannot express a judgement, possesses no truth-value, and makes no reference to anything in the natural world. The name "δ: Margaret Thatcher" does, however, have a reference: it refers to the sense of the name "Margaret Thatcher" as it occurs, e.g., in 1. Likewise 2 as a whole refers to the thought expressed by 1. Existential generalization is not possible on 2. And yet, if we accept Michael Dummett's suggestion,[31] the *sense* of expressions 1 and 2 is the same; only their reference changes.

If this is right, then I think we can construe Husserl's use of inverted commas as analogous to, if not identical with, our use of "δ": it is a device for cancelling assertoric force ("suspending judgement"), and for "neutralizing" the normal referential relation in which expressions stand to items in the natural world. And these, as we have seen, are the two major effects of the phenomeno-logical reduction. But if so, we have to interpret Husserl's text with a certain amount of charity; for he actually *says* that terms used in phenomenological description "have undergone a radical modification of sense". If this is literally the case, then it is clearly incumbent upon Husserl to specify exactly what the new sense of such expressions is to be, and this he spectacularly fails to do. With-out such a specification, however, phenomenological language will be strictly unintelligible. In practice, of course, Husserl continues to formulate his descrip-tions in what he admits "sound like statements about actuality". What he *should* perhaps have said is that post-reduction language does not change its sense — it is therefore just as intelligible as a natural language, German, say, is to its native speakers. Rather, it changes its reference. This, at least, is the only way in which I can make sense of his claim that "... we do not tolerate any judgement which makes use of the positing of the 'actual' physical thing". This, it seems, *is* possi-ble in a way which still leaves us something to talk about: senses.[32]

My suggestion, then, is that Husserl's phenomenological programme — or at least one aspect of it — can be understood as the provision of a fact-preserving redescription. It is fact-preserving in that it leaves everything as it is; it requires no alteration of anything *in* the world. After the epoché, the blossoming apple tree is still there in the garden and "has not lost the least nuance of all the moments, qualities, and characteristics" which it in fact possessed as a material object. We can, that is, understand Husserl as asking, in effect, What would the world be like if it and everything in it were merely an intentional object? To which his answer would be that it would be exactly as it is: not a single *fact* would change. As with the solipsism we examined earlier, if the antecedent to our question were true, this would require no change in our attitude to any matter of fact whatsoever; but it might well require a change in our metaphysics.

Programmatic though they are, the foregoing remarks indicate, I hope, something of the interest that fact-preserving questions may have for philosophy. As Neil Wilson said: "the question originally posed about Caesar and Antony does not concern just an isolated puzzle, but rather is an example of a general technique which might be expected to take us quite a long way in quite an interesting direction".

Notes

1. N.L. Wilson, "Substances without Substrata". *Review of Metaphysics* 12 (1959), pp. 521-539. All quotations from Wilson are from pp. 521-525 of this article.

2. S.A. Kripke, "Naming and Necessity", in *Semantics of Natural Language,* (eds) G. Harman and D. Davidson, Dordrecht, 1972, p. 289.

3. There are a number of readings on which 3* would be intelligible, indeed true: it might for instance be taken to mean that Antony was *also* called "Julius Caesar" (i.e. in addition to being called "Mark Antony") that he changed his name in later life; that his nickname was "Julius Caesar"; and so on. But none of these possibilities is relevant in the present context. For Wilson's argument to go through, 3* must be read in exactly the same way as 3, i.e. as asserting that Mark Antony's *name* was (not "Mark Antony" but) "Julius Caesar".

4. There are, in fact, good reasons to believe that Wilson has failed even to envisage a *possible* world, if, that is, Caesar and Antony are required to exchange their essential properties. However, like Wilson, I shall simply ignore problems concerning essential attributes.

5. Given, that is, that in 3' and 5' the expression "is called" is taken as short for "is called by us".

6. In the first place because the suggestion originated with Clifford; and in the second place because the example Wilson cites from Bridgman is itself faulty — Bridgman's question is not in fact a Bridgman question.

7. Leibniz's correspondence with Clarke, Third Paper, Section 5; in (ed.) G.H.R. Parkinson *Leibniz: Philosophical Writings,* London, 1973, p. 212.

8. L. Wittgenstein, *Tractatus Logico — Philosophicus,* translated by D.F. Pears and B. McGuinness, London, 1972. (References are by proposition-number.) See also *Notebooks 1914-1916,* translated by G.E.M. Anscombe, Oxford, 1969. (References are by date of entry.)

9. Here I follow Norman Malcolm, 'Wittgenstein and Idealism', in (ed.) G. Vesey *Idealism Past and Present,* Cambridge, 1982, p. 249.

10. William James, *The Principles of Psychology*, p. 289.

11. Alice Ambrose (ed.) *Wittgenstein's Lectures, Cambridge 1932-1935*, Oxford, 1979, p. 22.

12. See, e.g., L. Wittgenstein, *Philosophical Remarks*, Oxford, 1975, pp. 88-89; *Philosophical Investigations*, Oxford, 1958, §403; *Blue and Brown Books*, Oxford, 1975, pp. 57-61; and F. Waismann, *Wittgenstein and the Vienna Circle*, Oxford, 1979, pp. 45-49.

13. See, e.g., G.E. Moore, "Wittgenstein's Lectures in 1930-33", in his *Philosophical Papers*, London, 1959, p. 309.

14. See, e.g., P.M.S. Hacker, *Insight and Illusion*, Oxford, 1972, pp. 201-214; J.W. Cook, "Solipsism and Language" in (eds) A. Ambrose and M. Lazerowitz, *Ludwig Wittgenstein: Philosophy of Language*, London, 1972, pp. 37-72.

15. The quotations are from *Philosophical Investigations*. §§246, 302 and 293 respectively.

16. Although there are occasional indications that Husserl distinguishes these notions, I shall here treat them as the same.

17. Dorian Cairns, *Conversations with Husserl and Fink*, The Hague, 1976, p. 14.

18. Edmund Husserl, *Ideas Pertaining to a Pure Phenomenology and to a Phenomenological Philosophy*, First Book (henceforward: *Ideas*), The Hague, 1982, §32. See also *Cartesian Meditations*, The Hague, 1973, §3.

19. "Husserl's Inaugural Lecture", in P. McCormick and F. Elliston (eds) *Husserl Shorter Works*, Notre Dame, 1981, p. 15.

20. *Ideas*, §50.

21. *Ideas*, §88.

22. *Ideas* §64 (my italics).

23. *Ideas*, §90.

24. *Ideas*, §89.

25. Of whom one was, of course, Husserl himself.

26. G. Frege, *Begriffsschrift usw.*, in *Translations from the Philosophical Writings of Gottlob Frege*, (eds.) P.T. Geach and M. Black, Oxford, 1970, p. 2.

27. *Loc. cit.*

28. "On Sense and Reference", in *Translations . . from Gottlob Frege*, P.T. Geach and M. Black (eds.), p. 64.

29. *Op. cit.*, p. 63.

30. *Op.cit.*, p. 59, my italics.

31. M.A.E. Dummett, *Frege: Philosophy of Language*, London, 1973, pp. 268f; also *The Interpretation of Frege's Philosophy*, London, 1981, pp. 87-102.

32. Recent work on the relation between Husserl's notion of noema, or noematic sense, and Frege's notion of sense is clearly relevant here. See, e.g., R. McIntyre and D.W. Smith, "Husserl's Identification of Meaning and Noema", *The Monist*, 59 (1975), pp. 115-130.

Particular Actions

Robert W. Binkley

1. Introduction

I have two main concerns in this paper: one is Action Theory, the other is Ontology.

Actually, my chief interest is Action Theory. I could pass ontology by except that I find it thrust upon me. It is commonly felt that actions are a species of event, that events form a troublesome ontological category, and that this matter must be cleared up before action theory can proceed. I cite as instances two recent books on action theory, near the beginning of each of which one finds chapters on the ontology of events. Michael Zimmerman's *An Essay on Human Action*[1] has this as Chapter 1: "Events as Abstract Entities". Myles Brand *Intending and Acting*[2] puts this off until Chapter 3: "Events as Spatiotemporal Particulars". "Let no one enter here who has not an ontology of events" seems to be the watchword.

I do not share this view. Ontology, I believe, is the part of philosophy that characterizes the various categories of entity with respect to which we feel obliged to use singular terms. While we do use singular terms for events and actions, and find this very convenient, we are not obliged to, I hold, and so there is nothing in that area for ontology to do. I concede that it would be gracious of us to explain to ontologists why it is that, despite appearances, we are not so obliged, but that would be a secondary matter, finding its place in an appendix, not an initial chapter.

In this paper I examine a few of the ingredients that would be required for a complete defense of this view. The immediate stimuli for it were Brand's book and reflection on some of Neil Wilson's semantical and ontological views, and I will limit my discussion, for the most part, to areas related to one or the other of these sources. Brand's view is that events are spatiotemporal particulars, and he compares events to physical objects, which, he says, are also spatiotemporal particulars. A good bit of the paper will be taken up with showing that Brand is wrong about this, and in carrying out this attack I will find additional support in some of Wilson's insightful arguments. That is the negative side of the paper, but it leads to the positive side, for if events are not what Brand says they are, what are they? Here two things must be considered: What is it proper to say about events and actions when we are using the forms of speech which suggest that there are such things? and How, in the cool hours of ontology, are we to avoid using those forms of speech? On both of these questions, but especially the second, I will again find support in some of the things Wilson has said.

The focus of the discussion will be on events in general rather than actions in particular, but the implications of my conclusions for actions will be fairly obvious.

2. Base and superstructure

I begin with some general remarks about the reductionistic, nominalistic and physicalistic framework within which I move. It can conveniently be expressed in terms of a contrast between two levels of language which I will term *base* and *superstructure*.

Consider this example of recent radio humor: A customer brings a pair of pants to an establishment known as Philosopher's Drycleaning, and says that he wants to have them pressed. The clerk, naturally enough, asks Why? After some discussion, the ultimate end of the customer is clarified and finds expression in the words "What I really want is to have the wrinkles removed from these pants". "But where", asks the clerk, "are we to put the wrinkles once we have removed them?"

The clerk, on my analysis, is suffering from base-superstructure confusion. In the base language there are no such things as wrinkles; one simply says that the pants are wrinkled. But we are not limited to the base language.

One of the forms our language gives us for representing information is that built on combining names for individuals with predicates for characterizing them and their relations to other individuals. These forms, and certain logical devices, give us the formal resources that are systematized in elementary logic.

We have this linguistic pattern at the base level and, since it is simple, powerful and useful, we recycle it to generate the superstructure. The adjective 'wrinkled' is converted into the common noun 'wrinkle', and we suppose, that is, speak as if, there are individuals falling under it — 'this wrinkle' and 'that wrinkle' — and we then go on to characterize these individuals in various ways. Some of these ways are legitimate, as when we say that one wrinkle is longer than another, but others are not, as when the clerk supposes that the wrinkles, like cockleburs, could be somewhere in the absence of the wrinkled pants.

I am not at all opposed to superstructure; this way of talking is useful and, at least in practice, indispensable. Still, there is a philosophical danger in its use. The key move in erecting the superstructure is nominalization, the move in which we convert linguistic structures which are not individual terms into forms which are. The individual terms of the base language are associated with the entities we take to exist; from the perspective of common sense, these are physical objects, and, I at any rate would like to add, the places and times at which objects are or may be located. When we move to the superstructure we give to notions which at the base level are not associated with existing entities a grammatical form which suggests that they are. This is what misled the clerk.

Putting the point more generally, at the level of superstructure we have grammatical forms which invite us to say more things than are legitimate, and the way to discover where the limits of legitimacy lie is to forego the convenience of superstructure modes of speech, and return to the base. Legitimate superstructure remarks will be ones that, directly or indirectly, translate back to the base level.

Events, I believe, are like wrinkles, and are creatures of the superstructure. At the base level we describe events by referring to and characterizing objects, places and times. We move to the superstructure when these descriptions are nominalized. We nominalize "John fried an egg", for example, to "John's frying an egg", and then proceed to use this nominalization in such sentences as "John's frying an egg astonished his grandmother". This is all quite innocent, as is our talk about wrinkles, provided it is not taken to have ontological implications. However, it sometimes *is* taken to have ontological implications, and this, I believe, is what brings ontology into action theory.

3. Brand's account

The impulse to take events seriously is not gratuitous; there are genuine pressures at work, a number of which have been brought out in papers by Donald Davidson, especially "The Logical Form of Action Sentences" and "The Individuation of Events".[3] We may characterize these pressures broadly as variations on the theme that there are things that need saying, in general and in action theory in particular, that are better said in an event superstructure, base language equivalents being difficult or impossible to find.

Endorsing the event superstructure means endorsing singular terms referring to events, and for Davidson this meant treating events as concrete particulars.[4] Following up a suggestion made by E.J. Lemmon in his commentary on Davidson's paper,[5] Myles Brand has taken this idea further by holding that events are not only particulars, but spatiotemporal particulars. This theory first appeared in articles in 1976 and 1977,[6] there has been controversy about it in the journals,[7] and it appears now in his new book virtually unchanged.

Brand does ontology by supplying identity conditions, in this case for events and also, by way of comparison, for physical objects. Since his *identity* conditions have this ulterior ontological motive he distinguishes them sharply from mere *identifying* conditions. Conditions of the latter kind, for example, the rule that persons are the same if they have the same parents and siblings, serve mere epistemological and pragmatic functions. By contrast, identity conditions proper "encode the nature of an ontological kind" by "specifying conceptually significant properties of objects of that kind".[8]

Brand encodes the essential information about physical objects and events in the following identity conditions: Two physical objects are one if and only if, in point of fact, they occupy the same spatiotemporal regions. On the other hand, two events are one if and only if they occupy the same spatiotemporal regions by logical necessity.[9]

To illustrate this idea, consider a metal sphere that comes into existence at a certain time, and vanishes a short time later. (I should say in passing that objects such as metal spheres make appropriate examples because Brand limits his account to the familiar macro objects of the common-sense framework, spheres, automobiles, houses, human brains and bodies, and so on; by this reckoning, atoms and molecules are not physical objects.[10] This seems a reasonable approach, at least for the purpose of action theory, which has an inherent common-sense orientation.)

The sphere occupies a certain spatiotemporal region, and by this identity criterion, no other physical object can occupy that same region. Suppose now that during this period the sphere increases in temperature. Then that same region is also occupied by an event, the event of the sphere getting warmer. So, while two objects cannot occupy the same region, an object and an event can. Now suppose that the sphere also rotates during this period. The rotation of the sphere is a second event in the region, but it is not identical with the first since it is logically possible that there could have been a rotation there without a warming, or a warming without a rotation.

The introduction of a necessity operator into the criterion raises certain issues about rigid and nonrigid designation, and Brand deals with these by introducing a supplementary semantical principle for interpreting the condition; though these problems have formed the main issue in published discussions of Brand's theory, I shall here pass over them, restricting myself to purely ontological considerations.[11]

4. The All-At-Once fact about objects

Brand's identity criteria are supposed to encode information about the nature of the ontological kinds Physical Object and Event; if we seek to decode this message I think we get the result that objects and events are two species in a common genus, that of essential occupiers of spatiotemporal regions, entities which do occupy such regions, and whose very identity depends on which regions they occupy. The difference between the two species is the modal feature just noticed, which permits distinct events to share regions with other events, on a contingent basis, and with objects, but prevents objects from sharing regions with other objects.

I believe this all to be very wrong. The general thrust of my criticism will be that neither physical objects nor events belong to that genus, and that even if they did, the difference introduced by Brand would not properly distinguish them. I will first argue that physical objects are not occupiers of spatiotemporal regions, let alone essential occupiers of them. I shall next use an argument of George Schlesinger's to show that Brand's introduction of logical necessity into the identity conditions for events does not satisfactorily distinguish events from objects since it is a mistake to introduce necessity into such conditions at all. And I will conclude my criticism by attempting to remove events as well from the spatiotemporal regions to which Brand has consigned them. In a good bit of this I will be able to make common cause with Neil Wilson.

I begin by considering how Brand's criterion would apply to objects that merge and separate.

Suppose I enter a shop in which something I want is on sale for 50 cents, but I have only a quarter to my name. Attempting to gain by metaphysical subtlety what honest commerce would deny me, I take my quarter from my pocket and announce to the clerk that it is in reality two quarters occupying the same space; since every quarter is worth twenty-five cents, I have fifty cents in change, though, as I make a point of adding, the coin would be worth considerably more to a collector.

The clerk hefts the coin and inquires why, if it is a double quarter, it doesn't weigh any more than a single, so I explain that it is quite possible for a physical object to maintain its integrity through weight loss and gain; otherwise, people would not go on diets. No doubt, I suggest, my quarters would acquire full weight if they were separated.

He is unimpressed. Being familiar with Brand's identity criterion for physical objects, he complains that he knows of no spatiotemporal region occupied by one of my two alleged quarters that is not occupied by the other; my two quarters, he asserts, are really one.

In response, I *could* claim that one of my quarters came into existence at a later time than the other, but did so at a place then occupied by the older quarter, and that the two have been together ever since. If this were accepted, the clerk's defense would have to shift, for the verdict of Brand's identity criterion would be quite clear; there now would *be* spatiotemporal regions (in my pocket, for example, for a stretch of time before the arrival of the second quarter) occupied by one quarter but not the other; therefore, they would be distinct.

However, this approach would allow the clerk an appeal to legal technicality. He could say that since my alleged second quarter was not made in the mint it could not be a true twenty-five cent piece; it would be counterfeit, and by knowingly proffering it to him I would be committing an indictable offense. So I would say instead that I once had two genuine quarters, but that at a certain time they merged.

Or again, should the clerk be of the opinion that I never really had two separate quarters in the first place, I could redirect these considerations to the future. Soon, I could suggest, one of the quarters will cease to exist, leaving the other in sole possession of the space, (though not before there has been an opportunity to get to the bank). Or better, since the use of a temporary quarter might be thought a shady business practice, I could say that my coin will soon separate into two ordinary quarters.

The point I want to make about these stories, which are admittedly barefaced lies, is that on all of them, while the distinctness of the quarters is preserved because of non-coincidence of spatiotemporal region, the time of the non-coincidence is either in the past or in the future. Yet surely it is a mistake to suppose that I must look to the past or the future to determine how many quarters I now have. How many quarters I now hold in my hand must depend exclusively on what I have in my hand now, and identity conditions which make the determination depend on the way things are at other times have got to be mistaken.

This is a consequence of an important fact about physical objects which I will call the All-At-Once fact. This is a fact about the way we apply the part/whole concepts to physical objects, and can be expressed by saying that the whole of a physical object exists at every time at which the object exists at all. Objects, that is to say, do not have temporal parts, and so are not extended in time. They do, to be sure, endure through time, but that is quite different, and refers to the existence of the whole of the object at all the moments in a stretch of time.

This is why it is wrong to say that physical objects occupy spatiotemporal regions. They don't; what they do instead is to occupy spatial regions at times. The whole of my quarter is in my hand now, and if I have another quarter, the whole of it is there as well. Neither quarter has parts at other times that need to be checked before assessing identity or distinctness.

This fact is related to a second important fact about physical objects which we may call the Always-Somewhere fact; at every time at which a physical object exists there is a spatial region which it occupies. (It is often said that an object must occupy a continuous spatial region, but I agree with Brand in allowing the possibility that this region might be discontinuous.)[12]

The damaging implications of the All-At-Once fact for identity conditions based on coincidence of spatiotemporal region are masked, however, by a third fact, or near fact as I should prefer to describe it, for I believe it to be almost but not quite true. This is the claim, which I will call the No-Overlap thesis, that distinct objects cannot occupy the same place at the same time. This claim is true of quarters, at least in the ordinary course of events, as the clerk would no doubt have been happy to point out.

When the No-Overlap thesis is true it hides the clash between the All-At-Once fact and identity conditions based on the occupation of spatiotemporal regions because we then do not have to look beyond the present to find distinct regions for distinct objects; the Always-Somewhere fact requires that there be a space for each object and the No-Overlap thesis ensures that the spaces are distinct.

I will later be seeking to unmask the impact of the All-At-Once fact by undermining the appeal of the No-Overlap thesis, but first it is worth noting that even writers who accept that thesis still find it possible to give proper attention to the All-At-Once fact, and to resist putting objects into spatiotemporal regions. One such is Neil Wilson, to whose account I now turn for an independent argument against the spatiotemporal region approach.[13]

5. Objects and space-time asymmetry

In a very early paper, "Space, Time and Individuals",[14] Wilson considers two types of language, Space-Time languages, in which individuals are associated with locations in four dimensional space-time, and Substance languages, in which individuals have location in three dimensional space at various times. Ordinary language is firmly of the Substance type, he says, and there is no escaping it, so he lays down axioms for the individuation of substances in such a language, and among these we find the No-Overlap thesis, a version of the Always-Somewhere fact and other axioms including a preliminary formulation of a criterion of identity for individuals at different places and times based on the idea that they are identical when they have existed along a continuous path connecting the two times and places. While he does not formulate the All-At-Once fact, it is implicit in his other formulations, for example, in the continuous path criterion.

The continuous path approach to the identity of objects seems to me to be right just where the approach based on spatiotemporal regions is wrong, since it preserves the All-At-Once fact. The formulation of such a criterion is admittedly made easier if the No-Overlap thesis is assumed since the problem of crossed paths does not have to be considered, but I do not believe that assumption is essential since, as we shall see, identity of objects whose paths cross can be preserved by appeal to intrinsic properties of the objects and to unactualized potentialities for path diversity. But I shall not attempt to formulate a path identity criterion here.

Wilson develops this Substance language idea further in his later account of the roles of times and places in elementary facts. For example, in "Facts, Events and their Identity Conditions"[15] he finds himself discussing a sentence which I will number

(1)   Philip is drunk.

This has no truth-value and does not report a fact, he says, because the time is not specified. Facts such as facts about people being drunk require three components; an individual, a property and a time. (1) is incomplete, 'truncated', as he says, because a necessary component, the time, is missing. It can at best be taken as elliptical for

(2)   Philip is drunk at some time.

However, he warns, the impulse to completion which led us from (1) to (2) might tempt us to go farther, and demand that place be included as well as time. This would be a mistake, says Wilson, and I agree, for it leads fairly quickly to the placing of objects in spatiotemporal regions. If we yield to the temptation we will be compelled to say that such a genuine and complete fact-reporting sentence as

(3)   Philip is drunk at noon on August 31, 350 B.C.

is itself really elliptical for

(4)   Philip is drunk at noon on August 31, 350 B.C. at some place.

This would be wrong; Wilson argues that (4) is properly to be 'regimented' as

(4')   There is some place such that Philip is drunk at noon on August 31, 350 B.C. and Philip is at that place at noon on August 31, 350 B.C.

(4') is not something that (3) is elliptical for; it is instead something that (3) implies in virtue of a principle which Wilson describes as a 'universal metaphysical truth',

(5)   If x has property Q at time t, then there is a place P such that x is at P at t.

This metaphysical truth is one of the axioms of the earlier paper, and is very close to what I have termed the Always-Somewhere fact, though not identical with it.[16] Further, since the object x which has a property at a time is presumably the *whole* object x, this metaphysical truth is congenial with, even if it does not strictly entail, the All-At-Once fact which I am wielding against Brand.

This approach involves an asymmetry between space and time as they relate to physical objects. Facts about objects, that is, Wilson's kind of atomic facts, include times as constituents, but do not include places. Places are related to these facts only through a metaphysical truth which ties them to some of the constituents of the facts.

Wilson defends this asymmetry in another, less frequently cited article, "Notes on the Form of Certain Elementary Facts".[17] He there admits the presence of an element of *petitio* in his position, which arises in the following way: Wilson wants to say that the form 'x has property Q at time t' is complete, and that the suggested expansion to 'x has property Q at time t and place P' is a mistake. The opposition challenges the completeness of the first form, and in replying Wilson has appealed to a metaphysical truth, if object x has property P at time t, then etc., whose antecedent is of that very form, and which would therefore be rejected by the opponents. So we have a stand off.

However, Wilson holds that there are additional considerations which, though not decisive, still carry substantial weight. I will mention one of these which seems to me to be particularly nice, and which shows Wilson at his most adroit. It is an argument that time really does have the preferred status. Since time is an essential ingredient in the fact of Philip's being drunk but place is not, Wilson will convert the question "Where was Philip drunk?" into the question "Where was Philip when he was drunk?". Suppose that the correct answer is "in the agora" because Philip was sober on every day but Wednesday, and was in the agora on Tuesday, Wednesday and Thursday. Those giving equality, or even priority, to place will want to play the same game by converting "When was Philip drunk?" into "When was Philip at the place he was drunk at?", and will get the answer "Tuesday, Wednesday and Thursday", which is wrong since he was only drunk on Wednesday.[18]

This generalizes to the point that an object can be at the same place at different times, but cannot at the same time be at different places, (though the place at which an object is at a time may be discontinuous.) Wilson does not introduce this parallel, but we might compare this to the fact that while an object can be red and green at different times, it cannot at the same time be both red and green. For an object to be at a place at a time is thus like its having a quality at a time, and so place should be treated as a component of special placing facts, not an additional component in all facts.

6. Overlapping objects

I now return to the clash I see between the All-At-Once fact and the spatiotemporal view of objects, and the way it is obscured by the No-Overlap thesis, which I will now attack in two ways. My first attack aims at showing that the thesis is false. However, if that should fail I will fall back on a second claim which is that even if the thesis is true, it is not a *central* truth about objects, but rather a more or less accidental and peripheral feature that is easily thought away. As such, I claim, it is not something that should be encoded in identity conditions intended to have ontological significance.

To see the weakness of the No-Overlap claim consider objects that merge and split, such as drops of mercury. Suppose I begin with a drop of mercury in each hand. I combine them in one hand, and they merge into a big drop. Later, I split that drop so that again I have a drop in each hand. We have a way of talking about this case which preserves the No-Overlap thesis; we refuse to identify the pre- and post-merge drops and the pre- and post-split drops. We say that my two little drops cease to exist when the merge occurs, and are replaced by a big drop, which in turn, ceases to exist when the split occurs and is replaced by two new small drops.

But we do not always use this device to preserve the No-Overlap thesis; sometimes we will preserve identity at the cost of permitting overlap. Suppose I pull on a heavyweight knee-length wool sock, and wade out ankle deep into Lake Simcoe. After the water penetrates the sock, it seems plausible to say that there are certain spatial regions — just off the end of my big toe, for example — occupied by both Lake Simcoe and my sock. After a while I return to shore and wring out my sock into the lake. It would be eccentric to say, following the mercury drop pattern, that the episode has given me a new sock, even if there was shrinkage. And it would pass belief to claim that it has given Ontario a new body of water. Far better to say that for a short time my sock and Lake Simcoe, or parts of them, shared a certain spatial region. If this example is accepted, it shows that in some cases we abandon the No-Overlap thesis, and let distinctness of object rest on factors other than non-coincidence of region.

David Wiggins, a defender of No-Overlap, has considered the similar case of a sponge and the water it soaks up, and points out that one could preserve the claim by appealing the micro-structure of the wet sponge — molecules of water here, molecules of sponge there.[19] Of course, this is not available as long as we remain committed, as Brand is, to the common-sense framework. However, Wiggins believes that the thesis has deeper roots than this, and in the end rests it on such claims as that if there were overlap then it would not be possible to tell the objects apart. David Sanford[20] has criticized these claims, in part by developing a plausible example in which we distinguish two billiard balls even though they occupy the same space.

For my second argument I shall make a similar point with a similar imaginary example; it is probably not really possible for the case I describe to occur, but the impossibility is merely technical, not deep, to use Derek Parfit's terms,[21] and a conceptual analysis which cannot accommodate it must be held to be deficient.

We are familiar with stacking chairs — chairs molded out of plastic and shaped in such a way that one will fit into another for efficient storage. I want to imagine a technological breakthrough which carries this one step further; for storage purposes the chairs are made to occupy the very same space. I suppose that when two chairs are put together in this way we call the result a TwinPack. I suppose that they are manufactured as TwinPacks and, at least in the ordinary course of events, are separated for the first time by the dealer at the time of sale. Thereafter they are combined and separated by the owner as often as desired. I suppose that there is never room inside one chair for more than one other chair.

I do not mean this to happen by magic. I am supposing that the technology of it is to fit the atoms of one chair in between the atoms of the other. A TwinPack will weigh twice as much as a single chair. I suppose that such properties as color merge. That is, if you pack a yellow and a blue chair together the TwinPack will be green. I also suppose that at least a good many of the properties of individual chairs are preserved through the packings. If you scratch your initials on a chair and pack it with another, your initials will be on the chair when it is later unpacked. If you scratch your initials on a blue chair and pack it with a yellow chair, then on the TwinPack your initials will appear as yellow on a green background.

When we contemplate novel situations such as this we may well find that our present linguistic conventions do not dictate how we are to speak. Some conceptual innovation may have to take place and we may have to decide, rather than discover, what forms of speech are to be used. However, it seems to me that the way of speaking about this case in which we say that the same chair persists through the periods in which it is packed with another is very natural, has many advantages, and would in fact be adopted. The alternative, mercury drop, approach, in which two chairs are destroyed, their place being taken by a Twin-Pack which is later itself destroyed, to be replaced by a two new chairs exactly similar to the first, seems to me quite artificial.

So when we see a TwinPack we will say that we have two chairs packed together; we admit overlap. Brand's identity criterion is not yet in trouble; the chairs are still two because at other times they are separated, and thus are provided with distinct spatiotemporal regions. But the mask which hides the trouble is now removed, since we must now look to times other than the present.

To bring this out, suppose I am a dealer unloading a shipment of never yet separated TwinPacks. I say to myself that I have eight TwinPacks, and so sixteen chairs. I mark down "16 chairs" in my inventory. I am confident in this count because the things are too heavy to be single chairs. But then a fire breaks out in my warehouse, and everything is destroyed. When I make my fire insurance claim it is challenged. There never were sixteen chairs in my warehouse, I am told, but at most only eight. My alleged pairs of chairs were really single chairs since every spatiotemporal region occupied by one member of a so-called pair was occupied by the other.

This is a most unsatisfactory consequence of Brand's criterion, but it can be avoided only by abandoning the spatiotemporal coincidence conception of identity.

7. Necessary coincidence and conceptual priority

Faced with this insurance problem, my own inclination would be to press the following argument, among others. While my chairs were never *in fact* separated, I would urge, at any time they *could* have been separated. The spatiotemporal coincidence was an accidental, not a necessary truth about my chairs. This *possibility* of distinct regions establishes the distinctness of the chairs, I would say, and so I am entitled to compensation for all sixteen.

In making this move, which seems to me very natural and reasonable, I would appear to switch from Brand's identity criterion for objects to his criterion for events. If that were so it would be very damaging for, whatever else may have gone on, there is nothing in this story to suggest even remotely that the fire turned my chairs into events; two chairs packed together are not at all like the warming and rotating of a metal sphere.

But it is not so; there is equivocation on the word 'possible'. When I speak of the possible separation of my chairs before the fire I mean physical or technical possibility — I really could have separated them if I had wanted to. But, as we have seen, Brand's criterion is couched in terms of the logical modalities, so that mere logical possibility of distinctness of spatiotemporal region is enough to establish distinctness of events. It would take more than that for distinctness of chairs.

Brand stresses that it is indeed *logical* necessity he has in mind. Physical necessity would not do because, for example, one could not then distinguish the increase in temperature and the increase in pressure of a gas undergoing compression.[22]

It is important to see that Brand's criterion for event identity uses, and needs, logical necessity because the appeal to logical necessity is its undoing, according to a very instructive argument offered recently by George Schlesinger.[23] This argument applies whether or not we believe that objects and events occupy spatiotemporal regions. It shows that no matter what objects and events may be, it is unhelpful to distinguish them by appealing to a contrast between a contingent and a necessary coincidence.

Notice first that if we are prepared to frame identity conditions for events in terms of the logical necessity of a coincidence, then almost any coincidence will do; there is no particular reason to pick on spatiotemporal coincidence. For example, we could say that two events are the same when it is logically necessary that a certain person, Helen, is amused by the one if and only if she is amused by the other. However, supposing Helen to be amused by two events, how is it to be determined whether this coincidence of amusement is necessary or merely contingent? Reflection leads us to see that it is not any feature of the events themselves that determines this nor any feature of the mode or degree of Helen's amusement; it is rather that *given* the identity of two events then the coincidence of amusement for Helen will be logically necessary, and *given* distinctness, it will not be. We decide on identity first, and decisions about the necessity or contingency of coincidence follow.

It is therefore wrong to employ the necessity of coincidence in identity criteria; to do so violates the rule that, as Schlesinger puts it, "The definiens must be conceptually prior to the definiendum".[24] It is like offering "*x*'s wife has become a widow" as a definition of "*x* has died".

The penalty for breaking this rule is not falsehood. It is true that wives become widows if and only if husbands die. And it is true that two events are one if and only if they are necessarily coincident. The penalty is that no information is conveyed. The one statement tells us nothing about the nature of death. The other tells us nothing about events; it encodes no information about conceptually significant features of that ontological kind.

8. Events not extended in space

I have argued that it is wrong to say that physical objects and events are two species within the genus of occupants of spatiotemporal regions because objects do not occupy such regions. I now wish to add the claim that events do not occupy such regions either. Just as objects do not have temporal parts, I claim, events do not have spatial parts. Events can be located in space through the locations of their participating objects, but they do not fill volumes of space at times the way physical objects do.

Brand acknowledges the difficulty in fixing the spatial boundaries of many events — he cites the instance of a long distance phone call — but dismisses it as of merely pragmatic or epistemological importance, and comparable to the difficulty we face in defining the spatial boundaries of a complex physical object, such as an automobile,[25] but the difficulty is more serious than that.

P.M.S. Hacker[26] is among those who have claimed that events lack spatial dimensions. Events, he says, occur at places, but do not fill space.[27] He uses this to explain how the rotating and the getting warmer of the metal sphere can be located at the same place without competing for space; neither fills the space.

This same spatial overlap feature was seized upon by Brand to account for the difference between events and objects; he would say that the events fill the space, but do not *fully* fill it, do not fill it to the exclusion of other things. The difference, then, is that between not filling space at all and filling it in a nonexclusive way, but what does that difference actually come to?

There is at least this. Brand is committed to making sense of the idea of assigning spatial volumes to events, and so to the project of indicating for every case how in principle these volumes might plausibly be defined. Hacker is excused from that task, and can regard such problems as "nonsense problems".[28] He can say that we locate events in space only indirectly and in various ways through the objects that participate in them, but this does not require defining spatial volumes for them. It is not enough for Brand to wish these problems off on pragmatic and epistemological considerations, for then the idea of the spatial volume of an event is doing no work, and it must do work if it is to justify its place in ontologically significant identity conditions.

Consider an example. In March of this year there was a performance of the St. Matthew Passion in Leipzig to celebrate the Bach Tricentennial. It was broadcast via satellite to many countries in Europe and to North America. During a pause between a recitative and an aria someone in the audience coughed. This cough no doubt involved a vigorous agitation in the breathing apparatus of the cougher. It resounded throughout the concert hall, was heard around the world, and very probably leaked out into the solar system at large. What spatial volume, exactly did it occupy? Do we take the large view, and try to include all the spaces on which the transmission had an impact? Or do we think small, and locate the event in the body of the cougher? But then the whole body, or only the parts actively involved? Suppose the cougher's feet were firmly planted on the floor throughout, and did not move; should the space they occupy be included in the cough? And would it be different if, in the paroxism, there was a certain amount of violent kicking?

Surely Hacker is right to say that it is nonsense to attempt to answer such questions.[29] We know, or can in principle know, where the cougher was, and what went on in his body, where the concert Hall was, where the satellite was, where the radio listeners were, and so on. We can even know in principle which locations in space were affected by the radio transmission and which were not. But if these things are known, what further point is served by deciding which places are in and which outside the cough?

I conclude, then, events do not fill space, but rather are located in space indirectly, usually through participating objects. Objectless events, such as the fading of the odor of fried bacon from the kitchen, do occur, but can be handled by allowing spatial regions themselves to participate in events. While typical event descriptions, such as "John's running", arise from nominalizations of sentences in which the subject names an object, Brand, rightly, I think, allows the case in which the subject of the sentence generating an event description names a spatial region.[30] "(The region of) the kitchen's smelling less of fried bacon" might qualify. But even so, I think we would want to say that the walls of the kitchen define a volume filled by a certain odor, a different odor at different times; they do not define a volume filled by the change in odor.

9. Return to the base level

Objects, I am saying, *are* spatiotemporal particulars in the sense that they occupy spatial regions at times, though they do not occupy spatiotemporal regions. Events, by contrast, though they occupy 'temporal regions', that is, they go on for various lengths of time, occupy neither spatial regions nor spatiotemporal regions, are not spatiotemporal particulars, and are quite unlike objects. One begins to wonder whether they are any kind of particular at all. This is an issue on which Neil Wilson had some constructive things to say, but I fear he has not always been rightly interpreted.

P.M.S. Hacker characterizes Wilson's analysis in these terms: "A different, slightly bizarre, view conceived of events as 'truncated facts', shorn of one of their constituents", and proceeds to summarize it by saying, "The event of Columbus discovering America is, according to this conception, an abstraction from the fact that Columbus discovered America in 1492".[31]

But it is not altogether accurate to attribute to Wilson the view that events are truncated facts. He does indeed develop such a theory in "Facts, Events and their Identity Conditions", but in the end he says of it that, though it is a splendid theory, "its main flaw is that it is almost totally and irredeemably false", which is hardly strong endorsement.[32]

On the truncated fact theory, the *fact* that Columbus discovered America in 1492 is a four-element complex made up of Columbus, America, 1492 and the action of discovery, this last item viewed as a sort of Platonic property. The two events, the discovery of America in 1492 and the discovery of America by Columbus are three-element complexes, the first dropping Columbus from the fact, the second dropping 1492. The truncated fact theory will say that these two events are actually identical since they are "carved out of the same fact";[33] yet this cannot be, says Wilson, since the three-element event complexes have different constituents.

His actual view seems to be that (a) events cannot be distinguished from facts (full, non-truncated facts, that is), event descriptions being merely truncated fact descriptions, and (b) event talk can and should be 'paraphrased away'. I have trouble with part (a) of this doctrine since I do not believe in the complexes which Wilson says facts are; the action or property constituent, in my view, belongs to the superstructure. But I can endorse part (b), seeing it as a recognition by Wilson that at least events are of the superstructure.

So both Wilson and I are committed to showing how event talk can be translated from superstructure down to base. This is a large project, and I shall not attempt to accomplish it here.[34] I shall just offer a few examples, and draw a general moral, one of some importance for ontology in general.

Wilson has supplied a very nice way of handling certain event identity statements. Roughly, we can translate "The discovery of America by Columbus is identical to the discovery of America in 1492" down to the base level sentence, "There is just one time and just one person such that (a) Columbus discovered America at that time and (b) that person discovered America in 1492 and (c) Columbus discovered America in 1492".

So far, at base level, we remain within the limits of elementary logic, but not for long. Here, in approximation, is how Wilson would handle Davidson's famous example in which he tempts us to say that x's flipping the switch is identical with x's alerting the prowler: "There are two times such that x flipped the switch at the first time and the prowler became alert at the second time, and the prowler became alert at the second time *because* x flipped the switch at the first time". This non-truth-functional 'because' takes us beyond the limits of standard logic.

However, I will not pursue this reduction process further here, except to observe that it does not appear to be hopeless.

Instead, I will conclude by defending it against a particular sort of charge. As is already evident, any reduction of events to base language will require logical resources at that level going beyond ordinary first order logic. We will need adverbs. We will need non-truth-functional connectives such as 'and thereby' and 'because', and who knows what else. This provides a weapon with which the friends of events may attack the reductive enterprise.

We are motivated to engage in reduction, ultimately, by considerations of parsimony; it is with Occam's Razor that we cut away the superstructure entities. But Altman, Bradie and Miller[35] urge that there is also something they call

Russell's Razor to be considered; it tells us not to multiply logical apparatus beyond necessity. With which razor, then, are we to shave?

I believe that we are indeed faced with the choice between a rich logic and a rich ontology. But it seems to me that when we face this choice the balance of considerations favors the rich logic. We might put the point this way; God determined what ontological kinds there are but we invented the language in which we talk about them. To encroach upon God's domain for the sake of making our language simpler would be presumptuous. And to this it might be added that I do not wish to forbid the use of the logically simpler superstructure language, but only to urge that we do not rely on it when we are seeking to say what kinds of things God has given us.

Or rather, since the common-sense framework which is here in question is not the final authority on anything, we may bracket the above by saying that the common-sense framework supposes that God or nature has determined the ontological kinds, etc., and that when we are seeking to explicate the ontology of that framework we should multiply logical devices rather than entities. Events, and so actions, must go.

Notes

1. Michael J. Zimmerman, *An Essay on Human Action* (New York: Peter Lang, 1984).

2. Myles Brand, *Intending and Acting: Towards a Naturalized Action Theory* (Cambridge, Mass.: MIT Press, 1984).

3. Donald Davidson, "The Logical Form of Action Sentences", in N. Rescher, ed. *The Logic of Decision and Action* (Pittsburgh: University of Pittsburgh Press, 1967), 81-95, and "The Individuation of Events", in N. Rescher et al. eds., *Essays in Honor of Carl G. Hempel* (Dordrecht-Holland: D. Reidel, 1969), 216-234.

4. Alternatively, the singular event terms might be taken to refer to abstract entities, the line pursued by Zimmerman, developing the well known view of Roderick Chisholm. I shall not consider that possibility here.

5. E.J. Lemmon, "Comments on D. Davidson's 'The Logical Form of Action Sentences'", in N. Rescher, ed., *The Logic of Decision and Action*, (Pittsburgh: University of Pittsburgh Press, 1967), 98-100.

6. Myles Brand, "Particulars, Events and Actions", in Myles Brand and Douglas Walton, eds., *Action Theory* (Dordrecht-Holland: D. Reidel, 1976), 133-157; "Identity Conditions for Events", *American Philosophical Quarterly*, 14 (1977), 329-337.

7. For example, Michael Tye, "Brand on Event Identity", *Philosophical Studies* 35 (1979), 81-89; Myles Brand, "On Tye's 'Brand on Event Identity'", *Philosophical Studies* 36 (1979), 61-68.; Terence Horgan, "Nonrigid Event-Designators and the Modal Individuation of Events", *Philosophical Studies* 37 (1980), 341-351; Peter M. Simons, "Brand on Event Identity", *Analysis* 41 (1981), 195-198.

8. Brand, *Intending and Acting*, p. 59.

9. For objects we have: $(o_1.)$ $(o_2.)$|if o_1 and o_2 are physical objects, then $o_1. = o_2.$ iff $(r)(o_1$

$Or = o_2 Or)$]. (p.59) For events: $(e)(f)$ [if e and f are events, then $e = f$ iff $\Box$ $(r)(eOr =fOr)$]. (p. 65) In each case r ranges over spatiotemporal regions, and O is #"...occupies——'.

10. Ibid., p. 58.

11. For discussion of these issues see the articles by Terence Horgan, Michael Tye and Peter Simons, as well as Brand's reply to Tye, all cited above.

12. *Intending and Acting*, p. 59.

13. Other writers who resist that approach include Anthony Quinton, "Objects and Events", *Mind* 88 (1979), 197-214, and P.M.S. Hacker, "Events and Objects in Space and Time", *Mind* 91 (1982), 1-19.

14. N.L. Wilson, "Space, Time and Individuals", *Journal of Philosophy* 52 (1955), 589-598.

15. N.L. Wilson, "Events and their Identity Conditions", *Philosophical Studies* 25, 303-321, especially pp. 311-312.

16. The difference is that for Wilson an object must have a property at a time before it is required to have a place. Since I would say that objects, when they exist, must always have properties as well as places, this small difference reduces to nothing.

17. N.L. Wilson, "Notes on the Form of Certain Elementary Facts", in Paul Welsh, ed., *Fact, Value and Perception: Essays in Honor of Charles A. Baylis* (Durham, N.C.: Duke University Press, 1975), 43-51.

18. Ibid., pp. 49-50.

19. David Wiggins, "On Being at the Same Place at the Same Time", *Philosophical Review* 77 (1968), 90-95.

20. David Sanford, "Locke, Leibniz and Wiggins on Being in the Same Place at the Same Time", *Philosophical Review* 79 (1970), 75-82.

21. Derek Parfit, *Reasons and Persons* (Oxford: Clarendon Press, 1984), p. 219.

22. Brand, *Intending and Acting*, p. 66.

23. George N. Schlesinger, "Events and Explicative Definitions", *Mind* 93 (1984), 215-229, especially pp. 216-220.

24. Ibid., p. 219.

25. Brand, *Intending and Action*, p. 56.

26. P.M.S. Hacker, "Events and Objects in Space and Time".

27. Ibid., p. 13.

28. Ibid., p. 10.

29. Brand's writings on this issue show an interesting development. In "Particulars, Events and Actions", p. 146, Brand says that "problems of locating events are weakened" by letting the relation between event and region be 'occurs within' "rather than some relation requiring precise location", such as 'exactly occupies', which suggest an attempt on his part to get way from the commitment to definite spatial volumes. But this theme drops out of later statements, and in the book we have an unabashed 'occupies'. And this is right since once you take seriously the idea of *all* spatiotemporal regions, you will, by a judicious consideration of possible subregions, arrive at the notion of a definite volume.

30. *Intending and Acting*, p. 73.

31. P.M.S. Hacker, "Events and the Exemplification of Properties", *Philosophical Quarterly* 31 (1981), 242-247, p. 242. The view that Wilson's is said to be different from is the view that events are on a par with states of affairs and processes as three different kinds of fact, which Hacker attributes to G.H. von Wright, *Norm and Action* (London, 1961), pp. 25 ff.

32. N.L. Wilson, "Events and their Identity Conditions", p. 314. In quoting I correct a typographical error.

33. Ibid., p. 314.

34. I made some modest moves in that direction in "The Logic of Action", in Myles Brand and Douglas Walton, eds, *Action Theory.* (Dordrecht-Holland: D. Reidel, 1976), 87-104.

35. Andrew Altman, Michael Bradie and Fred Miller, Jr., "On Doing Without Events", *Philosophical Studies* 36 (1979), 301-307. This is a reply to Horgan's "The Case Against Events".

Objects, Existence, and Reference:
A Prolegomenon to Guise Theory

Hector-Neri Castaneda

This is an investigation into the fundamental connections between the referential use of language and our rich human experience. All types of experience — perceptual, practical, scientific, literary, esthetic, ludic, ... — are tightly unified into one total experience by the structure of reference to real or possible items. Singular reference is essential for locating ourselves in our own corner of the world. General reference, by means of quantifiers, is our main tool in ascertaining the accessible patterns of the world. Both are primitive and mutually irreducible. (Often this has been denied.) The unity of total experience is constructed through the biographical unity of a person, and the sociological unity of the communications across a community. This unity of experience is wrought out by an underlying unitary system of reference. This system is unitary because the singular references it underwrites link each experience to thin objects (guises) from which the contents of *all* types of experience are built up. But it is one and the same world that we cognize, theorize about, act upon, suffer emotionally, and react esthetically to. This fundamental unity of world and total experience is the fact that the constituents of the world are thinkable contents of experience. The more thinkable they are, the thinner must they be. The thinness of the strict objects of singular reference accounts for the unified differences in types of experience: these consist in the diverse ways thin contents of experience are put together, whether by nature, by God, or by us, or a combination thereof. We need, therefore, a comprehensive theory of individuation, existence, predication, and truth. One such a theory is Guise Theory.

I. Introduction: The Fundamental Facts and Problems About The Connections Between Human Experience and General Semantics

The most trivial and fundamental facts about our human situation are straightforward. We exist in the midst of a world of real infinitely-many propertied massive objects. We have experiences of them, that is to say, we think and even talk about them. Because thinking is symbolic, the structure of our language somehow represents the structure of the world. This makes communication about the objects in the mutually shared world feasible. And it raises the profound questions as to how thinking, language and existence connect to each other.

Yet to all appearances we also think and speak of what does not exist — sometimes because, believing to be focussing on what exists, we are in error; sometimes because, for planning, for hypothesis framing, for decision, or for mere entertainment, we deliberately consider what does not exist. This raises the perplexing question about what it is to refer to non-existents.

Our thinking of the existing and our thinking of the non-existing seem, furthermore, to be of one piece. The property words and the logical vocabulary we use to distinguish existents from each other are precisely what we use when we consider mere possibilities or enjoy fiction. The language of reality and the language of the non-existing seem to have the same semantical dimensions. The contents of consciousness or of experience, embodied in our uses of words, are uniformly the same whether we think what exists or what does not exist. Yet there seems to be more than a mere semantic parallelism with a two-storied experience: there lurks a profound semantic unity, which grounds the comprehensive underlying unity of experience: existents and non-existents intermingle. We deal with non-existents in the midst of existents in ludic experiences, which have a profound psycho-therapeutic function. We illuminate the real in its contrast with the non-real, as in moral fables and historical novels. When we are in the process of expanding our scientific hypotheses and theories, we treat non-existents, even those which turn out to be contradictory, on the same footing as previously postulated existents. In deliberation we operate with non-existing objects, on a par with the existing ones we take for granted, when — fulfilling our metaphysical destiny of performing intentional action — we plan to create objects in the world. The duality between real and non-real objects seems to be a fundamental element shared by all types of human experience.

Of course, we need the sharpest distinction between existents and non-existents, so much that in a vital sense we are concerned with existents only. For instance, the basic needs of our life have to be fulfilled through interactions with real objects, indeed the more primitive our needs are the more real all their relevant satisfiers must be. On the other hand, the more distinctively human our living is, the more our living seems to be a continuous transaction with non-existents. Thinking seems to be impervious to the distinction between existence and non-existence. Therefore, our human condition seems to necessitate that the semantics of the language we use to think be unified and general so as to be indifferent to the privileges of the existing. But where, if not in thinking and in the semantics through which we carry out our thinking, do the privileges of the existing belong in our intellectual activity?

Yet non-existing objects are very obscure even perverse. Could it be that their wanton perversity is an appearance issuing from the well entrenched practice of anchoring semantics to contemplative *belief* about the world? Language is essentially a means of expressing, indeed of communicating, belief, and typically, true belief about the physical situations we share in our common world. But the very same language with its selfsame semantics seems to function *also* as the means of thinking in all types of experience. The sameness of semantics seems indeed to provide for the fundamental unity in the total experience of a human being. At any rate, we must delve under our doxastic semantics and construct a fundamental *thinking semantics*.

Doubtless, in all experiences we have appropriate beliefs or half-beliefs (to use H.H. Price's term for the doxastic attitude of acceptance involved in reading a novel through[1]). Yet beliefs about the real world are too rich and too structured to provide a serviceable semantic paradigm for all other types of experience, in which we are not exhaustively absorbed with the real truth about the world. A unified semantics of the means of thinking should, by operating at the minimum common denominators of experience, allow for reference to non-existents.

But can we really think of non-existent objects? Is to think of a non-existent object merely to think of a possible way a certain real object may be or might have been? Is it merely to think of a collection of properties? But can we think of impossible objects as well? How can we name non-existents? Is to think of a non-existent perhaps merely to think of a word or phrase, which might have denoted a real object? Can we refer to non-existents singularly, so to speak, in person? But can we refer to them generally through quantifiers? Can the phrase "there is" be ambiguous so as to range over non-existents? But what can "there is" mean over and above "there exists"? Don't we refer to existents and nothing but existents without quantifiers, for instance, when we say: "All trespassers will be prosecuted"? There may exist no trespassers, yet aren't we palpably speaking of existing persons who may be trespassers?

II. Non-Existing Objects Are Deeply Troublesome

Non-existing objects are worrisome, and rightly so. Their failing to exist is at bottom nothing else than their not entering directly, in person, the causal order of the world. This is bad enough. Yet not too much, since we do feel comfortable with numbers and other abstract entities, which do not enter the causal order directly, by virtue of their *own* causal powers. Non-existing objects have other, much more drastic deficiencies. They are surrounded by epistemological clouds: how can we know anything about them? But this is consequent upon their very bad misbehavior in other respects. They seem wantonly to violate common and elementary logical proprieties. This is their undoing in the ontological schemes of some philosophers.

For one thing, some, e.g., Meinong's celebrated objects the round square and its companion the existing round square, are inconsistent. That is their best reason for not existing. That inconsistency is somehow internal, as the singular "the round square" shows: it packs an inconsistency within itself. This inconsistency lies at the level of the constitutive differentiation of that alleged individual from all other individuals. It is, to be sure, bad enough. Nevertheless, what seems truly unforgivable is that that internal inconsistency spills over into our whole system of beliefs: those Meinongian objects seem ostentatiously to violate the most sacred law among them all: the law of non-contradiction. Since thinking is propositional, we cannot merely think *the round square*; we must think it as having properties, as a subject of predication. If we countenance such objects, we are certainly required to believe that:

(1)   The round square is round.
(2)   The round square is square.
(3)   Whatever is square is not round. Hence, we must, it seems, believe that:
(4)   The round square is not round.

And we seem to be committed to the contradiction (1)&(4).

The preceding contradiction may be thought to be a peculiar problem with Meinong's celebrated objects[2]. It might be adduced that the solution lies at hand: make consistency a necessary condition of objecthood: non-existing objects are genuine only if they are consistent.

This condition of objecthood is, however, obscurantist. We are capable of thinking non-existing objects that we want to make, or expect to encounter in some future adventure, thinking them to be self-consistent, without realizing that they involve subtle internal inconsistencies. Here we have as ultimate parameter the proved meta-theorems, based on Goedel's theorems about the essential incompleteness of arithmetic, according to which there is no decision procedure for implication in general[3]. However, we never need reach that limit. The more elementary psychological fact is this: no mental operation, act or state is closed under any type of implication. For instance, it is not merely logically possible, but psychologically possible that a proposition (or sentence) P implies Q and that some one believes — let alone thinks or considers — P without believing Q. This is an important law governing our basic *human condition of mental finitude.*

The requirement of consistency for all objects of thought cannot serve to explain how thinking operates in experience, and how natural language functions as the embodying instrument of thinking. The difficulty is too serious and the risk of inconsistency too grave for us to be content with half-measures. Either we acknowledge with full equanimity that some thinkable objects are internally inconsistent and propose a challenge to the law of non-contradiction, or we shun non-existing objects altogether and search for a different, but unified account of experience, thinking, and general semantics.

For another thing, the threat of contradiction lurks behind even self-consistent non-existents. All or most of the non-existing objects we can consider individually must be incomplete. Clearly, the King of France in 1982 is neither bald nor not bald. Similarly:

(5)   Don Quijote does not have a two-pronged mole on his right shoulder, and does not fail to have such a mole.

In the simplest logic we are used to employ, double negations cancel, so that (5) above is equivalent to the following contradiction:

(6)   Don Quijote both has and does not have a two-pronged mole on his left shoulder.

Here we face an immediate option. We can say that self-consistent non-existing objects do not violate the law of non-contradiction, but only the law of excluded middle, which, although a mighty law is still a lesser law than the law of non-contradiction.

That is not all. There is the even more scorching question: How can a non-existing object *have* properties? They are so obnoxious as to violate the absolutely fundamental requirement of having properties in the decent way in which Tyler Burge has the physical property of being tall and the psychological property of being a brilliant philosopher, James Tomberlin that of being a most powerful philosophical critic, Alvin Plantinga that of being the greatest example of the combination philosopher-theologian, the Usumacinta River the property of originating in Guatemala and ending in Mexico in the Gulf of Mexico, etc. A necessary condition for these individuals to have the properties mentioned, and others, is that they exist. More sharply, how can a non-existing object have the property of being self-identical — a property that any decent entity should have?

III. The Stunning Russellian Solution

Dealing with non-existing objects is patently an ordeal. They seem to require their own sense of predication and to demand their own exceptions to the laws of logic. Understandably, many philosophers quickly become impatient with them and banish them from their official worlds. Anybody with a little notion of philosophical respectability and some minimal sense of order can sympathize with the proscription of non-existents.

No wonder then that Bertrand Russell under the slogan "Only existents can have properties", which expressed what he, revealingly, called a robust sense of reality, proposed to solve all the perplexities that surround non-existing objects in one enormously simplifying stroke:

(*R.RSR*) *Russell's Robust Sense of Reality.*

EXISTENCE is tantamount to HAVING PROPERTIES is tantamount to BEING SELF-IDENTICAL is tantamount to BEING IN THE REALM OF THINKABLES is tantamount to BEING IN THE DOMAIN OF QUANTIFICATION.

Russell proposed to reduce talk about non-existents to talk about existents. To this effect he conceived the brilliant following analysis of the definite article "the" in its singular use:

(*R.ADD*) *Russell's analysis of definite descriptions*

A sentence of the form

The F (one) is G

is syntantico-semantically analyzable as:

There exists just one thing that is F and it is G.

It is of great importance to appreciate the fact that (R.RSR) and (R.ADD) do *not* include the following important thesis at the intersection of the philosophy of language and the philosophy of mind:

(Q.Q.Ref)   The fundamental, at bottom really the only, mechanism of reference (to particulars) is quantification. Proper names and all other singular terms are eliminable by reduction to quantifiers and predicates. Whatever may be picked out by a single term, or a use thereof, is picked out by the existential quantifier underlying the eliminative reduction of the term. Singular terms are only vicarious means of reference[4].

Russell's (R.RSR) and (R.ADD) are compatible with the denial of (Q.QRef). In fact, his view of language, at the time he adduced (R.RSR) against Meinong, included quantifiers as mechanisms of general reference alongside logical constants as independent mechanisms of singular reference. Because of his deep concern with the problems of the nature of experience, he assigned experiential primacy to singular reference, and fretted about its logical primacy, not about reducing singular reference to general, but rather the other way around. Experience, especially perceptual experience, consists of the presentation of objects, which Russell called objects of acquaintance. Such objects were the targets of primitive singular reference. Accordingly, he proposed that the only genuine logical constants in natural language are the different perceptual uses of demonstratives, especially "this" and "that." These views, which are to some extent defensible[5], led him to other views that amounted to assigning a mysterious non-experiential role to quantifiers. He held that the objects with which we had no acquaintance were known, and referred to, under definite descriptions. He also held other strange views, which are not germane to our present concern with the basic problems of singular reference[6].

Now, (R.RSR) and (R.ADD) and (Q.QRef) together constitute a powerful and simple view of language and reference. No wonder that Quine and many other great philosophers and their followers have endorsed that combination. The Russellian fourfold conflation of concepts recorded in (R.RSR) became one fundamental dogma of philosophical logic and philosophy of mind during the second third of this century. Russell's analysis of definite descriptions, (R.ADD), evolved into the archetype of philosophical accomplishment. To illustrate, the following were thought to be not merely logically equivalent but essentially synonymous sentences:

(7)   John exists.

(8)   Someone is the same as John.

(9)   John has some property.

(10)   There is a thinkable individual which is identical with John.

These are powerful conflations: They work havoc in our naive view of language and thinking. Thus, Russell's Robust Sense of Reality, even if it is not married to (Q.QRef), imposes arduous tasks: our pervasive talk ostensibly about non-existents must be analyzed away in every single type of experience where it appears. Palpably, not all cases are the same.

Many affirmative judgments of existence do seem simply to identify an object claimed to exist with an existent. For instance:

(11)   The Queen of England exists

does not seem to be unduly distorted by being interpreted as:

(11A) There exists just one individual that is identical with the Queen of

England.

Or as:

> (12) Among the existents there is just one individual that has the property of being a queen of England [now].

On the other hand, negative judgments of existence are not so pliable. To begin with consider:

> (13) The dangerous burglar we were expecting turned out not to exist after all.

Perhaps it is not wholly unreasonable to interpret (13), not as referring, singularly to *one* particular non-existing burglar, but rather as referring in a general way to *all* existing burglars, and perhaps to all existents. Thus, it may not be outrageous to consider (13) as saying very much the same thing as:

> (14) No existing individual is a dangerous burglar and an individual we were expecting, or more than one existing individual are dangerous burglars we were expecting.

Thus, (13) and (14) illustrate Russell's analysis of definite descriptions (R.ADD) above.

It is, however, not immediately obvious that we can without loss of meaning or information eliminate apparent references to the non-existing Napoleon Bonaparte's fifth son who was King of Bologna, by talking about all existents, or about the existents in the nineteenth century. In particular, consider:

> (15) Napoleon Bonaparte's fifth son who was King of Bologna never existed.

By the Russellian analysis, taking the negation to have the whole sentence as its scope, (15) is short for:

> (16) It's not the case that: just one existent is both Napoleon Bonaparte's fifth son and some-time King of Bologna and that existent existed.

Given the uniqueness condition built into being somebody's fifth son, (16) is, in accordance with the Russellian logic, equivalent to:

> (17) Among the existents nothing is — has the property of being — a fifth son of Napoleon Bonaparte and King of Bologna.

Patently, (17), as well as (16), like (14), places us inside the corral for existents and impels us to search for the presence of the properties being Napoleon Bonaparte's fifth son and being a King of Bologna. This is clearly a different picture from the one (15) presents: (15) seems rather to say something stronger, which merely implies (17), namely:

> (15A) *The* individual Napoleon Bonaparte's fifth son who was King of Bologna — somehow pre-constituted prior to the investigation about its existence — is not among the sometime existing individu-

als: *that* individual is not in the sub-corral of existents.

Of course, one can, moved by the trouble-making nature of non-existents, reject the picture of the world and experience presented by (15A) and then learn to think that (15) and (17) mean exactly the same. With that conditioning the semantic assimilation of (15) to (17) would not seem too much of a distortion of the sense of (15).

At the present level of generality in our discussion the issue is simply the contrast between the two pictures. We will deepen the issue by delving into the contrast in order to see the ontological, semantic, and cognitive structures that undergird the two pictures.

In any case we must record:

>(R.F.) *Russellian Fact:* There are cases in which it SEEMS feasible, i.e., not too distortive of meaning, to equate talk of a certain non-existent with talk about all existents, or all existents of a certain class.

There are, however, uses of singular terms that at first sight do not fall under (R.F.). For example, on Russell's analysis (R.ADD) all affirmative predicative sentences about non-existents are false. Yet there are reasons for thinking that some of them are true, and the reasons are of variegated sorts. For instance:

>(18) The present King of France is a king

is of the classical type that Kant regarded not merely as true, but as analytically true. From other quarters we have alleged truths like:

>(19) Don Quijote went on his first journey without Sancho Panza.

>(20) Santa Claus is a jolly good fellow.

>(21) Don Quijote is different from Sanson Carrasco.

>(22) Every contemporary Englishman is shorter than Gulliver.

>(23) Lyndon Baynes Johnson was more cunning than the ideal prince constructed by Machiavelli.

>(24) Jimmie Carter was somewhat more assertive than Hamlet.

>(25) The Browns are poorer than the average American family.

>(26) The man John says he saw is older than the man Mary says she saw. Obviously one is lying, and at least one of those men does not exist.

>(27) The book on action theory I planned to write was much more readable than *Thinking and Doing*.

This budget of proposed counterexamples to (R.RSR) is incomplete. We will have the opportunity of adding other instances. But because of space we will not discuss them in detail. We will concentrate on some of the major types of experience that seem to involve non-existents.

Our (apparent) reference to non-existents is so pervasive that Russell's Robust Sense of Reality (R.RSR) seems too sweeping. Thus, in the last years different efforts at breaking Russell's monolith (R.RSR) have developed. A very interesting effort, still very much Russellian, is so-called free logic.

IV. The Free Logic Solution: Two Semantic Postures

The standard Free Logic approach distinguishes between our use of singular terms and our use of quantifiers. With this distinction it breaks through the linguistic aspect of Russell's Robust Sense of Reality, (R.RSR), right at the middle. The semantic and ontological sides of (R.RSR) are, however, touched only slightly. The chief development is that singular terms are free of existential import. Not only the terms and their uses may fail to pick out existents, but the users themselves are free to use such terms without even purporting to refer (to existents). In brief, the main theses composing the standard Free Logic Solution to the problem of elucidating the language of non-existence are[7]:

(FL.1)   Non-denoting terms are legitimate singular expressions in meaningful sentences.

(FL.2)   Non-denoting terms in direct speech constructions are not substituends of the variables of quantification.

(FL.3)   The quantifiers in non-fictional direct speech range over (existing) objects. Non-denoting terms denote nothing that can be the value of a quantifier.

These theses allow as meaningful sentences apparently about non-existing objects. Such sentences can be assigned truth-values. In particular, sentences of the form "$a = a$" are all allowed to be true, whether a exists or not. Thus we have at least the appearance of attributing self-identity to all mythical heroes and literary characters. We can also, which is of the greatest importance, construct meaningful sentences relating existing to non-existing individuals, as in sentences like (22)-(27) above. Thus, the following Russellian equations are jettisoned in their linguistic aspect:

(R.RSR.1)   To be the subject of predication is tantamount to existing.

(R.RSR.2)   To be self-identical is to exist, and vice versa.

To theses (FL.1)-(FL.2) either of two alternative semantic complementations may be adjoined. One is the *Weak Semantic View of Non-existents.* On this view singular non-denoting terms may be said not to denote existents, but to denote non-existents, and, then, add that the ontology of non-existents consists of their isolation and the essentially atomistic nature of the truths about them. Each singular sentence about a non-existent can at bottom be assigned a truth-value more or less independently of the other sentences about it. Of course, intersubjective criteria for truth are not ruled out. This freedom of truth assignments captures at least part of the human creativity of literary and mythical truths. Once a novel is written the truths about the characters of the novel are there objectively. On this view the fiction writer does create non-existents. The isolation of non-existents from existents is deployed by theses (FL.2) and (F.3) above.

Theses (FL.1)-(FL.2) may, on the other hand, be complemented with a pragmatic *No Semantics View of Non-existents*, which accounts for the use of non-denoting terms by resorting both to purely syntactic features of discourses containing such terms and the purposes for which such discourses are produced. This view actually adheres to Quine's semantic tenet (Q.QRef) above: the bound (or bindable) variables of quantification constitute the fundamental mechanism of reference to particulars: to be is to be the value of a quantifiable variable. Free Logic, of course, does not accept Quine's reduction for the case of non-denoting singular terms. Nevertheless, on this view, because there are no non-existents that can be values of the quantifiers, we cannot truly refer to non-existents.

The dispute between the Weak Semantics View and the No Semantics View is not entirely verbal. Each view has different commitments to what counts as mind-independent or external — not necessarily spatial — objectivity. We have here, first, a shared recognition that we widely use sentences with terms that do not denote (existents), and, secondly, two degrees of weaving that recognition with a view of language. Granted the syntactic legitimacy of singular sentences with so-called non-denoting terms, the No Semantic View deprives that syntax of a semantics of non-existents by withholding from those terms all objective connections and any connection with quantification. This move is strong if it is erected on the objectual interpretation of quantification, conceived, furthermore, after Quine, as the fundamental mechanism of reference from which denoting singular terms derive their referential role. The Weak Semantics View postulates an isolated semi-objectivity that bestows non-existent referents upon so-called non-denoting terms. This view could assign an autonomous status to singular reference, yet it still assigns a more basic status in our grasping of reality to general reference through quantifiers. There is, thus, a fundamental difference concerning objectivity, the connections between language and objectivity, and the hierarchical order of the referential powers of the mind.

The preceding contrast of views is predicated on the normal objectual interpretation of the quantifiers as mechanisms through which thinking grasps objectivity collectively, especially infinite or indefinite collections of objects. In opposition some philosophers have proposed the substitutional interpretation, according to which the quantifiers are intralinguistic mechanisms connected, not semantically with values, but only syntactically with substituends. This interpretation robs Free Logic of a motivation to segregate non-denoting terms from quantification. Clearly, if the particular, so-called existential, quantifier "Some" or "There is" does not relate to objects — it being immaterial whether such objects are physical or mental, concrete or abstract —, but to *names*, then "There is a winged horse" is true: for we do have the linguistic instance "Pegasus is a winged horse." Obviously, the substitution interpretation makes the connections between thinking (and language) and reality a great mystery. Thus, we will put it aside in the following meditations[8].

On the No Semantics View we cannot really refer to non-existents. Hence, it is not clear that we can genuinely think of them. Nevertheless, to the extent that we can consciously use language with non-denoting terms to express beliefs, there is a minimal sense, shared by the two views mentioned above, in which also the Russellian equation below is *shunted:*

(R.RSR.3)   To be thinkable is tantamount to existing.

V. General and Singular Reference

The question before us now is whether Free Logic in either of the two semantic interpretations is an adequate account of our use of singular terms, especially non-denoting terms, and quantifiers in our different types of experience. In partic-ular, we must ascertain the roles of so-called non-denoting singular terms in experience, whether besides their apparent function of presenting identifiable items for thinking, they connect thinking with intersubjective thinkable contents, whether such contents function objectively enough to be values of quantification. If so, then Free Logic would seem to be a half-house in the way to a fuller theory of language, existence, and singular and general reference.

Undoubtedly, thesis (FL.1) is the full recognition of our linguistic practice, e.g., in daily life and in literature, of referring to non-existents. But the segrega-tion of proper names from quantification, understood objectually, is a drastic one. This is so even in the case of the Weak-Semantics View that allows reference to non-existents.

We cannot be happy merely with the rejection of Quine's thesis (Q.QRef), or even with its rejection and the mere adoption of the *Two-types of Reference View*, according to which *both* singular and general reference are fundamental and mutually irreducible. There is the unity of world and experience, hence, of language, too, to be taken into account. For this we need *bridging implications* that connect the two types of reference to each other. These bridging implications determine the way in which, on one hand, singular reference supports general reference, and, on the other hand, general reference complements singular reference. Singular reference, especially demonstrative perceptual reference, is the conceptual mechanism one has for finding one's place in the world and for acting on the objects and persons around. General reference provides us with the conceptual equipment for formulating, and hence investigating, the patterns of the world — regardless of how far beyond our perceptual experiences those patterns reach.

Hence, to the extent that proper names like "flogiston," "the man that I, mistakenly as it turns out, thought I saw," "Ossian," "(the planet) Vulcan," "Edda Hobbler," "Ivan Karamazov," "Saint Christopher," "The Virgin of Guadalupe," and "The Christ of Esquipulas," are not legitimate substituends for, because they do not name values of, the quantifiers "all," "some," etc., we are not thinking in a fully referential sense of what those names represent in our domain of discourse. (Recall that we are orthodox — perhaps old-fashioned here too — in adopting the objectual interpretation of the quantifiers.) This raises a question about the point or sense of our using such non-denoting terms. A naive believer in non-existing objects can say that we use such singular terms, as is the case when we use denoting terms, to introduce items for discussion, which, of course, give unity to pieces of speech. But what do non-denoting terms do if they seize nothing at all that can be in the domain of discourse and thought?

VI. The Unity of Cross-Referential Networks in Discourse: Semantic vs. Meta-Linguistic Unity

Undoubtedly, singular terms introduce *foci of discourses*. Consider, for the sake of concreteness, a paragraph in some study about *Don Quijote* where its author Cervantes is being described or discussed. The whole paragraph obtains its topical unity by its being an exposition about Cervantes. All the later uses, and some earlier ones, of the pronoun "he" receive a unitary referential character by their being cross-referring with the name "Cervantes." Thus, this proper name performs the role of unifying and holding up together, so to speak, a whole *cross-referential network,* which functions as a skeleton of the discourse in question. This holistic or structural function in discourse of proper names and of coreferring pronouns is of great importance. The skeleton of the discourse in the conjured paragraph can be diagrammed as follows, where the token of the name "Cervantes" depicts the focus-introducing token of the name, and the tokens of the pronoun "he" preceding the token of "Cervantes" represent coreferring terms proffered before that focus-introducing occurrence of "Cervantes":

(N) he ... he ... Cervantes ... this author ... he ... he ... he
Here we can have two different semantic views.

First, on the *Comb View* the skeleton (N) is certainly a syntactic network of coreferring singular terms unified by the proper name "Cervantes," but *each* occurrence of a term is semantically self-sufficient and independent, denoting directly the man Cervantes. Each term is like the tooth of a comb directly and by itself touching reality, the syntactic network being simply the structure that gives to the referential teeth their overall unity in the particular discourse under consideration. Thus, (N) is just a part of the referential comb:

(C.N) he —— he —— Cervantes —— this author —— he —— he —— he ——

(The man)   C E R V A N T E S

The Comb View is a natural view for philosophers inspired by formal logic. Each well-formed formula in a calculus is built up from the primitive symbols of the calculus, and the formal semantics proceeds by assigning interpretations to the primitive symbols. The pronouns of ordinary language that form a referential network, e.g., (N), can be easily conceived to be stand-ins for the focus-introducing term: the reason we use pronouns rather than iterate the focus-introducing singular term is to be explained by some pragmatic reasons of monotony avoidance or abbreviation.

The Comb View is almost perfect for those cases that P.T. Geach labeled "pronouns of laziness," which are almost mere stand-ins. For example,

(G.1)   Carlos was the last one to come, and he was the first to go
may be said to be a mere abbreviation of:

(G.2)   Carlos was the last one to come, and Carlos was the first to go.
Yet even here there are two crucial differences between (G.1) and (G.2). On the one hand, (G.1) expresses a unitary cross-referential network, whereas (G.2) doesn't. On the other hand, because of that lack of unity, (G.2) has an ambiguity not present in (G.1), to wit: each occurrence of "Carlos" may pick out a different person, or even a different part of one and the same person — in case the speaker believes that he is dealing with two Carloses. (For more on names see the paper mentioned in note 25.) (G.1) has a different ambiguity: if embedded in a paragraph, the pronoun "he" may refer back to another person mentioned earlier in the paragraph. But in each case the pronoun "he" in (G.1) will be part of a cross-ref-

erential network.

In brief, (G.2) is ambiguous. On one interpretation, there is in it no cross-referential network, but two separate referential prongs, each hooking up with its own denotatum. Any sameness between the denotata is external to the speaker's purview and statement. On another interpretation, on the assumption of co-reference (G.2) contains a cross-referential comb. In contrast, (G.1) contains at least part of a cross-referential network. Furthermore, in the case in which (G.1) expresses a whole discourse "he" refers back to "Carlos." Thus, in a sense (G.1) implies the corefential interpretation of (G.2). This bestows upon the pronoun "he" in (G.1) certain referential *autonomy.* Notwithstanding, because of the crucial unity of discourse, a holistic view is better: the skeleton "Carlos ... he ..." refers as a whole because "Carlos" in it refers: "he" refers through its linkage to "Carlos." This view is better yet in those cases in which a pronoun lacks referential autonomy, i.e., it cannot be substituted by its antecedent, as is the case with quasi-indicators. (See the materials mentioned in note 13.)

Second, on the discourse-holistic *Pointed Spear View,* none of the occurrences of the singular terms, except perhaps the occurrence of the proper name (or singular term whatever) that introduces a focus of discourse, is connected to the outside world. The focus-introducing occurrence of a singular term is, thus, the *ontological spearhead* of the whole cross-referential network. The network refers to something (existing or real, of course, according to those opposed to non-existing objects) through its spearhead, but only if this spears something. Thus, skeleton (N) is a very coarse picture of the double-stemmed spear:

(S.N)

$$\text{(the man)}$$
$$\text{C E R V A N T E S} \leftarrow \text{Cervantes} \begin{cases} \text{he — he} \\ \\ \text{this author — he — he — he} \end{cases}$$

Tyler Burge, in a most illuminating paper[9], has adopted the Pointed Spear View to provide a pragmatic justification of our use of non-denoting terms without allowing them a semantic or ontological dimension. For a singular term to be able to perform its structural cross-referential role it clearly does not matter whether the object denoted by the term exists or not. Thus, Burge has adopted Free Logic and follows the Russellian tradition in assigning to quantifiers the ontological role of ranging exclusively over what exists as well as over what can be referred to. Thus, in discourses about Don Quijote, or any non-existent, we have cross-referential networks like (N), and we have, according to Burge (but in my terminology), a pointed spear like (S.N), except that nothing is speared and the place corresponding to that of the man Cervantes in (S.N) is empty. The discourse stands by itself as a linguistic structure, whether the name "Don Quijote" spears something in reality, or not. This extralinguistic connection between the name "Cervantes" and the man Cervantes is presumably most important when our discourse is promoted by fact-finding purposes; but when we are engaged in literature or some other ludic activity, that connection is, or may be, irrelevant.

Palpably, there are many profound truths in the view just summarized. The unity of discourse needs to be highlighted — even for the innocent-looking cases of pronouns of lazyness as in (G.1); that language is used for a variety of purposes is a truth of the greatest importance often neglected in the study of syntax and semantics. Undoubtedly, the different types of experience represent profoundly different major purposes and needs in human existence.

Evidently, the cross-referential role of a proper name is a pragmatic role that unifies a strand in a discourse. But *that unification needs accounting for*. Obviously, the pragmatic unity of a discourse D as a whole consists precisely in that the proper understanding of D by a person P includes, and hinges on, P's thinking — upon the causation of P's unified perceptions of all the terms in each cross-referential network of D — the selfsame thinkable item as involved in the properties and relations mentioned in D. The cross-referential terms embody a unity of thinking of the *same thing* throughout the discourse. The pragmatic function that unifies the utterance of the whole discourse D under one purpose or goal, is too broad and too general to provide by itself an internal unity to D, in substitution of an underwriting thinking semantic unity for each cross-referential network in D. To be sure, a focus of discourse D need not be an existing object for D to gain its unity. A non-existing object characterized by a set of properties has both thinkable content and sufficient intrinsic unity to unify a cross-referential network. Of course, to say this is to shunt the Russellian equation of thinkable individual with existing individual, and is, also, to place singular reference alongside general, quantifiable reference.

The unity of the cross-referential network *needs* accounting for. If it is not accounted for in semantic terms, then we need something else that can determine that unity. The overall purposes of the discourse hang too loose around each cross-referential network in it to furnish the unity of each network. This is especially pressing in mixed cases in which we relate existents to non-existents.

The Meta-linguistic View of the Unity of a Discourse about non-existents.
An alternative view to the ontologico-semantical account of the syntactic unity of
a cross-referential network with non-denoting terms is the Meta-linguistic View.
On this view such a discourse unity is accounted for very neatly: it is the unity of
the spear of a cross-referential network: the network refers to its own spearhead,
the very same term introducing the focus of the discourse.

Here I will not pursue the meta-linguistic line. My reason is that I much
prefer a theory that preserves the ostensive object-linguistic character of our
discourses about non-existents. This is particularly important for the case of those
discourses in which we think and talk about objects that, even if we think they
exist, turn out not to exist. Our discourse is in such cases ostensibly object-linguistic, and for very good reason. It is anticlimactic and perplexing to be told *ex
post facto* that our thinking was really meta-linguistic, and that we actually used
words not intended to refer to something different from them, but words that
referred to themselves, that we mentioned, not used proper names for objects —
in spite of whatever pains we might have taken to avoid the confusion of use with
mention, and in spite of how successfully it may seem to us that we have avoided
that confusion. Patently, that alleged use-mention confusion would be utterly
unavoidable, because it would depend solely on the empirical knowledge, *ex
hypothesi* not available at the time of thinking, of whether a putative object exists
or not. This is very perplexing. Yet it is even more perplexing in the case of
mixed discourses relating existing to non-existing objects as in the case of examples (22)-(27) above. In particular, it is desirable to avoid committing ourselves to
the view that such discourses merely relate existing objects to words[10].

So far we have discussed singular reference. Because of the bridging implications linking singular and general reference, it would seem a natural consequence to suppose that quantification is just ready at hand. For instance, why
shouldn't we not be able to think of non-existents as members of classes, and
even to think of *all* or *some* member of such classes? But lest this may seem too
aprioristic, we must examine our use of both singular and general reference, to
determine whether we quantify explicitly over non-existents, before we decide to
depart from Free Logic in its adherence to the Russellian semantics of quantification.

VII. Singular and General Reference to Non-Existents Needed In the Experience of Planning and Acting Intentionally

Even a cursory but attentive canvassing of the sentences through which we have experiences of the most common garden variety reveals that quantification having non-denoting terms as substituends is just as frequent and crucial to our lives as is the use of singular sentences containing such terms. Hence, there is a reason for treating non-denoting terms as substituends of variables of quantification, namely: otherwise we both throw away extremely important sentences (important because of their roles in our lives), and dislocate the semantic and syntactic structural relationships of sentences with non-denoting terms to other sentences — especially those that relate existents to non-existents.

Let us proceed now to establish the empirical premise of the preceding argument. Consider the following situation:

(NE.1) *The non-existing houses of Academic Paradise.* Several professors of Indiana University have associated to form a construction company. They have bought a farm to build 300 houses of different types in a new subdivision, to be called *Academic Paradise.* The corporation has done all the necessary work. It has surveyed the land; partitioned the farm into lots, recreation areas and streets; posted landmarks, and made some paths; drawn maps and blueprints; bought some materials; published brochures with descriptions and artist's drawings of the different types of houses, etc. It has numbered all the houses and named the streets. In fact, lots and plans have been contracted with some clients who have selected their particular houses. The contractors are ready to start as soon as they obtain the bank loans applied for. But only one loan is approved. The economy collapses, and only ten of those houses are built. Yet the executives have discoursed about the different *numbers* of houses they will build of each different kind, style, design, type, location, quality, category, size, and price. Eventually the land will be divided up between creditors and on it a shopping center and some professional buildings will be erected.

This example is ostensibly rich in general references to objects that have not existed and will never exist. Behind that summary description of the situation lurk a good number of singular terms, besides the singular terms of the form "the house No. N", through which the executives, their clerks, their sub-contractors, their advertisers, their friends, their prospective clients, and many others have thought and communicated about all or some of those houses which were bound not to exist. Observe how the preceding sentence is a quantified sentence whose quantifiers range over non-existing objects. Many quantified statements about those houses have a mixed range of both existents and non-existents, for instance:

> (28) Each house of Academic Paradise is to be erected on a full acre lot.
>
> (29) None of the houses has less than three bathrooms.

Given the situation described in (NE.1), there was a fixed schedule of construction, and each house was carefully constituted as an entity with its own place in that schedule. Thus, the unbuilt houses have an individuation not affected by their failure to exist. That individuality transcends the period during which Academic Paradise seemed within reach: we can still now refer singularly to each of those houses, and generally to sets of them through quantification. Consider now the following lament:

> (30) The three-story house with the largest swimming pool was the first one that they failed to build.

The first stage in the Russellian analysis of (30) by (R.ADD) is:

> (31) There is just one existent object that is a house in [Academic Paradise] with three stories and the largest swimming pool [in Academic Paradise] and it is (or was) the first house [of Academic Paradise] that they failed to build.

Obviously, whereas (31) is false, (30) is true.

On the Russellian ontological view (R.RSR) and its concordant logical tenet (R.ADD), any set of unbuilt houses is identical with the null set. Since only real objects have properties, they cannot have the property of being a member of this or that set. On the other hand, the unbuilt houses of Academic Paradise remain as individuated as possible and have membership in genuine thinkable non-null sets with different numbers of members. For instance:

> (32) Altogether 290 houses were left unbuilt.
>
> (33) There were 100 houses with swimming pools and only 5 of those were built.

The case described in (NR.1) is, in spite of its naturalness, a rather high-flown one. The two points about singular and general reference are even more pedestrian than they appear in (NE.1). In fact, those two points are utterly pervasive in daily life. We need quantification over non-existents in our daily discussions of plans, which we formulate and discuss in direct speech sentences. If anything is central to life, in the biographical, not biological, sense, it is planning, i.e., the adoption of a network of interrelated general intentions to be successively specified with particular intentions, and ultimately carried out by a sequence of intentions of the *I-to-do-this-here now* type. And it is of the essence of intending and planning that what is intended *may* fail to exist, for different causes, including weakness of the will[11].

Planning is centrally included in the research activities of scientists. They must consider objects, which may turn out not to exist, for postulation in their theories or hypotheses, as well as for research and for computational activities. Scientists must consider them individually — as Free Logic has it — and generally, as values of their quantifiers in their research discourse — as the Meinongians and Guise Theorists have been insisting on.

Quantification carefully restricted to existents is useful in the formulation of a finished scientific theory, one that no further research will alter. Perhaps the following is worth stressing:

> (EROTICS) *Principle   of   Existential-Reference-Only   Tenable   in* Completed Science:

> The ultimate objective of science is to provide a total description of the empirical facts and of the order of the world; its *logical desideratum* is, thus, to formulate theories that because they are complete, have quantifiers ranging only over existents.

Nevertheless, the language of daily life with our planning and our ludic experiences, all fully integrated in our unified total experience lived through one and the same natural language, needs quantification over non-existents.
But what is really a non-existing object?

VIII. Ordinary Existential Quantification Presupposes Non-existents

A valuable datum about quantification was discovered by G.E. Moore in 1936[12]. Here it is:

> The sentence 'Tame tigers growl' seems to me to be ambiguous. So far as I can see, it might mean 'All tame tigers growl', or it might mean merely 'Some tame tigers growl', or 'Most tame tigers growl'. ... But I do not think that there is any ambiguity in 'Tame tigers exist' corresponding to that which I have pointed out in 'Tame tigers growl'. So far as I can see *'Tame tigers exist' and 'Some tame tigers exist' are merely two different ways of expressing exactly the same proposition ... It ['Tame tigers exist'] always means just 'Some tigers exist', and nothing else whatever.* (P. 117; my emphasis.)

Let us ponder Moore's observation. The assertive use of

(M.1)　Tame tigers growl

invites the request for elucidation of the sense meant. Suppose, then, that the statement (or proposition) declared is more perspicuously put:

(M.1a)　Some tame tigers growl.

Then we can ask: "Only some, or all?" This disjunctive question is left open by the statement (M.1a), and an informative answer may very well be:

(M.lb)　Just some tame tigers growl — the others don't.

Moore tells us that in the case of:

(M.2)　Tame tigers exist

the situation is different. It is pointless to ask: "Only some, or all?" In this case the second disjunct is ruled out by the semantics of existence. Hence, in the case of (M.2) we have no choice, but must travel the route which we *chose* for the case of (M.1), namely:

(M.2a)　Some tame tigers exist.

(M.2b)　Just some tame tigers exist — the others don't.

This is very straightforward. Affirmation of existence of the general type, by means of the particular, so-called existential quantifier, sits on top of the assumption of a general domain of discourse from which the existing objects under consideration are separated. This goes hand in hand with the picture of singular existential statements furnished by example (15) above: to deny the existence of an object is, not merely to fail to find some properties instantiated in the domain of existents, but to place the object outside the domain of existents.

The alternative thrown out by virtue of semantic considerations must be necessarily false. Thus, by Moore's datum the semantics of existence excludes the interpretation of (M.2) as:

(M.2c)　All tame tigers exist.

Therefore, it is necessarily false that all tame tigers exist. There must be some tigers that we can on formal considerations alone say that they do not exist, indeed, that they cannot exist. Any example? This is really easy and clear. Recall Meinong's contradictory objects. All contradictory tigers must fail of existence. For instance, the growling but not growling tame tiger must logically fail to exist.

On the other hand, the proposition (M.2) "(Some) tame tigers exist" is contingent and known to be true *a posteriori*. Its negation is also contingent and *a posteriori,* namely:

(M.4)　It not the case that some tame tigers exist.

If we interpet this as a sorted quantification, the sorted quantifier being *some tame tigers,* then (M.4) is of the form:

(M.4a)　not [(some tame tigers) exist].

We have the principle of double negation and the one below establishing an equivalence between sorted quantifiers:

(QN) *All ... are F* is equivalent to *Not [Some ...) are not F]*.

Hence, (M.4a) is equivalent to:

(M.4b)   All tame tigers are not existing.

Patently, given that the domain of existents is a sub-domain of the thinkables, that the property being a tame tiger is consistent, (M.4b) should be contingent. Necessarily some tame tigers fail to exist, but it is contingently true or false whether *all* tame tame tigers fail to exist.

Hence, underlying our existential use of the particular quantifier expressions "some," "any," "there exists," "there is," etc. is, not only a presupposed domain of thinkables within which all existents lie, but also the undergirding presupposition that *non-existents are, even if only tacitly acknowledged, necessary members of the domain of discourse.*

IX. Perceptual Reference, Thinking Semantics, Doxastic Referents, and Existence as a Form of Predication

In the preceding chapters we discussed reference to non-existents in ordinary non-perceptual contexts. But perceptual experience is a locus of non-existence. Not only are all our perceptions surrounded by illusion, but sometimes we even hallucinate. Here is a Pandora's box of problems, *all of which must be taken up and given a solution in any worthy,* comprehensive theory of reference. But we will steer very carefully not to deviate from our topic: the nature of reference and the nature of the underlying semantics of reference. The task for us here is to disentangle the different strands of reference in perceptual judgments. In perception we are caused to consider information which purports to come from the external world, and we react to it both by thinking and by believing. Because what we perceptually think rests on a huge doxastic pedestal, perception provides a natural screen for separating doxastic from thinking reference.

In perception we confront a portion of reality and typically we confront it as an arrangement of particulars *qua* particulars. To perceive is to make singular reference. Furthermore, to perceive is to make singular references to items *presented* as parts of a whole and unified perceptual field. That presentedness is the nuclear element in the meaning of demonstratives[13]. Since that presentedness is crucial for our confronting the world in realistic or contemplative experience, here we can have a glimpse of the irreducibility to believing of the sensuous core of perception, the irreducibility of singular reference to general reference, and the irreducibility of demonstrative reference to singular or general third-person non-presentational reference. Though tempting, we just cannot go into these issues here[14].

Let us turn to *perceptual demonstratives*. Often these appear in communicational utterances of indexical sentences. By focusing on communication contexts, the usual approach to the problems of reference seems initially to adopt a hearer's point of view. This permits setting aside the subjective aspects of the speaker's indexical references — as well as the hearer's — by quickly moving our attention to the shared public, intersubjective topic. This is a quiet move away from strict semantico-pragmatic reference to doxastic reference and, worse, to doxastic semantics, the coarse semantics of the massive objects of the real world. That doxastic semantics has sometimes fostered an existential view of reference: that all reference is to existents. We must, therefore, subject that initial posing of the problem of demonstrative reference to some exegesis.

To begin with, even in dialogue the first-person thinking point of view is fundamental: a dialogue is nothing but a gappy sequence of alternations of the required first-person thinking point of view. The gaps are filled in by processes that cause the ensuing alternations. Patently, language must be *spoken*. Even when it is heard, it must have been spoken before; and then it has to be interpreted: a speaker has to make sense of what he or she hears. The larger semantics of the communicated message presupposes the thinking semantics of the thought of content. In any case, let us comply with the requisite second-person initial setting. Consider the following four-prong story.

(P*) *The Drowning Man in the Quarry Adventure.*

Hiking near some quarries I hear, or it seems to me as if I hear, repeatedly the noises "I am drowning." The hearer's point of view is fully applicable. The semantical rules of the first-person pronoun "I" tell me that each use of "I" denotes its user. Upon hearing the quoted sentence I proceed to search for the source of the noise. After some turning and twisting I come to what I take to be a large hole on the ground full of water, surrounded by a thick mist; I see something like a man that looks to me as if he were drowning.

Against this background we must distinguish several cases of thinking and reference. For our philosophical convenience let us make the subsidiary assumption that my thinking is irremediably out loud.

Case (A). I exclaim, thinking out loud, pointing to the vague silhouette behind the mist, expressing my perceptual judgment:

(1) THAT *is* a man drowning!

In this case there is in fact (out there in the world) a man drowning, and I am pointing to him.

Case (B). I have exactly the same perceptual experience as in Case (A), and declare out loud the self-identical perceptual judgment, i.e., judged content:

(1) THAT *is* a man drowning!

But, unknown to me and unthought of by me, this time there is no existing drowning man (out there in the world); I am hallucinating.

Case (C). I have exactly the same perceptual field as in Case (A), but I am suspicious about the veridicality of my perceptions. It is of no consequence whether my suspicions are well grounded or not. The point is that my perceptual judgment is a *sceptical* one:

(2) THAT *appears to be [looks like]* a man drowning.

As in Case (A), THAT man exists. The world beyond contains, unbeknownst to me, a real man suffering a real drowning.

Case (D). As in all preceding cases my perceptual field is the same, but my total current, sensual and doxastic experience is the same as in Case (C). Thus, I once again cry out my perceptual skeptical judgment:

(2) THAT *appears to be [looks like]* a man drowning.

This time, however, as in Case (B) there exists no such man, but unlike Case (B) this time I am not taken in by the appearances.

Let us reflect on the semantic aspects of the differing situations. To begin with, the indicator "THAT" has *exactly* the same meaning in all four types of assertion with sentences (1) and (2). The *thinking referent* of "THAT" is in each case an internal perceptual content presented to the speaker in his visual field. Of course, beyond "THAT" lies the rest of sentences (1) and (2). Clearly, although these sentences differ radically in the type of judgment they express, they show that in all four cases the thinker makes a *claim* about the physical world: affirmative in Cases (A) and (B), sceptic in Cases (C) and (D). In all four cases the thinker-speaker is concerned with an external target of his thinking. In cases (A) and (C) such an external target exists; in cases (B) and (D) it doesn't. That external target functions, however, as *the* target of his whole thinking episode only in Cases (A) and (B); in Cases (C) and (D) the thinker is deliberately and conscientiously *not* aiming at it. The external, physical, massive target is, thus, not only not what the use of demonstrative "THAT" harpoons, semantically or otherwise; it is, besides, what the perceptual judgment may or may not aim at, regardless of its existence. The external target is, not the thinking referent of the perceptual judgment, but the subject-matter of the perceiver's *claim:* the external physical object is, if you wish, a *doxastic referent.*

It is of the utmost importance that the doxastic referent of the perceptual judgment as a whole not be expressed in the subject of the judgment, or even in the strict predicate of the judgment. The allusion to the doxastic referent is carried forth by the copula *is* in perceptual judgment (1) and *appears to be* or *looks like* in judgment (2). And only the former, the existential copula *is* of (1), represents the speaker's doxastic commitment to there existing a real drowning man. Apparently, then, doxastic reference is not so much a matter of reference, but a matter of judgment, and as such its habitat is a *form of predication.*

To sum up, individuals, whether existing or not, are the objects of reference; the finite, presentable ones are objects of singular reference; classes of them, especially indefinite or infinite classes of them, are the objectives of general reference. Existence is, it seems, thinkable primarily as a form of predication, a way in which individuals can have properties; therefore, its chief expression is a copula — through verbal inflections. Let us call the form of predication that depicts existence *existential predication.*

Consequently, there is a sense in which Russell's Robust Sense of Reality is correct. There is, then, a sense of having properties in which only existents can have properties. Then, we must, on the one hand, reject the Russellian equation (see p. 44 above):

(R.RSR.O) To be thinkable is tantamount to be existing.

On the other hand, we must give him *nearly* full credit for the following equations encompassed in (R.RSR), understood, of course, in a restricted way, thus:

(R.RSR.1*) To be the subject of existential predication is tantamount to existing.

(R.RSR.2*) To be existentially self-identical is tantamount to existing.

In all four cases the speaker expresses a thought content that commands his assent. It lies *internally* within his perceptual field, and he takes it to be *true or false.* He puts it forth non-committally in sentence (2); he formulates it endorsingly in sentence (1), as something he believes. This has some most important philosophical morals we cannot dwell upon here.

X. Universal Quantification Over Existents Alludes to Non-existents: It is Default Quantification

Quantification over non-existent objects seems here to stay. Moreover, as observed above, we need quantification over both existents and non-existents. We have exegesized Moore's datum and seen how the particular quantifier over existents presupposes quantification over a larger domain that includes non-existents. Against Moore's datum we have what I will call, perhaps anachronistically:

> (R.D) *Russellian Datum.* Ordinary universal quantification seems to be a *default* existence quantification, ranging over existents.

This datum is surely behind the Quinean doctrine that quantification is the fundamental mechanism of reference and that all reference is to existents. Consider, for instance, the following sentence:

> (QU.1) All men in the big corral like milk.

When in normal life we use (QU.1) to make a most natural statement, we do seem to be thinking *only* of existing women and men, an existing corral, and existing persons who like milk. In that use (QU.1) should be equivalent to the following, where the italicized words should feel utterly *redundant:*

> (AU.1a) All *existing* men in the big corral are *existing* persons who like milk.

Indeed, the attribution of existence in (QU.1a) does seem redundant. This conforms to datum (R.D). Yet (QU.1) has a slit through which the possibilities can be seen at varying distances. Obviously, (QU.1) allows of an ambiguity concerning milk. In normal speech situations probably (QU.1) is intended to refer to real milk. However, because liking is a psychological state it must be open to possibles: a person may like something that does not exist. Here we see again how *our human condition consists in possessing powers to transact with non-existents.* The reference to milk here is as a mass, but masses can be parceled out into chunks or pieces, which are individuals. Thus the reference to massive non-existing milk signals quantification over non-existents. Of course, the example could have instead referred to the men in the big corral liking to hunt zarmadillos, a mythical species of delicious armadillos sung in the folktales of Southern Arizona.

Let us consider another example:

> (QU.2) All women are mammal.

Again, as typically used this sentence speaks only of existents. Hence, it should also comply with the redundancy datum:

> (QU.2a) All *existing* women are *existing* mammals.

Here we have a weak feeling that the sense of (QU.2) is not exhausted by the sense of (QU.2a). The proposal that they are equivalent invites the rejoinder:

(QU.2b) Well, even non-existing women are mammals.

What happens is at least superficially clear. Even though we typically speak of existing women, (QU.2) is necessarily true and hence overruns reality, and this can be put by saying that it is true also of non-existing women. Thus, underneath the skin of (QU.2) lies a modal statement. *Modal statements, like psychological ones, openly demand quantification over non-existents.* Possible-world semanticians will correct the above formulation, but not the point: they will say that we would implicitly refer to possible worlds in which the objects not existing in our world exist there. This is fine for our purpose here: existence in other merely possible worlds merely collects and orders the non-existents.

Patently, we must develop an account of objecthood that assigns to non-existing objects their proper place in the scheme of thinkables.

XI. Universal Quantification Over Existents Stands On A Contrast Between Existential and Non-Existential Predication

Let us return to (QU.1a) and (QU.2a). The redundancy datum they make explicit is impressive. If one disregards psychological states and logical modalities, one can feel that the redundancy datum shows that in basic factual discourse one just quantifies over existents. (That's why Quine has been set against modal logic, and is somewhat annoyed by psychological modalities[15].)

But why disregard? Here are important methodological issues. Nevertheless, we cannot digress to tackle them. There is one crucial issue, however, that must be mentioned, especially when we are discussing the logical structure of language. Mathematical logicians do wonderful things with their formal systems. For instance, they prove completeness theorems, which establish isomorphisms between formal systems. Typically such theorems have an enormous value: in the study of a formal system one can use those isomorphisms as external detours to construct internal theorems. Now, those completeness theorems hinge on certain assumptions of closure, particularly, that the well-formed formulas of the system under study are all of certain types *and not of other types.* These closure principles, which are great for mathematical logic, are poison for philosophical logic and general semantics. The fundamental truth about language is that because it is the axis around which experience revolves, and each experience is always subsumable under a more comprehensive experience, fragments or types of language are *not* closed. In general the tremendous deductive value of completeness theorems does not carry along a matching semantico-philosophical value.

The closure principles for well-formed sentencehood are the first ones to be jettisoned when we progress in our study of comprehensive structures. Here we are precisely engaged in such a comprehensive study: we are not setting limits to ordinary reference to the objects in our environment: we are subsuming that kind of reference under larger experiences in which reference to existents can show fully what it is[16].

Philosophical logicians who see quantification as a part of a language that has non-denoting terms are doing the right thing. Because the attribution of existence is redundant, especially for the case of (QU.1), many philosophical logicians have pressed their insight into a modification of the rule of universal instantiation by adding an existence condition, thus:

(Ex.Un.Ins) 1. All A's are B's.
2. *a* is A.
3. *a* exists.
Therefore, *a* is B[17].

The addition of premise 3 to the regular rule (Un.Ins) is a definite improvement. (Ex.Un.Ins) brings out into the open the presupposition mentioned above (pp. 43) that the possession of the property of being a great philosophical theologian by Alvin Plantinga, that of being a tall brilliant philosopher by Tyler Burge, that of originating in Guatemala by the Usumacinta River, etc. in the *way* they possess these properties implies that they exist.

Nevertheless, something paramount is missing in (Ex.Un.Ins). Since it is the *way* in which existents have those properties that requires that they exist, what we need is a much stronger premise that analyzes further that relevant way of having properties. To make this sharper consider the following background to an application of (Un.Ins) involving (QU.1), which we have stipulated to have full existential import:

(B.QU.1) *Background for (QU.1)*:

We are considering a range of corrals. The big corral is the main milk corral where our best milkcows are in exhibition. There are in it two huge statues: one man and one woman: they are perfect likenesses of the founders of the multi-million dollar corporation, and represent a catalogue of financial values which we do not care to enumerate. The fact of language use is that we all refer to these statues as *the big man* and *the big woman* who protect the corral and its contents. In short, we have the following true statements as far as our relevant experiences go:

1. (QU.1): All men in the big corral like milk.
2. The larger statue in the big corral is a man, obviously, in the big corral.
3. The larger statue in the big corral exists.

Patently, it would be a mistake to infer that the larger statue in the big corral likes milk. Existence is *not* the problem. The trouble lies in that the larger statue in the big corral is a man, but not in the relevant existential sense we need. Here we are confronting *two* forms of predication, and only one is relevant to the existential interpretation of (QU.1). This duality of forms of predication is palpably brought forth by the way the predicational premise 2 is formulated: we do not say, instead:

2'. The larger statue in the big corral is a man in the big corral.

We need a wider understanding of (Un.Ins) as follows:

(G.Un.Ins) 1. All things that are-existentially A are-existentially B.

2. *a* is-existentially A.

Hence, *a* is-existentially B.

(Ex.Un.ins) misses the predicational location of the problem of the existential interpretations of (Un.Ins), and also loses the simplicity of the syllogism, which requires just two premises. Here we find full satisfaction for the Russellian datum (R.D.). Furthermore, we find here an impressive connection with our discussion of perception in Ch. VIII. The distinction of forms of predication is gaining support and by gathering different problems under it it sheds light on the structure of our thinking of reality.

XII. Contextual Quantification

We do not have much room for a discussion of the semantics of quantifier expressions. But one additional remark is opportune. We have seen how the quantifier expressions apply to different sortal nouns to form sorted quantifier expressions. Sometimes it is the context of speech and thought that intervenes to specify a domain of quantification. This was the case with the larger domain of existents we took for granted in the case of (QU.1) and (QU.2).

Apparently, then, the general meanings of quantifier expressions, i.e. the meanings they have as part of the language system, shared by those who speak the language, are *neutral* with respect to existence. It is the pragmatic constraints, i.e. the varying implicit assumptions about their use in different types of speech contexts, that limits the domains of quantification to existents, or to both existents and non-existents, or to selected sets of them. Thus, the semantics of the quantifier words "all," "every," "some," "nothing," "no one," etc., assigns to each of them an undetermined *contextual slot* for the specification of the relevant domain of quantification in each context of speech. Then there is the pragmatic principle that the *default domains of quantification,* the domains with which we automatically fill in the contextual slots of the quantifiers we use, are domains of existents.

The contextual slot in the meaning of each quantifier expression is not, of course, a variable of quantification. Nor is it like a demonstrative pronoun or adverb that in the speech act receives a particular thought of referent. It is like a hook with which we seize domains of values for the quantifiers in the context of speech. Those domains need not be thought of explicitly. The hooking is *doxastic:* it is the setting in readiness our propensity to tap a reservoir of individuals representations of some of which are stored in the memory banks of the thinker-speaker. Here we can see how indexicality (characteristic of demonstratives) is different from contextuality.

XIII. Quantification Over Non-Existents Within Fiction

Quantification in special contexts is perplexing. Perhaps as the principle (EROTICS) above hints, everything we say belongs within a special context, or a special language game — if you like. Within special contexts, fictional contexts occupy a most distinguished place. After all we have enjoyed and will continue to need the enjoyment of fiction to maintain our sanity. Of course, we must reckon with the obvious fact that there is a very large number of professionals and merchants of fiction. Academic experts on literature are actually only a minority within the vast multitude of fiction-dealers. (We leave out the politicians and the advertisers of products or services.)

The most perplexing view about quantification is the *diffusive* version of Free-Logic, which interprets every quantifier as ranging over the domain of existents, regardless of the context in which the quantifier occurs. The perplexity is of great magnitude, because quantifiers do in fact occur in fiction and often they seem to have non-existents in their domains. Just consider "All the brothers of Ivan Karamasov" and "All the maids tending to Don Quijote's needs while he was the Duke's guest." The diffusive view will have: either (i) to deny that such quantifiers are what they, from every corner one considers them, appear to be, or (ii) to hold against all other appearances that such quantifiers have existing objects as values. Either alternative seems to distort the character and nature of our experiences involving fiction.

There is the less radical view that all quantifiers in pieces of fiction belong fully in the scope of fiction operators, like "According to the relevant myth" or "According to Cervantes' *Don Quijote* (*Part I*)." These quantifiers are, thus, sealed off from direct speech and, therefore, involve no commitment to the existence of such fictional characters as are mentioned in the sentences containing them. Yet we must still ask: "But what are the values of such quantifiers?" A reasonable answer is that those quantifiers range over the possible objects fostered by the piece of fiction in question. Then a semantics of possible worlds may be promoted for the possible worlds determined by the narrative. This is fine. But then we are in fact condoning quantification over non-existents, even if within sealing-off literary operators.

Notwithstanding, we cannot be happy with the simple view that quantifiers within fiction are so sealed off that the fictional entities they posit are also all sealed off from reality. This sealing off might be taken by a hard-nosed quantificational existentialist to argue that quantification within fiction deals with the same existents of factual quantification. This view would be interesting if fiction and fact were neatly compartmentalized with nothing being shared between them. Fortunately for the richness of our experience, many quantifiers within fiction also apply to existents. Some of the non-existing individuals may also be self-contradictory, like Meinong's existing round square. Mixed quantification is bound to appear in historical novels, fables, satires, and pedagogical stories. Such quantifiers present obdurate difficulties for a purely existential view of quantification. If, on the other hand, the quantifiers are allowed to range just over non-existing objects, then they are not semantically uniform. We need, therefore, at least a carefully worked out theory of fictional quantification, and one that can illuminate the mixed cases in which fiction and reality intermix. Let us discuss a bit further the mixture of fiction and reality.

XIV. Fiction And Reality Require Not Different Individuals, Not Different Properties, But Different Forms of Predication

Evidently, the same language with the very same meanings appear in literature as in descriptions of daily life. The literary discourses are segregated from ordinary descriptive or scientific discourses. Typically the word "Novel," or the phrase "Short Stories," or some other expression appears at the beginning of a book. And there are other devices to both segregate and announce a piece of fiction, e.g., "Once upon a time," "Did I tell you the story (joke) ..."

But we want to theorize about the harder, more significant data. The fact is that typically a story assumes a large amount of empirical truth about the world in which we carry on our normal pursuits. The outer border consists of our capacity to understand behavior in terms related to our own behavior which occurs within our psychological make-up. A lot about human nature is tacitly presupposed by our literary experience. This provides an implicit background from which empirical truths are brought in for literary effect to be mixed with the genuinely fictional truths created by the writer.

There are diverse quantities of explicit truths about existents intermixed in pieces of fiction. These truths, understood as such, are fundamental for the unity and purpose of many a literary work. A satire, for instance, disintegrates if the alleged truths it is ridiculing are not posited as truths, or possible truths. Consider, for illustration, a statement like the following, which we presume to be part of a novel about the late President Kennedy depicting his courage and generosity in the fact of an invented meeting with Fidel Castro, at which the two leaders openly and with total frankness discussed the international problems affecting the relations of the United States with Latin America:

> (L) Kennedy had been staying at the White House the entire week. He had been enjoying a few-days vacation in the midst of his most intimate family. And ... THEN he received Fidel Castro in secret. He shook hands with him, looking at him intently with sympathetic openness, even a wisp of admiration. ...

The construction is this: all the statements in the first part down to "THEN" are factually true; the ensuing statements are fictional. It is of the essence of the novelesque account of the events treated that the historical context, partly captured by the factual conjunct of (L), be wholly accurate: they belong to the most accurate biography of President Kennedy. On the other hand, the fictional part is not empirically true, yet even it is meant to depict a possibility conceived by the author; it is of no consequence that the possibility be for the worse or for the better for the United States, or for Latin America, or for the world.

In (L) we have conjunctions of the form:

(L.1) Kennedy was F and did A,

where the first conjunct is meant to be factually true and the second is a fictional truth proposed by the novel.

In attempting to provide an account for the differences and connections between literary and factual language we have these main theoretical alternatives, among other more contrived approaches:

> A) Fictional statements are confined within literary or mythical operators;
>
> B) Fictional statements differ from factual statements by being about different entities: Fictional vs. actual individuals;

C) Fictional statements differ from factual ones by their predicates;

D) Fictional statements differ from factual ones in their form of predication.

Obviously, there is an important truth in A). Yet to propose that the difference between literary and factual language consists simply of the fact that the whole of the narrative is insulated from reality by a literary operator, say, "In the novel Such and Such" is to run against the grain of experience. There are literary operators; but they do not help us understand the duality of fictional statements of the form (L.1).

Approach B) will force us to distinguish the Kennedy in the novel from the Kennedy in real life. Since the two are connected, the theory has a nice problem to deal with. Furthermore, if the Kennedy in the novel is not the same as the one in reality, we must make sure that real truths are properly mapped into fictional truths. This approach should be developed[18].

Approach C) postulates an ambiguity in predicates like the schematic "is F," which appear both in the novel and in the history that grounds the novel. The problem of literary semantics becomes more pressing, and the fact/fiction duality within fiction becomes a serious research topic.

Approach D), even though it seems recondite to our standard fashions of philosophising, has several virtues. To begin with, it allows that real persons and objects appear in fiction: the univocity of both reference and meaning of singular terms is maintained. Secondly, the univocity of predicates and logical machinery is preserved; that is, all predicate and abstract vocabulary has the standard ambiguities of ordinary factual language, and no more: there is no special fictional ambiguity in predicates. Thirdly, the factual truths also appear, so to speak, in person in fiction, exactly as they appear in history. Fourthly, the intimate connection that satires, fables, historical novels, etc., have with facts is highlighted: those facts can appear in the satires, fables, and historical novels themselves.

In brief, the *Two-Types of Predication View,* one type of predication for alleged factual truths, and another for fictional statements, seems to be the most promising approach to the connections between fiction and reality and the total unity of experience. We could call factual predication *consubstantiation,* to signal that the real entities are substances; we could in general call the fictional predication *consociation* and then introduce indices signalling the works in which those predications were created, or indices pointing to the creating authors.

What are the subjects of literary predication?

Response: All the thinkable possible objects. Literary creativity has no other limit than the creator's powers to think.

The preceding is a very fast discussion of the syntax, the semantics, and the ontology of literature and other fiction. Elsewhere I have presented additional data on the underlying unity of fiction and reality and of the special semantic and logical problems created by the mixture of fact and fiction in one work of art[19].

The distinction in forms of predication arrived at here to account for the mixture in fiction of real truths and fictive truths raises one question: How is this distinction related to the one uncovered in IX in the context of perception? We cannot go into this here, but perhaps a simple remark about Guise Theory may not be amiss. Guise Theory at present includes the thesis that fictional predication is a co-species of the form of non-existential predication distinguished in IX-XI. Both are subsumed under the label *Consociation*.

XV. The Culturization of Literary, Mythical, All Theological Personages

As explained elsewhere (note 19), we must reckon with the fact that many a fictional character refuses to stay within the confines of the story — hence, in the scope of the corresponding story operator — in which it was created. For instance, Don Quijote very early migrated from its original birth-home *El Ingenioso Hidalgo Don Quijote de La Mancha* (1605), which was the aging Miguel de Cervantes' first literary success. During Cervantes' own life time Alonso Fernandez de Avellaneda (allegedly a pseudonym) published in 1614 a continuation of the adventures of Don Quijote. Cervantes was flabbergasted and became very angry, but had time to include some sharp mockery of the codicious imitator in his own Second Part, published in 1615. Don Quijote and Sancho are very much transformed, for the worse in the apocryphal narrative, for the better in the authoritative *Segunda Parte del Ingenioso Caballero Don Quijote de la Mancha*. Since then Don Quijote has had a very lustrous career. He has visited other artistic media, and has matured and enriched his personality. Don Quijote is not just imprisoned in Cervantes' original novel about the *hidalgo* of La Mancha. Literary critics and exegetes write about him as if he belonged to the world at large. He is an institution.

Similarly diversified and rich histories have been woven around the great literary heroes and heroines. Oedipus, Medea, Dido, Hamlet, Lady Macbeth, Faust, Nora, Anna Karenina, Madame Bovary, and their colleagues belong to our culture at large, no longer prisoners but honored visitors in the original stories in which they came into literary existence. They have somehow become our friends or our enemies, our guides or our anti-models. We find inspiration in them, they

excite our emotions and our judgment. Some of them are in a sense no less important to us than the real persons we encounter anonymously and opaquely in our
daily social interactions.

Influential literary or mythical personages are like institutions. On Jeremy
Bentham's expression, institutions are legal fictions. These are important
precisely because they are fictions we take into account; their legality consists of
the nature of their influence upon us. To be sure, institutions exert their power
through other individuals; and thus in our normal transactions with them they
exhibit their quasi-reality: their social reality. On the other hand, literary or legen-
dary figures exert their influence directly through the persons who treat them with
the appropriate attitude of respect, or hatred, for that matter. Thus, they exhibit a
psychological quasi-reality.

At this juncture it may be useful to recall Anatole France's wonderful story
Putois. Putois was invented by a woman who didn't want to visit a stuffy relation
of her husband's. She begged to be excused on the grounds that she had made an
appointment with Putois, who would do some special work on her garden. Putois
became more and more useful with the passing of time. Other members of the
community began to have dealings with him. The plot thickens to the point where
the inventor of Putois had an experience that she could not describe otherwise
than the effective presence of Putois in her house. The moral of the story is, in
France's own words:

> ... it is not the real beings, but rather the imaginary ones that exercise
> the most profound and the most durable influence ...[20]

This is an exaggeration. The fundamental and trivial point is that the influence
that a person, whether real or imaginary or fictional, exerts upon us in the sense
that we intentionally react to it, is an influence that proceeds from our internal
conception of the person.

A related point is this. It is only a contingent matter that certain literary
figures become our friends even companions. In principle all literary characters
can transcend their literary jurisdiction of origin.

Consequently, many statements about a fictional character belong, not to this
or that story, but to the natural language in which we compare stories and the
characters are treated as personages that move from story to story, from art
medium to art medium, maintaining a core of identity. Obviously, there is a very
complicated system of networks of anaphora — built patiently along the centuries
by a multitude of readers, critics, imitators, and admiring artists of different
types   —, which maintains the thematic unity of all the discourses about such

fictional characters.

To say that there is such a multi-personal anaphoric structure underlying all literary criticism is simply to point out the datum that needs philosophical elucidation. To elucidate this datum and the nature of literary discourse we need a theory of literary reference embedded within the large theory of reference in general; and we need this general theory with its embedded department of literary reference in order to make sure that the theory of reference to existents gains its proper depth and perspective.

More widespread and more deeply-seated and more comprehensive is the network of dispositions to act on thoughts involving theological non-existents. We know quite well how important to other persons are their religious beliefs in non-existing gods, demi-gods, prophets, saints (like Saint Christopher), guiding spirits, transcendental principles, and their likes. It is only he who lacks any faith whatsoever who can pretend to be indifferent to the vital and cultural significance of our favorite non-existents.

XVI. Quantification Over Fictional Individuals Without Fiction

The view that quantification in direct speech is only over real objects faces a special hurdle in connection with fiction. Reality and fiction are not two isolated realms of discourse. In preceding sections we have noted how quantifiers within fiction seem to range over both existents and non-existents. The story (N.1) in VII, about the bankrupt builders of Academic Paradise, has shown how outside fiction and myth, in the pursuit of our plans, we need singular reference to non-fictional non-existents (the unbuilt houses), as well as general reference to sets of non-fictional individuals some of which exist (the few houses that were built) and most of which do not exist. Analogously, outside fiction and myth we must sometimes pay attention to the relations between reality and fiction. On such occasions we need quantification in direct speech, ostensibly within the perspective of the real, that has either fictional individuals as values, or has a mixture of fictional characters and historical figures among their values. Let us consider some very general cases.

    Tomberlin's Example[21]:

        (NE.2) Every wholly mythological character is admired by both Alvin
              and Peter.

Clearly, (NE.2) is not a statement within any piece of fiction. No applicable operator of the form "According to the myth ..." has that sentence in its scope. Alvin and Peter are not mythical characters — yet. (NE.2) is a statement made from the perspective of our basic experience of the world, and we seem to be quantifying, very liberally, over all possible objects of discourse, maintaining our neutrality with respect to existence. Recall that, as our above discussion of Meinong's Round Square established, being a possible object of discourse or thought does *not* logically imply being a logically possible object.

Free Logic has no problems with the singular terms that Alvin and Peter, but Tomberlin too, are ready to use to instantiate (NE.2). Free Logic allows them the meaningfulness of the following singular sentence:

(S.1) If Hercules is a wholly mythological character, then Hercules is admired by both Alvin and Peter.

Free Logic does not, however, allow that (S.1) be an instantiation of (NE.2). It holds that (NE.2) does not logically imply (S.1). Presumably we could speak as follows:

(NE.3) Hercules, Zeus, ... are all the wholly mythological characters in Greek mythology.

Presumably also, (NE.3) is a statement within the operator "In Greek mythology." But we could not infer from (NE.2) and (NE.3) that:

(S.2) Alvin admires Zeus.

On Free Logic we could infer only that:

(S.3) If Hercules *exists* and is a wholly mythological character then Alvin admires him.

This seems a very harsh stipulation. Clearly, Hercules' existence may be wholly irrelevant to Alvin's admiration. In fact his admiration may be grounded precisely on Hercules being a non-existing object, e.g., in being capable of serving as an ideal of the highest combination of loyalty and physical strength. Thus, in normal experience, in which (NE.2) and (NE.3) together do imply (S.2), we can convey a good deal of information about Alvin (similarly about Peter) very succinctly. This is not a trivial matter. Given the finite capacity of our minds we *need biologically* to store information in the most compact ways so that by the use of logical rules — especially possessed as habits of thinking or propensities to think, built into our hardware as the practitioners of Artificial Intelligence may put it — we can derive and use implied pieces of information that we need *not* store by themselves.

Logical implications are vital. Here we have the beginnings of a transcendental argument for the need by finite minds of a full logic — let alone quantification — of non-existing entities. We have seen how crucial non-existents are for our lives. Obviously, the more interconnected the non-existents are to each other and to the existents, the more useful they are in playing their crucial roles in our lives. We must, therefore, for our own sakes, place them alongside the existents with equal rights as members of the total domain of discourse. Consigning them to a glorious isolation of a separate and unequal singular reference, as Free Logic does, is both to cut off very drastically their usefulness and, as a consequence, to emasculate our own powers of enjoying a rich biography.

Michael McKinsey's Example[22]:

In a high-school class a teacher has been discussing several individuals. And then he makes the following statement by way of introducing the topic of the connections between fiction and reality:

(NE.4)   We have studied three Arthurs. Two of them are real, but one is fictional. The fictional one is King Arthur, the chief Knight of the Round Table.

This is also a statement made from the ordinary perspective of the world, in which we lump together real and non-real individuals, treating the real ones as constituting a proper sub-domain of the large domain of individuals in our discourse. As remarked above, in VIII-XI, a search to determine which individuals exist or not requires that we think of both the existing and the non-existing as lying in precisely in the same boat — with the same status in our discourse.

Obviously, statements about fictional characters may be made outside the context of stories about them. These statements can be quantified. Fictional characters can be counted, classified, and compared with real persons. Comparative literature is the result of the attempt to create a professional discipline with such activities.

Evidently, the quantification involved in counting non-existents, or mixed domains of existents and non-existents presupposes that in order to have properties it is not necessary to exist. We are dealing with the notion of object close to Meinong's and definitely non-Russellian.

XVII. What is a Non-Existent Object After All? What is an Object? A Glimpse Beyond: Forms of Predication and Guise Theory

The debate about possible objects
Recently an energetic many-sided polemics has erupted in the professional journals concerning the status of merely possible objects. With the development (in the 1950's due to Saul Kripke, Richard Montague, and Jaakko Hintikka) of so-called possible world semantics, possible objects have multiplied, and there are also possible worlds to deal with. Some philosophers are content with all possibles. David Lewis, for instance, has been celebrated as well as chastized for his candid commitment to all possible worlds. He has said that actuality[23] is merely our belonging to our world. This is too much Platonism for many philosophers.

Some philosophers, possessing a Russellian robust sense of reality, find the talk of possibles obscene. Some wish that all talk of possibles and modal concepts which involve possibles should be banished altogether. Others hold that talk of possibles and possible worlds is merely a way of talking about the actuals. Some, spiritual descendants of the nominalists, recommend meta-linguistic analyses in order to reduce all talk and thought to actuals, including among actuals words and their uses. And so on.

I am anxious not to enter that dispute. As I see it, actuality is the overall property of the actual world, and existence is what individuals in the actual world have. But in my old-fashioned metaphysics existence is irreducible and the concept of existence is a most primitive and fundamental one. Truth is a generalization of actuality, for many propositions are true even though they say nothing about actuality. No harm need result from saying that *reality* in its most general sense is the totality of truths. There are less comprehensive senses of "reality" including the totality of all contingent truths about the actual individuals, and the totality of all existing individuals themselves. Hence, I have adopted as fundamental the categories of individual, property, predication, operators of different types, and proposition, which is the truth-valued unit of thinkable content[24]. Hence I have all along held that possible worlds are nothing but sets of propositions governed by certain closure principles, a notably interesting case being that of maximally consistent sets of propositions. Of course, set-theoretical modellings are just *that:* modellings, useful for establishing methods for testing for implication, but not ontological accounts of the fundamental concepts of individual, property, etc. (See note 16.)

Thinkable individuals vs. Russellian individuals

Within that categorial framework we ask: What is an individual? This question is nowadays seldom asked. For the most part philosophers simply adopt the stand that individuals are subjects of predication, especially the subjects of the lowest type. This is of course not intelligible by itself if an understanding of the hierarchy of types of entities and of predication is missing. Thus, in the last analysis the notion of individual turns out to be primitive and unanalyzable. The content of the notion is provided by our experience of examples. This is crucial in our learning our ontological vocabulary. The examples of individuals we start dealing with are actual, existent individuals. Hence, the working notion of object or individual that most philosophers have is essentially a Russellian mixture of at least the notions of individual and existence. Consequently, the concept of a non-existent object feels self-contradictory. At least it feels empty: it lacks the existential core of the examples in our learning history.

The situation is aggravated under certain pressures, e.g., from the identity of the subject of change, or the need to distinguish the subject of predication from its properties. These pressures may lead to the postulation of an underlying substrate. Of course, each substrate somehow packs the existence of an existing object. Then the notion of a non-existent object becomes very taxing.

Properties and thinkable individuals

Some philosophers, e.g., Alvin Plantinga, have proposed a property solution to the problem of non-existents. All the individuals there are exist. This is a basic axiom. But apparently we think and talk about non-existing individuals. Yet there are no such individuals. What happens then? The response is simple: In such cases we are thinking of sets of properties. A non-existing individual is equated with a set of properties.

That solution is in the right direction. But it is not satisfactory. It is certainly right in that, as we learned from Plato, the contents of thinking (and consciousness) are universals, i.e., properties and other abstracts. Furthermore, that proposal can account for our thinking of impossible objects.

But the equation of non-existents with sets of properties cannot be helpful unless we *also* equate existents with sets of properties. The key datum here is the one discussed abundantly above, namely: we can think of objects we want to construct or we anticipate finding in experience, and they turn out to be non-existent, even impossible; thus the content of our thinking is mixed: some objects exist and some don't, and this difference is *external* to what we have before consciousness and is *ex post facto* and perhaps *entirely beyond our ken*. The correct theory of thinking requires that the thought content as such be impervious to existence. Hence:

(Ind*.1) If non-existing objects are sets of properties, then all existing objects are sets of properties.

However, no object is a mere set of properties. We think of sets of properties without thinking of objects. Let us, for instance, consider the set of properties shared by Keith Lehrer and Jonathan Cohen. This set of properties is certainly not an individual we are thinking of. To be sure, we may go on and think of the non-existing individual that somehow is constituted by those properties. Likewise, we may think of the set of properties such that each one is exclusively possessed by just one member of the philosophy faculty of Oxford University in 1980 and is the first property through which one differentiates the philosopher in question from his colleagues. We are not thinking of that set of properties as an object instantiating those very properties, which may exist or not. In fact, in the sense in which sets are objects, that *set* may be said to exist; but we may even think that such a set is incapable of composing an *object*. Clearly, then:

(Ind*.2) Mere sets of properties are not the thinkable individuals to which we attribute properties or existence.

At the very least we must say that a thinkable individual, whether it exists or not, is a set of properties *conceived* in a certain way, perhaps, as being in principle, if the set is consistent, jointly exemplifiable. Thus, we can have a minimal psychologistic view of thinkable individuals: the individuality would consist in the way the set of properties is conceived *concerning exemplifiability*. Obviously, we will have to provide a recursive characterization extending individuality to inconsistent and logically valid sets of properties, say, as super-sets of individuated sets. In any case:

(Ind*.3) Thinkable individuals are at least sets of properties unifiedly *embellished* by being conceived as units, or super-units, of exemplification.

Let us use the symbol c to signal individuation, i.e., our attitude before a set of properties as a unit or super-unit of exemplification. Then a thinkable individual, whether existing or not, is of the form:

(Ind*.4) c P1, P2, ...

Since sets are somehow abstract individuals, our new individuals may be called *concrete individuals*. We shall refer to c as the concretizer operator.

The preceding introduction of the operator c is *a priori*. We have pretty much offered, in Kant's terminology, a transcendental deduction of it. We must find, therefore, a realization of that operator in natural language. This search for expressions of c in ordinary experience corresponds to Kant's metaphysical deductions.

A little reflection shows that the operator *c* is precisely what the definite article *the* in its singular uses expresses. That is why — as we have seen *ad nauseam* — *this article represents a singularity that* transcends existence: it presents to consciousness a unified uniquely demarcated unit of thinkable objectivity. Hence:

> (Ind*.5) The thinkable individual denoted by an English expression of the form *The F, G, and H* is representable as the individual *c* Fness, Gness, Hness .

Evidently, being conceived is an item for rational cognitive psychology to deal with, but joint exemplifiability is an ontological aspect of a set of properties composing a possible individual. Furthermore, the thinkability of the set is another of its ontological features. This requires that a set of properties be finite for us to think of it in person, running through all its members, as having the special function of purported unified joint exemplifiability. These ontological aspects provide the operator *c* with more than a pscyhologistic dimension.

Still there is an idealistic aura to the above characterization of concrete individuals. This is unavoidable when we are discussing the *contents* of thinking and believing. Internally, *de dicto* as is often said, all contents are alike, particularly in being, *qua* contents, indifferent to existence. Furthermore, existence is external to those contents. But here is only a *structural idealism:* the structure of the world is what we find it to be from inside our experience of it.

A thinkable concrete individual is, thus, a unique complex with the structure depicted in (Ind*.4) above, which has the ontological role of having properties and the logical role of being a subject of predication. This is the case, whether the individual exists or not. In any case, the thinkable individuals are very *thin objects:*

> (Ind*.6) Concrete objects, with the structure (Ind*.4), are objects of thought, whether they exist or not. But only if their core sets of properties are finite can they be objects of singular reference. We suppose that there are objects having as cores infinite sets of properties. Such objects must be collectively referred to through quantification.

The individuator *c* is of course a primitive concept. That is why the Russellian analysis (R.ADD) (P. 44 above) of the singular "the" is ultimately incorrect. We have partially explained the meaning of "c" by the role in thinking of special sets of properties. In part also the role of *c* is ontological: it carries a relation to exemplification.

But what is exemplification?

Substrates, Co-actuality, Existential predication

Undoubtedly, exemplification is the being there in the real world of the exemplified properties. Here the notion of *substrate* or *substance* intrudes: properties are exemplified when they somehow are inserted in a substrate. Now we find a tension. Substrates must be adequately parcelled out so that they can, on the one hand, accept properties and, on the other, be distinct from each other in the way objects are distinct. This problem of the unity and distinctness of substrates is often neglected. Yet it is a serious problem. Of course, nowadays few philosophers write on the basic ontological problems; the issues of individuation, predication, distinctness, and the like are not taken up.

The unification of the set properties considered for exemplification guarantees distinctness. That is precisely the whole point of considering the set of properties as a unified exemplifiable item. (This grounds Leibniz's principle that total indiscernibility implies identity.) At any rate, the differentiating role is supernumerary on substrates, but then exemplification cannot be inherence in a substrate specially demarcated. We can instead postulate a massive undifferentiated substrate, if we wish. Then exemplification would be inherence in that massive substrate. But what can a massive world-filling substrate be? What role would this ontological ether play? Only the role of assigning existence to exemplifications.

Why not discard that ethereal substrate and conceive of existence as a special, existential relation between thinkable individuals? Then we can drop the massive substance in which existents allegedly inhere, and adopt a relational view of substance, say:

> (Ind*.7) Substances are systems of (thinkable) individuals clustered together by a special relation of co-actuality.

The special relation of co-actuality through which individuals constitute substances may be called *consubstantiation*, to underscore our relational view of substance.

Reduction of existential predication to consubstantiation

Now one problem jumps into view: How does the existential predication we discovered before in VIII and IX relate to this consubstantiation? The answer I like is: identity. The schema supporting this answer is this:

> (C*.Pred) A proposition expressed by a sentence of the form *The F is-existentially G* is the same as the one expressed by the corresponding sentences of the form: *The F is-consubstantiated with the GF*.

Adding to the canonical notation developed above the symbol "C*" to denote consubstantiation, we can capture the point of (C*.Ex) as follows:

(Ind*.C*) Sentences of the form *The F thing is-existentially G* expresses
propositions of the form C*(*c* {Fness}, *c* {Gness,
Fness}).

Here we have a reduction of existential predication to the predicational copula of
consubstantiation, which is a form of *contingent sameness*, the one that holds
between the (thin) individual the morning star and the (thin) individual the
evening star: C*(the morning star, the evening star). We also have propositions
of the form C*(Venus, the morning star). I say "propositions" advisedly, because
the proper name "Venus" is a kind of variable that ranges over thin thinkable individuals, typically different ones in different contexts of speech and thought. At
this juncture we need a detailed phenomenological analysis of the semantics and
pragmatics of proper names[25].

Non-existential empirical predication and sameness

Earlier, in IX and XIII, we saw that existential predication contrasts with another
form of predication pertaining to mental activity. Perceptual objects, whether
existing or not, have properties in perceptual fields, which are contingently
possessed as a result of the perceiving activity. Likewise, fictional objects,
whether existing or not, possess properties through the fiction-maker's creative
activity. Perhaps these two forms of having properties are one and the same. The
hypothesis that they are is a simplifying one worthy of exploration. Let us call it
consociational predication. Of course, we also have statements of identity to the
effect that a certain perceived item is the same as another perceived item, and that
a certain fictional character is another character, perhaps in the same work of art.
For instance:

(C**.2) That plum tree over there is what's killing that evergreen.

(C**.3) In *Don Quijote:* Don Quijote is the same as Alonso Quijana, and
the same as the Knight of the Sad Countenance.

Here again we can reduce property predication to the sameness predication. Let
us introduce the symbol C** with subscripts indicating the source of mental activity engendering consociational statements. Thus:

(C**.Pred) Sentences of the form *The F is-consociationally-according-
to-M G* express the selfsame proposition as the corresponding
sentences of the form: *The F is-consociationally-the-same-ac-
cording-to-M as the GF*, that is, the selfsame proposition as is
expressed by: C**M(*c* {Fness}, *c* {Gness, Fness}).

Internal predication and existence

The two (or perhaps more) types of predication discussed above are external. They are, as shown, senses in which thinkable individuals are said to be the same. There are other types of external predication. But they all contrast with a fundamental form of internal predication.

Recall the conflicting views of Kant and Russell concerning example (18), in II:

(18) The present king of France is a king.

For Russell sentence (18) can only be used by us to make false statements, empirically and contingently false because whether there *exists* a king of France or not is a contingent and empirical matter. On the other hand, for Kant (18) expresses a true proposition, and a necessarily, analytically true proposition because the predicate is included in the subject. Obviously, the two philosophers are not joining the issue: they have different conceptions of truth and talk past each other.

Discussing sentence (18) in isolation slants the dispute in Russell's favor: we focus on one purpose of speech and lose the unity of discourse. There is no useful point to be made in an ordinary life situation by the assertive utterance of (18) — given that we know so much about the political situation of France. But as we have seen in the preceding discussions, we must not deal with isolated sentences but with *discourses*; we also have seen the need to distinguish our beliefs and knowledge about the world from the semantics of the language we use to acquire and change beliefs — and to live other experiences, besides. We need, *not* a doxastic, but a general *thinking semantics*. Thus, we have seen that BOTH Kant and Russell are right in what they want to stress. Hence, we must accommodate both points of view. Therefore, we must recognize the two truths involved:

(18.K) The present king of France is-Kantially a king.

(18.R) It is not the case that the present king of France is-Russellianly a king.

We know that (18.R) is a statement about existential predication. On the other hand, (18.R) needs its own special recognition:

(Int.Pred) Some sentences of the form *a is G* formulate propositions to the effect that the property Gness belongs to the core set of the individual *a*. We can canonically represent them in the form *a* (Gness).

We must stop.

XVIII. Conclusion

The preceding is only the beginning of a comprehensive account of objecthood, predication, identity, sameness, etc., and of the general semantics of the language through which we live a rich but unified experience. We can see how the different distinctions distilled from the investigation come together at different junctures. The pattern begins to emerge. Its full development constitutes Guise Theory[26].

Notes

1. H.H. Price, "Half-Belief," in *Belief* (London: George Allen & Unwin, New York: Humanities Press, 1969).

2. For the original discussion of Meinong's round squares see Bertrand Russell's: "Meinong's Theory of Complexes and Assumptions," *Mind*, n.s. 13 (1904): 204-219, 336-354, 509-24, "Review of Meinong *et. al., Untersuchungen zur Gegenstandstheorie und Psychologie*," *Mind*, n.s. 14 (1905): 530-538, and "Review of Meinong's Uber die Stellung der Gegenstandstheorie," *Mind*, n.s. 16 (1907): 436-439; Meinong's *Uber die Stellung der Gegenstandstheorie in System der Wissenschaft* (1907), in *Alexius Meinong Gesamtausgabe*, V, ed. by Roderick Chisholm (Graz: Akademische Druck-und Verlagsanstalt, 1971): 197-365. For commentary on the Meinong-Russell debate see, among others, Roderick M. Chisholm's Introduction to his anthology *Realism and the Background of Phenomenology* (Glencoe, Illinois: The Free Press, 1960), Reinhardt Grossmann, "Non-Existent Objects: Recent Work on Brentano and Meinong," *American Philosophical Quarterly* 6 (1969): 17-32; Hector-Neri Castaneda, "Thinking and The Structure of the World," *Philosophia* 4 (1974): 3-40; Karel Lambert, "Impossible Objects," *Inquiry* 17 (1974): 303-314; Terence Parsons, *Nonexistent Objects* (New Haven, Connecticut: Yale University Press, 1980), pp. 2, 11, 21, 30, 38-42, 118-120, 93; William Rapaport, *Intentionality and the Structure of Existence* (doctoral dissertation presented to Indiana University at Bloomington, 1976): pp. 92ff, 132-137.

3. Kurt Goedel, *On Formally Undecidable Propositions of* Principia Mathematica *and Related Systems* (1931), (Edinburgh and London: Oliver & Boyd, 1962, transl. by B. Meltzer).

4. Thesis (Q.QRef) is, I believe, original with Willard Van Orman Quine. See, e.g., *From a Logical Point of View* (New York: Harper & Row, revised edition, 1963): pp. 70ff.

5. For an ontological analysis of the objects of perception and the ontologico-epistemological functions of perceptual demonstratives, which captures some of Russell's insights, see Hector-Neri Castaneda, "Perception, Belief, and the Structure of Physical Objects and of Consciousness," *Synthese* 35 (1977): 285-351.

6. See, e.g., Wilfrid Sellars, "Acquaintance and Description Again," *The Journal of Philosophy* 48 (1949): 496-505.

7. Free logic has been energetically promoted by Karel Lambert and developed by him, Bas Van Fraassen, Richmond Thomason, Robert R. Meyer, and others. See, e.g., K. Lambert, "Existential Import Revisited," *Notre Dame Journal of Formal Logic* 4 (1963): 288-292; Alonzo Church, "Review of 'Existential Import Revisited'," *The Journal of Symbolic Logic* 30 (1965): 103-104; Robert K. Meyer and Karel Lambert, "Universally Free Logic and Standard Quantification Theory," *The Journal of Symbolic Logic* 33 (1968): 8-26. Here a universally quantified logic is a free logic that allows for logical validity in the empty domain of discourse. This still leaves the quantifiers ranging over existents, as is instituted by the following two Meyer-Lambert

axioms, whereas for Russell "E!x" means that x exists, and A(x//y) is the formula resulting from A(x) by replacing all free occurrences of x in A(x) with free occurrences of y:

103. (x)A(x)—> (B! —> A(x//y)).

104. (x)E!x.

Lambert and others have developed a free description logic, which formalizes some strategies within free logic for dealing with the denotation of non-denoting definite descriptions, e.g., allowing them to denote something outside the domain of quantification, or nothing. The issue here is mainly the uniqueness of the denotatum. Since the quantifiers continue to be existentially interpreted, we still have here a Russellian view with his Robust Sense of Reality only slightly mollified. See Karel Lambert "Notes on Free Description Theory: Some Philosophical Issues and Consequences," *Journal of Philosophical Logic* 1 (1972): 184-191; Dana Scott, "Existence and Description in Formal Logic," in Ralph Schoenman, ed., *Bertrand Russell: Philosopher of the Century* (Atlantic-Little, Brown, 1967); Richard B. Grandy, "A Definition of Truth for Theories with Intentional Definite Description Operators," *Journal of Philosophical Logic* 1 (1972): 137-155.

8. Concerning the substitution interpretation of the quantifiers and its contrast with the objectual interpretation, the following studies are especially important: J. Michael Dunn and Nuel B. Belnap, Jr., "The Substitution Interpretation of the Quantifiers," *Nous* 2 (1968): 177-185; Robert Binkley, "Quantifying, Quotation, and a Paradox," *Nous*, 4 (1970): 271-277; Leslie H. Tharp, "Truth, Quantification, and Abstract Objects," *Nous* 5 (1971): 363-372; Leonard Linsky, "Two Concepts of Quantification," *Nous* 6 (1972): 224-239; Ruth Barcan Marcus, "Quantification and Ontology," *Nous* 6 (1972): 240-250; Saul A. Kripke, "Is There a Problem about Substitutional Quantification?," in Gareth Evans and J.H. McDowell, eds., *Truth and Meaning* (Oxford: Clarendon Press, 1976); Martin Davies, "A Note on Substitutional Quantification," *Nous* 14 (1980): 619-622.

9. Tyler Burge, "Russell's Problem and Intentional Identity," in James E. Tomberlin, ed., *Agent, Language, and the Structure of the World* (Indianapolis, Indiana: Hackett Publishing Company, 1983). In this volume there is also my "Reply to Tyler Burge: Reference, Existence, and Fiction."

10. Yet perhaps here is a juncture at which different master theories of the world and experience can be developed. Their full development must, certainly, be attempted so that dia-philosophy may become a professional reality. To be sure, a purely substitutional interpretation of the quantifiers creates what seems an impassable hiatus between language and reality. Yet I am not posing that hiatus as a fatal objection, but only as a supreme task for views of the world and of language built on such an interpretation. I hope, for the sake of dia-philosophy, that a skillful philosopher may construct the sturdy bridges required to make that hiatus surmountable. On the need for philosophical pluralism see Hector-Neri Castaneda, *On Philosophical Method* (Bloomington, Indiana: Nous Publications, 1980).

11. For an account of intended content, intentional action and its causation, and weakness of the will, see Hector-Neri Castaneda, *Thinking and Doing: The Philosophical Foundations of Institutions* (Dordrecht: Reidel, 1975), chs. 6, 10-12, "Intentional Action, Conditional Intentions, and Aristotelian Practical Syllogisms," *Erkenntniss* 18 (1982): 239-260, and "Reply to Michael Bratman: Deontic Truth, Intentions, and Weakness of the Will" in James R. Tomberlin, *op.cit. in Note 9.*

12. George Edward Moore, "Is Existence a Predicate?" *Aristotelian Society Proceedings*

Supplementary Volume 15 (1936), reprinted in G.E. Moore, *Philosophical Papers* (London: George Allen & Unwin; New York: The Macmillan Company, 1939. The ensuing page references are to the latter.

13. On the experiential role of indexical reference see Hector-Neri Castaneda, "The Semiotic Profile of Indexical (Experiential) Reference," *Synthese* 49 (1981): 275-316, and "Perception, Belief, and the Structure of Physical Objects and Consciousness." This experiential role is precisely the main difference between David Kaplan's excellent semantics for indicators and my views. See Kaplan, "Demonstratives," unpublished, but widely circulated monograph (Department of Philosophy, University of California at Los Angeles, 2nd. draft 1977), and Hector-Neri Castaneda, "Direct Reference, Realism, and Guise Theory: Constructive Reflections on David Kaplan's Theory of Reference," in Howard Wettstein and John Perry, ed., *Studies on Kaplan's Themes* (forthcoming). As I see it, in the example of the Drowning Man Adventure discussed next, the speaker expresses a thought content that lies *internally* within his perceptual field, and he takes it to be *true or false*. He puts it forth non-committally in sentence (2); he formulates it endorsingly in sentence (1), as something he believes. But the strict, thinking semantics of demonstratives is the same and reveals that demonstratives have an irreducible experiential meaning. It also reveals that there are irreducible indexical truths. Furthermore, these truths are contentually subjective, although structurally intersubjective. This provides the need for what I have called *quasi-indexical* reference. All this cuts across the existent/non-existent categorical cleavage. Hence, all of that has to be brought to bear in the best theories of reference as well as in any comprehensive treatment of non-existence.

14. See the papers mentioned in Notes 5 and 13.

15. See, e.g. W.V.O. Quine, "Reply to Dagfinn Follesdal" in Donald Davidson and Jaakko Hintikka, eds., *Words and Objections: Essays on the Work of W.V. Quine* (Dordrecht: Reidel, 1974).

16. On these points see *On Philosophical Method*, cited above in Note 10.

17. See Note 7 above.

18. This is so for dia-philosophical reasons. William J. Rapaport, who has developed a Meinongian semantics from my Guise Theory, has a suitable different view of fictional discourse. See his "Review of Terence Parsons *Nonexistent Objects*," Nous 19 (1985): 255-271 and "Meinongian Theories and a Russellian Paradox," *Nous* 12 (1978): 153-180. Edward N. Zalta develops a theory of objects along Rapaport's lines, but his account of fiction seems to be different. See his *Abstract Objects: An Introduction to Axiomatic Metaphysics* (Dordrecht: Reidel, 1983). A different Meinongian view of fiction appears in Terence Parsons, *Nonexistent Objects*, cited above. Other views are deployed in *Poetics*, 8 (1979), special issue edited by John Woods and Thomas G. Pavel on formal semantics and literary theory, by Richard Routley, Jens F. Ihwe and Hannes Rieser, John Heintz, Nicholas Wolterstorff, Robert Howell, Thomas G. Pavel, Lubomir Dolezel, Merrie Bergmann, Robert A. Schultz, and Gottfried Gabriel. Also see William J. Rapaport's "Meinongian Semantics for Propositional Semantic Networks," 23rd Annual Meeting of the Association for Computational Linguistics, University of Chicago, (1985).

19. See Hector-Neri Castaneda, "Fiction and Reality: Their Basic Connections," *Poetics* 8 (1979): 31-62.

20. Anatole France, "Putois."

21. Reported to me verbally by James Tomberlin, and discussed first in "Reply to Tyler Burge" mentioned above in Note 9.

22. Michael McKinsey presented this example in his comments on Burge's paper mentioned in Note 9, when this paper was presented at the 1979 University of Cincinnati Colloquium.

23. David Lewis, "Anselm and Actuality," *Nous* 4 (1970): 175-180. See also Robert M.

Adams, "Theories of Actuality," *Nous* 8 (1974): 211-231.

24. See *Thinking and Doing*, Ch. 3, and "Perception, Belief, and the Structure of Physical Objects and Consciousness," cited in Notes 11 and 5, respectively. The notions of *propositional guise* and of *PROPOSITION are introduced in this latter paper.*

25. For an inquiry into the phenomenological linguistics of proper names see Hector-Neri Castaneda, "The Semantics and the Causal Roles of Proper Names," *Philosophy and Phenomeno-logical Research* 46 (1985): 91-113. See also the essay by Tyler Burge and Castaneda's reply in the Tomberlin volume cited in Note 9. One crucial point that emerges from the examination of our experience of proper names is that — in spite of Plantinga's claim to the contrary — no proper name can harpoon an individual essence. Just as the use of the demonstrative "this," whose funda-mental role is to refer to items presented in experience *qua* presented, cannot in its normal uses pick out individual essences. The *haecceity* or *thisness*, which Duns Scotus postulated for each individual, is a hypostasis built on the experiential use of "this"; it has been revivived by Robert K. Adams and Alvin Plantinga and transposed to the category of quality. See Note 13.

26. The original complementary expositions of Guise Theory are Hector-Neri Castaneda, "Thinking and the Structure of the world," *Philosophia* 4 (1974): 4-40, and "Perception, Belief, and the Structure of Physical Objects and Consciousness," *Synthese* 35 (1977): 285-351. Alvin Plantinga's "Guise Theory" and Romane Clark's "Predication Theory: Guised and Disguised," and Castaneda's replies to these, in the Tomberlin volume cited in Note 9, both provide good introductions to Guise Theory and further develop it, especially in its more sophisticated version of Ordered Guise Theory. Further valuable discussions of it are: Jay Rosenberg's "Castaneda's Ontology," David Woodruff Smith's "Mind and Guise: Castaneda's Philosophy of Mind and World Order," and Jeffrey Sicha's "Castaneda on Plato, Leibniz, and Kant," all in James B. Tomberlin, ed., *Profiles: Hector-Neri Castaneda* (Dordrecht: Reidel, 1985). Another interesting study is Jig-Chuen Lee, "Frege's Paradox of Reference and Castaneda's Guise Theory," Philo-sophical Studies 46 (1984) 403-415.

Predication: The Copula[1]

Romane Clark

Introduction

Philosophical theories of predication are often determined by views antecedently held concerning the natures of the terms predicated. What philosophers have said about the relation between what is ascribed to an object and the object to which it is ascribed has often been pretty much a function of their views about what objects are and about what properties and concepts are.

The question naturally arises: Are there any independent grounds, grounds not based in antecedent views about the natures of the terms of predication, for characterizing predication itself? Turned this way around, we might ask, say, whether there is any evidence for thinking that predication is in fact a copulation of what is referred to together with what is ascribed to what is referred to. We ask this question now quite naively, quite without commitment to any special views concerning the ontological characters of the terms involved. Answering our question may itself provide some grounds which are based in the nature of predication for the views we come to hold concerning the natures of the terms involved, rather than the other way around.

So there is, then, some interest for us in this natural question. It has not been the usual question, however. To motivate things that follow we consider some recent remarks made by distinguished philosophers about the nature of predication. We exploit these to draw some conclusions useful in answering our question. The conclusions we draw are at odds with what these philosophers have maintained.

First (negative) Consequence. Despite what Professor Geach has said, the copula is NOT a predicable forming operator on predicables.[2]

Professor Geach has written:

> We need not say anything so brutal about the poor copula as Frege did;
> that it means nothing at all. In many Greek sentences the copula may be
> indifferently inserted or omitted: this I think suggests that we should
> regard it not as meaningless but as a trivial predicable forming operator
> on predicables. ... The 'is' operator is like adding zero or multiplying by
> one.

Straight off, it is clear that Geach's remarks ought not to be taken literally. At
least, they ought not if they are understood as characterizing the copula of
English. A predicable forming operator on predicables yields a predicable when
applied to one. The result then is an expression to which the operator also applies.
But the 'is' operator of English is not like this. The 'is' operator does not iterate.

Further, the copula of English is not a trivial identity operator on predicables.
It is not one whose presence adds nothing to the significance of the sentence in
which it occurs. This is clear for deleting the copula from an English sentence in
which it correctly appears does not leave, as Geach's account suggests it should,
an altered sentence of equivalent sense. It leaves no significant sentence at all.

Geach's characterization if applied literally to the copula of English is
wrong.

Second Consequence. The predicate does NOT seem to effect a specification
of a concept.

Professor Strawson characterized simple subject-predicate utterances as
discharging in their use three functions:[3]

> That of specifying the object represented as falling under the concept;
> that of specifying the concept under which the object is represented as
> falling; and that of indicating the propositional or predicative mode of
> combination.

Geach, in the paper from which our earlier quotation was taken, sharply criticized
this account of Strawson's. Geach charged Strawson with a tripartite analysis of
simple predications. He accused Strawson as analyzing them as having, logically,
the form: subject-copula-predicate.

Strawson replied saying that while he *characterized* such utterances as
fulfilling these functions, he did not *analyze* them in this way. In fact, he said,
"the second and third of these functions [i.e., the function of specifying a concept
and the function of indicating the mode of combination involved] are discharged
by a single part of the utterance, viz. the predicate."[4]

There is a certain tension in Strawson's reply to Geach. If, after all, the predicate does discharge the twin functions Strawson assigns to it, then, natural language and "surface grammar" to one side, it is plausible to suppose that a perspicuous display of the logical form of simple subject-predicate utterances *should* be tripartite. And, given the functions satisfied in the production of such an utterance, it is plausible to suppose that a perspicuous logical display *must* be copular. All that is necessary to make what seems plausible quite explicit is to assume on the one hand that discrete semantical functions are, in perspicuous logical display, discharged by syntactically discrete expressions. And, on the other hand, the claim that this display must be copular requires only, it seems, an assumption making explicit what is involved in the specification of concepts.

Strawson does not develop these points, but we can say a little about them. Ordinarily, or so we tend to think, we specify concepts by making abstractive references to them. We exploit in English a familiar range of nominalizing operators to take so-called general terms into singular ones. To the adjective 'red' there is the suffix, 'ness', and the singular term, 'redness', etc. We specify the concepts which we ascribe to things by forming nominatives from the general terms used in such ascriptions. We ascribe concepts to things by using general terms. These occur, appropriately modified and inflected, but unnominalized.

So, if the ascription and specification of concepts are as we tend to think of them, then there is an underlying tension in Strawson's characterization of the predicate and its functioning. If the predicate specifies a concept, then a perspicuous display of that function should involve an abstract singular term. Presumably then the mode of combination indicated by its occurrence would be copular, joining the specified abstract entity to the object referred to by the subject. But if the predicate indicates the ascriptive mode of combination of concept and object, then a perspicuous display of that function should involve an unnominalized general term occurring with appropriate verbal auxiliaries as part of a larger predicate. But there is not in the predicate dual occurrences of the general term, once nominalized but once not.

So far it appears that the copula of English is not trivial in the way Geach suggests. And the predicate of English is not important in the way Strawson suggests. We wonder whether matters are as they appear here.

A 3rd Consequence: The copula is *not* a modal expression of mood.

Professor Stenius, exploiting Wittgenstein's example of the boxer, wrote:[5]

A picture as such has no mood. ... A sentence depicts how things stand, if it is true. And it asserts that they do so stand. ... The picture of a boxer is a sentence-radical; it indicates ... the matter of a sentence, but is not itself a sentence, because for a sentence to be formed there is needed besides this matter a definite 'function' in which the picture is to be used.

Sentences in the different moods are different sentences. They may share the same descriptive content, but the mood of a sentence expresses what I do with that content. The mood is not itself part of that content. We display the picture and say, "Here's how he did it," or "Here's how you are to do it," or ask, "Was this how he did it?"

Evidently the display of a picture is not ordinarily part of what is pictured in a display. Since the mood of what I say expresses what I do with the descriptive content of my utterance, it is not ordinarily part of the descriptive content of my utterance. Rather, the expression of mood is, according to Stenius, a modal element. It is that which, attached to a sentence-radical expressing the descriptive content of the sentence, yields a sentence. Since, in English, the copula is a linguistic expression by which we express the mood of what we say, it is logically a modal expression if Stenius is right.

Stenius is not right in this. A little reflection makes it pretty clear that our expressions for the moods are not, after all, modal expressions. Modal expressions iterate, but our expressions for the moods do not. And a modal sentence ordinarily remains significant when its modal element is deleted, but a moodless sentence does not do so. A sentence in no mood is no sentence at all. Further, there are speech acts for the moods but not for modals. Uttering my sentence I may thereby assert or query what is the case. But uttering my sentence I do not and cannot necessitate that which in the performance of the act I may state to be necessary.

Cop-Mods

So it is clear, I think, that moods are not modals. It is interesting to note that the moods can themselves be modified by modals, as of course can sentences as wholes and general terms also be. Modals, however, cannot be modified by moods. This interesting asymmetry in fact affords a certain unexpected and independent test for the philosophical significance, or lack of it, of the copula — as we shall see a bit later.

For now we can exploit the simple negative consequences gathered from the references to Geach, Strawson, and Stenius to remind ourselves of an obvious but often ignored fact. The predicate of English is a grammatically complex entity consisting of a verb or verb phrase with associated verbal auxiliaries and trappings. Unless this complexity is logically irrelevant, it is ill-served by the logician's jejune juxtaposition of singular and general term.

In fact, however, some of this complexity is logically relevant. General terms come modified and inflected with expressions for mood, tense, gender and the agreement in number of subject and predicate and the like. Certainly the expression of mood, for instance, carries a distinction of fundamental logical and semantical import. And tense substantively determines the truth-conditions of our assertions of fact. So it seems clear that the grammatical complexity of the predicates of our natural language is at least in part a reflection of relevant logical and semantical complexity. And it is clear that the grammatical copula in English is a vehicle which carries our expressions of mood and tense. The copula is not, after all, an otiose operator like "multiplying by one".

The issue is not whether the copula has logical significance. Of course it has. The issue is rather whether it has philosophical significance for our theories of predication. But with respect to this issue, the situation is not so clear. Mood, for instance, reflects not so much the relation of concept to object, as what we, in the production of a sentence, do. We assert, or request, or query what is or is to be the case. We do not in the production report what it is we do. Rather, by exploiting expressions of mood, we perform those speech acts whose occurrences are separately reported (by ourselves or others) using speech-act operators. (Stenius' account perhaps conflates these related but different things, identifying the speech-act operators on sentences with the related, but distinct expressions of mood.)

But if expressions for moods display, but do not state, what it is we do in the production of an utterance, then, whatever the logical and semantical significance of these expressions may otherwise be, they may well be thought to have little significance concerning the connection of concept to object. (Perhaps this is the charitable reading to be given the quotation taken from Geach above.)

It is not then in terms of the primary function of the copula or of its verbal surrogates, that of expressing the mood of an utterance, that a non-tendentious characterization of predication is to be found. It is, somewhat surprisingly, the secondary function of the copula as a rack upon which are hung various modifications and inflections which has special philosophical interest.

There is a range of ways in which we, in English, modify the expressions we use to express mood, like the copula. We inflect them, expressing tense, and gender, and number. We modify them with negative particles. Old English once contained a contracted negative tensed copula as it now contains the tensed one. 'nis', 'nam', and 'nil' once occurred, and 'willy-nilly' even now remains. We have in English adverbial forms of modality, tense, and negation, positioned at the copula. In particular, we have not only sentential and general term alethic modal modifiers, but copulative ones as well. We may say: It is possible that John is a candidate; or, John is a possible candidate; or, John is possibly a candidate.

Of the verbal trappings that go often with our expressions of mood, some are substantive, like negation and tense, and some are broadly structural, like number and perhaps gender. It is familiar logical practice to ignore the structural inflections of the copula as irrelevant or redundant. And it is familiar logical practice to express the substantive modifications of the copula, like negation and tense, as exportable operators which, prefixed to a sentence, yield a sentence.

Generalizing, we wonder whether it may not be that *all* of the various substantive grammatical inflections and modifications of the copula trivially give way in adequate formal representation to other forms of modification? We wonder whether the grammatical positioning of modifiers at the copula has logical and semantical significance or not? To ask whether the mode of combination expressed in an act of predication is anything more than an indication of the speech act effected by the production of the utterance, is now to ask whether the grammatical occurrences of adverbial mood modifiers collapse, logically, always into ones perspicuously represented as sentential or general term modifiers.

If they do not, then despite Geach and Frege, there may reasonably be thought to be some semantic point to the occurrence and positioning of the "connecting tissue" present in our acts of predication. It has, it may be thought, some content of its own significant to the predication beyond merely displaying the mood of what is said.

But if the mood modifiers do, universally and in principle, collapse logically into sentential or general term modifiers, then it may plausibly be thought that whatever it is which indicates the mood of our utterances is of no special or interesting philosophical significance. Geach, if this is so, had it quite right. So far as predication is concerned, the copula is a vacuous operator like "adding zero or multiplying by one."

In what follows, we consider the predicate to be a logically complex expression, consisting of a general term (a verb, perhaps, or adjective or common noun) together with a verbal auxiliary expressing mood (perhaps a literal occurrence of the verb 'to be' or verbal surrogates to similar effect.) Given an expression of at least this much complexity, there are in principle at least three possible points of modification. Modifiers governing the predicate as a whole, if any, we call "pred-mods." Modifiers governing the general term, we call "term-mods." Modifiers positioned at the expression of mood, governing the verbal auxiliary, we call "cop-mods."

We ask: Do cop-mods, the modifiers of mood, modify them in an interesting way, a way with discrete semantical import, or do these modifiers merely collapse into pre-mods or term-mods?

Scope

In attempting to answer this question, it is natural to think in terms of the scope of the modifiers which occur. This is particularly so in the case of the alethic and psychical modal modifiers. We know occurrences of these modifiers can render the expressions they govern opaque to the application of standard logical principles. The Substitution of Identities, The Interchange of Equivalents, Existential Generalization upon terms occurring within the scope of alethic modal operators, all may fail in these modal contexts, as we know.

What is of special interest now is the fact that, grammatically at least, the adverbial, copular modal modifier does not govern the occurrences of either the subject term or the general term of the utterances in which the modifier occurs. If such cop-mods do not collapse, logically, into other modifiers, separately placed in the utterance, then there exists a modal sentence of a quite special sort. It is one which is neither a *de dicto* nor yet a *de re* modal sentence with respect to either its singular or its general terms. Yet it is a sentence which is not equivalent to its matching non-modalized sentence. Sentences like these, if they exist, carry modal force. They do so however without creating those intensional contexts which inhibit the correct applications of the familiar formal rules which govern our ordinary extensional discourse. Accordingly if such sentences exist, there is presumptive evidence that the copular mode of predication is semantically significant. The question of whether, in this case, its significance is in particular connexive would remain then as an important next question.

The positioning of modifiers, and the positioning of adverbial modifiers, have always raised interesting questions of scope. The distinct occurrences of adverbial modifiers suggest the possibility of reasonably subtle semantical distinctions. We say, for instance, things like these:

1. Formerly, the chief of staff was a presidential candidate.

2. The chief of staff was a former presidential candidate.

3. The chief of staff was formerly a presidential candidate.

Depending upon the context of their occurrence, one or more of these sentences may strike us as ambiguous. But it is easy to imagine contexts in which their meanings seem clear and clearly distinct. 1., for instance, might in suitable circumstances be used to assert that it used to be, perhaps before some constitutional change, that the chief of staff, whoever that might have been, was a presidential candidate. 2., by contrast, even in those same circumstances, says something quite specific about the present chief of staff: there was a time earlier than the utterance relative to which, at an earlier time, the chief of staff was a candidate. 3. says simply that the chief of staff, the present one, was at an earlier time a presidential candidate.

So the positioning of the modifier apparently matters. It matters in fixing the reference of the subject term. It matters in fixing the time of a predication relative to the occasion of utterance. It is a commonplace that different positioning, even within the predicate, may issue in different things said.

It is reported, perhaps, that at the testimonial dinner,

4. Tom rudely gestured during the presentation ceremony.[6]

This is not to be confused with

5. Tom gestured rudely during the ceremony,

for 5. implies 4. but not conversely. And 5. suggests an act performed with certain evident intent — Tom "flipped the finger" perhaps. But 4. is compatible with naive social ineptness — Tom perhaps just didn't know enough to sit still.

We can try now to abstract a bit from examples like these. The examples suggest that the positioning of modifiers can matter a good deal in determining what is said on a given occasion. And they suggest that there is an interesting range of locations for these modifiers with discrete import.

We suppose that predicates are formally characterized recursively as those members of the class of expressions which result from the concatenations of certain specified operators upon antecedently specified general terms. (The operators are the formal representation of the verbal auxiliaries and expressions of mood of our natural language.) The complexity of the resulting predicates makes available a certain range of positions at which we can place our adverbial modifiers. These are the positions marked by the presence of the distinct syntactical elements of the predicate. In addition to familiar sentence and singular term modifiers, we have now as well modifiers which, in their separate ways, attach to the predicate. Some of these attach to the predicate as a whole, our "pred-mods." These are modifiers which take predicates into predicates. (I construe 'rudely' in 'rudely gestured' of example 4. as an instance of a pred-mod.)

There are modifiers internal to the predicate as well. Some of these, when applied to a general term, yield a general term. (There are lots of familiar examples of these, some of which radically alter the sense of what is predicated. Consider, e.g., the effect of modifying the term 'candidate' with the modifier 'ineligible'. Others, like 'rudely' in 'gestured rudely' of example 5. are adverbs of manner; adverbs used to express the way in which an action is done.)

But there are other internal predicate modifiers as well, our "cop-mods." For the verbal auxiliaries by which we take general terms into predicates are themselves capable of modification. In English, those auxiliaries come inflected, indicating tense, or come with negative particles attached. Thus, the general term 'run' occurs suitably inflected in the predicates occurring in 'John run*s*' and in 'John *is* runn*ing*.' The 's' in 'runs' and the 'is ——ing' in 'is running' are operators each taking the general term into a predicate, but doing so with different temporal significance. These operators are in turn capable of further modification, as when we say, e.g., that John is *not now* running.

So we have at least three distinct ways to position modifiers with respect to the syntactical complexity of the predicate. And we have as well some informal reinforcement for doing so in the grammatical distinctions implicit in examples. These examples suggest that the different positioning of modifiers is not only syntactically relevant but semantically important as well. The important formal question is whether or not sentences with modifiers positioned at the copula are equivalent always to sentences with those modifiers displaced to other positions.

Our few earlier examples already suggest that modifiers cannot in general be repositioned *ad lib*. This earlier suggestion is strengthened when one considers compounded modifiers, stacked together at some given position. Transfer of modifiers to other positions may rupture the scope relationships of the nested operators. Adverbs of manner, for instance, have long been known for their sensitivity to negation. Repositioning here may yield not just altered sense but nonsense. John may be running to the scene of the accident, or he may not. He may be running quickly there, or he may not. But John cannot be quickly not running there. The copular negative operator cannot, in an instance like this, be correctly repositioned as a general term modifier. We understand why it cannot, for not running is not a form of running; therefore, quickly cannot be the manner in which John does it.

More generally, if less spectacularly, repositioning of negative operators often yields altered sense. To say, for instance, that the chief of staff was not formerly a candidate is to say something true just in case he never has been. But to say that he formerly wasn't, is to leave open the possibility that he may also at some time have been.

Negation sensitive adverbs of manner suggest that copular negation does not collapse with equivalent sense into general term negation. Temporal modifiers compounded with negation suggest that copular negations do not collapse into sentential negative operators. Russell, long ago, in his theory of definite descriptions, provided the resources for providing in a single example an occurrence of the negative modifier which collapses neither into a sentence or term modifier.

To say 'John's oldest son did not run quickly to the accident' is not, given the adverb of manner, to say that he quickly did not run there. The negative particle cannot be repositioned to the general term. But neither is it to say 'It is not true that John's oldest son ran quickly to the scene of the accident.' It implies this last, but this last does not imply it. This of course was a circumstance to which both Russell and Strawson, in their differing ways, were long ago sensitive. For his part, Russell, in developing his theory of descriptions, was sensitive to questions of domination given occurrences of over-arching operators, negative and existential. The first sentence could be used to say something true in case the boy did not run, but walked; or ran, but not quickly; or ran quickly, but not to the accident. The second would be true in each of these circumstances all right, but true as well if John had no son. We have accordingly a case in which a sentence with a negative copula does not collapse either into an equivalent sentence with the negative operator repositioned at the general term or to one in which it occurs as a sentence operator of largest scope.

One can of course generalize these questions of scope domination to any set of operators, even modal cop-mods as we soon will do. But it is possible to generalize as well over the complex and indirect specifications we give of the concepts we predicate, quite as much as we do over our descriptive references to the subjects which fall under them. For there are definite ascriptions quite as much as there are definite descriptions.[7] The concepts which are specified by definite ascriptions vary quite as much with the occasions of their productions as do the references of definite descriptions in the varying contexts of their employment. 'My true love's hair is the color of the sands of our beach' varies in its reference, ascription and truth depending upon the speaker, location, and the occasion of the production of the sentence. My true love, for instance, will on the occasion of the utterance turn out to be a blonde or brunette as we stand on the Pacific shores at Laguna or on the black volcanic sands of an Hawaiian beach.

Definite ascriptions have a special interest for us here, with our interest in the scope relationships of modifiers of predicates. It is plausible to analyze definite ascriptions rather as definite descriptions have been analyzed. To define in use an occurrence of a definite ascription like 'the color of the sands of our beach' is, in Russellian fashion, to make explicit that there is a property, which is uniquely the color of our beach, and which is how the object of our reference is. Any such ascriptions coupled with occurrences of copular modifiers will, quite as much as do definite descriptions, raise questions of the primary or secondary occurrences of the various operators relative to the existential specification of the ascription.

There is a certain gain in exploiting definite ascriptions for our purposes. In the first place, their use obviates one of the possible redeployments of copular modifiers. There are no distinct general terms to serve as a location for the repositioned modifier. More important is the fact that definite ascriptions permit a literal reading of Strawson's statement, quoted earlier, of the functions discharged by the use of a predicate. It was difficult earlier to understand how the use of a predicate served at once both to specify a concept and to ascribe it to an object of reference as well. Specification seemed to require some form of abstractive reference, a nominalization of some general term. But only a single instance of a term occurs in simple predications; it is unnominalized general terms which standardly appear. Now, however, definite ascriptions appear to introduce variables ranging over properties, to quantify over them, and to place them in both subject and predicate positions in the contextual characterization of the ascription. The twin functions of specification and attribution are now explicitly and separately manifest. They are so, but at the price of singular reference to what is ascribed by their use. If black is what the sands of the beach are, on the occasion of my utterance, then blackness is what I in that use specify and is the color which I, on the occasion, ascribe to my true love's hair.

World-theory

To accommodate formally the full range of cases and yet preserve the necessary distinctions of scope, we mark all terms, singular and general, simple (like proper names and adjectives) and complex (like definite descriptions and ascriptions), with explicit representations of their scope. In mimic of those which Russell introduced for definite descriptions, scope markers are silent prefixes. They indicate nothing of the nature of the expression whose scope they mark. They add nothing to the content of what is expressed. They function instead as a sort of punctuation device, making explicit what otherwise might be tacit in the use of a term.

Lower-case 's' will be our syntactical variable for any singular term, simple or complex. Bracket '[s]' is its associated scope-marker. Upper-case 'G' is a syntactical variable for any general term, simple or complex. Bracket '[G]' is its associated scope-marker. As a representation, indifferently, of occurrences of the copula or its verbal surrogates, we introduce the special operator, 'cop'. 'Cop' flanked left and right by a general term and a singular term respectively, each carrying its associated scope-marker, enclosed in parentheses, constitutes a sentence.

For unmodified, extensional sentences the scope-markers of the terms may be brought forward in any order and equivalently prefixed to the sentence as a whole. But with the presence of modifiers a textured range of scope distinctions becomes available. This is particularly pointed with appearances of non-extensional modifiers, ones the presence of which render the contexts which lie in their scope opaque to the application of certain standard logical rules.

Consider now some modal operator, M, sprinkled across sentences with terms of varying scope. Consider the example we mentioned earlier as an instance of this. There are grammatically distinct expressions of possibility like these:

6. It is possible that John is a candidate.

7. John is possibly a candidate.

8. John is a possible candidate.

It is natural to view the modal operator of 6. as having largest scope. If so, its use yields an assertion *de dicto*. The singular term 'John' and the general term 'candidate' lie internal to the modal operator. 6., then, has the logical form:

10. M[s][G] (G cop s).

Equally, it is natural to view 8. as containing a "transparent" occurrence of its singular term; it is a *de re* sentence with respect to its subject, having the form:

11. [s] (M[G]G cop s).

7. is a *de re* sentence with respect to both of its terms, singular and general, and has the form:

12. [s][G](G M(cop) s).

Indeed, exploiting these scope distinctions, it is natural to add as well:

9. With respect to being a candidate, it's possible John's one;

this last being an instance of

13. [G]M[s](G cop s),

a sentence which is *de re* with respect to its general term only.

The effect of positioning modifiers with respect to scope markers is quite like that, e.g., of combining quantifiers with other operators. We recall Russell's definite descriptions in the presence of negation. We think of the Barcan formula and its converse, where modalities occur nested with quantifiers. It remains only to show that the scope relationships displayed in the different positionings of the modifiers relative to scope markers of the terms may have explicit, distinct semantical interpretations. These interpretations will show that possible distinct sentences stand logically in distinct inferential relationships. In particular, sentences with the modal cop-mod do not then collapse into equivalent sentences with the modal modifier positioned elsewhere.

We can establish these results by exploiting the familiar "possible worlds" interpretations of modal sentences. We do so for ease in making our case, quite without philosophical presumptions concerning the appropriateness of taking literally these interpretations of modality.

We think, then, of possibility as truth in some world "accessible" from our own. We embed this interpretation in a conservative extension of standard first-order logic. We think of the use of ordinary modal sentences as mundane[8] assertions true or false of the actual world. To each mundane assertion of modality there exists a certain unique transcription which is a sentence of standard first-order logic supplemented with some special predicates and constants and with some specific assumptions governing these. Mundane modal logical truths are those which have provable transcriptions in this extended 1st order logic.

For these purposes we introduce the following special terms. 'TwA' says that the proposition that A is true in the world w. 'Rww*' says that the world w* is accessible from w. 'BwI' expresses a membership relation. It says that an individual, I, singular or general, belongs to the world w.

Mundane truths are first relativized to the actual world, represented here by the special constant 'o'. Where 'M' is the modal operator expressing possibility, we have first 'To(MA)' for the mundane modal assertion of the possibility that A. The truth-in-a-world predicate, T, is then confined across formulas in accord with the following, familiar, stipulations:

$$Tw(MA) \quad to \quad (Ew^*)(Rww^* \& Tw^*A),$$

where 'M' is the expression of dominant scope in A. The truth-in-a-world predicate is further confined across binary truth-functional operators, as follows:

Tw(A # B)   to   (TwA) # (TwB);

and across negation,

Tw-A   to   -TwA.

For the quantifiers, confinement proceeds thusly:

Tw(EI)A   to   (EI) (BwI & TwA).

for individual variable, I, singular or general, and

Tw(I)A   to   (I) (BwI then TwA).

Finally, the truth-in-a-world predicate is confined similarly across occurrences of scope markers.

Tw[I]A   to   (BwI & TwA),

where 'I' is a term constant, singular or general.

To each mundane modal assertion we have by these principles a matching world theory transcription in which each occurrence of the truth-in-a-world predicate is confined to atomic formulas. Depending upon assumptions laid down for the accessibility relation, R, various standard modal systems result. Their theorems have provable transcriptions in our extended lst-order logic.

More relevant here, depending upon assumptions laid down concerning the membership relation, B, various distinct implicative relationships holding among sentences with the modal operator variously positioned have provable transcriptions as well. These assumptions are "population principles", principles distributing individuals and concepts across possible worlds.

On a certain population assumption, for instance, the mundane modal sentence with copula modifier implies, but is not implied by, an otherwise similar sentence but with just a general term modal modifier. And this sentence in turn, with its transparent, *de re* occurrence of the subject term, implies, but is not implied by, the matching *de dicto* sentence with its modal modifier of largest scope.

This is to say that sentences of the form 12., [s][G](GM(cop)s), imply but are not implied by those of the form 11., [s](M[G]G cop s). And this last implies but is not implied by those of the form 10., M[s][G](G cop s), on this certain assumption about membership in possible worlds. This is so, for the transcriptions of these stand in these implicative relationships, on that assumption, in standard 1st-order logic.

For instance, the world-theory transcription of 12. above is

Bos & BoG & (Ew) (Row & Tw(G cop s)).

The transcription of 11. above is

Bos & (Ew)(Row & BwG & Tw(G cop s)).

The former transcription implies the latter on an assumption of "increasing population", the assumption that any individual, singular or general, which belongs to a given world also belongs to any world accessible from it. That is, the implication holds on the assumption that:

(w)(w*)(I)(Rww* & BwI then Bw*I).

The converse assumption of "decreasing population", the assumption that any individual, singular or general, which is a member of a world accessible from another is also a member of that other world, is an assumption sufficient to support the converses of the implications above. These population principles may well strike one as implausible; certainly, the principle of decreasing population seems wildly so.

The general point, regardless of the plausibility of the population assumptions, is this: the patterns of inferential relationships and failures show that sentences involving copula or verbal modal modifiers do not in general collapse into equivalent sentences with those modifiers repositioned. These formal consequences reinforce the informal and intuitive suggestions which the grammar of commonsense examples anyway provides.

The upshot then is that copula modifiers have an integrity of their own.[9] They make an independent contribution to the significance of our sentences. The copula is not just a vehicle for expressing the mood of what we say, although it is also that. It is also a syntactical element upon which modifiers can be positioned with unique effect. The copula, in this secondary function, makes a necessary and substantive contribution to predication.

Even so, even if one grants the fact, there remain the questions: What shall we make of all this? Precisely what is the contribution of the copula to predication? Further, if distinct positionings of modifiers contribute distinct significance to sentences which are otherwise the same, then we have it seems not multiple occurrences of a single modifier but occurrences of paronymous modifiers. 'Rudely' in 'gestured rudely' is an adverb of manner. It has to do with how certain acts are performed. But 'rudely' in 'rudely gestured' is a predicate modifier and has to do with the occasion of the behavior. Evidently, although the semantic values of these operators are quite different, the modifiers share a common lexical core of meaning. And we have not discussed here how to accommodate paronyms.[10] So, both questions of the point and of the detail of all this remain and have, for me at least, some urgency. What reasonably can we conclude from the exercise?

Certainly, there are a few negative things we can say. We know at least that certain views are not right. They are not for they do not as yet systematically accommodate the special role the copula seems in fact to play. And there are some positive things to say as well. For the outcome seems at least to support a certain presumption. It is a presumption which is most easily and directly accommodated by the simplest but most flagrant of philosophical theories of predication. It is most simply accommodated by the view that the copula indicates a connexive mode of combination between certain entities which are specified in our acts of reference and attribution.

The important thing about presumptions is not that they can be overridden, although of course they can be. The important thing is that a presumption sheds the onus of proof to the opposite side. We need not seek additional reasons for accepting what is presumptively true. But we do need to provide special reasons for rejecting a presumptive truth. We need reasons for overriding what is presumptively so. Otherwise, lacking these, the presumption is the thing to accept.

In this instance, the natural, presumptive view is that the copula indicates a mode of connexion between discrete sorts of entity. It is worth emphasizing that this presumption is not overridden by simple appeals to its ontological excessiveness. To suppose so would beg the question. For this presumption resulted from an attempt to find independent, non-metaphysical grounds for the dispensibility of the copula. (Not to be coy, it was my anticipation before attempting this exercise that the copula would turn out to have at best only linguistic significance as an expression of mood. Since I now believe this is not the case, I face the task of trying to marshall additional, less simple and direct reasons for overriding the presumption that the copula in doing more functions connexively.)

However that may be, so long as the presumption remains intact and the grounds upon which it is based remain operative, the natural conclusion is that Strawson was after all quite right. The predicate does, not only grammatically but logically, discharge two basic functions: it does specify a concept under which an object of reference is, in the predication, said to fall. And it does indicate its mode of combination with that object. And Geach was right, too, at least about one thing: Strawson's characterization of predication is indeed tripartite. It is indeed logically of the form: subject-copula-general term.

Notes

1. This is a slightly altered version of a paper presented at the University of Iowa, Illinois University, and Northern Illinois University as well as to a faculty reading group at Indiana University. It benefits from the comments and criticisms which followed its presentation at each institution. The sins of commission and omission which remain are, of course, my own responsibility.

Part of the material for this paper was the result of work done under the auspices of a Fulbright grant, 1981-82. My thanks go to the Australian-American Foundation, to the Research School of Social Sciences, the Australian National University, and to Indiana University for their support during that year.

Finally, it is a pleasure to acknowledge the help and intellectual companionship of many friends. Of these, the examples, suggestions and criticisms offered recently by Tim Day, Tom Ernst, Barry Miller need special mention. Longer term, Robert Binkley, Hector Castaneda, Roger Fleming, Everett Hall, and John Heintz, have each influenced my views on the topics of this paper and related issues.

Neil Wilson, whose memory we honored on the occasion of these presentations, was a special intellectual companion and friend.

2. *Philosophical Subjects: Essays Presented to P.F. Strawson* Zak van Stratten, ed. See P.T. Geach, "Strawson on Subject and Predicate," p. 182. The present paper attempts to develop a suggestion made in my review of this festschrift for Strawson. See *Nous,* XVII, #4, (1983) pp. 694-701.

3. *Op.cit.,* pp. 292-293, "Replies."

4. *Ibid.* p. 293.

5. E. Stenius, *Wittgenstein's Tractatus: A Critical Exposition of Its Main Lines of Thought,* pp. 158-160.

6. Examples like these, as well as a range of others to other effect, are gratefully borrowed from Tom Ernst. See his *Towards an Integrated Theory of Adverb Position in English,* doctoral dissertation, Indiana University, 1983.

7. I borrow the term from John Heintz who, so far as I know, coined it. Heintz has investigated interesting issues turning upon apparent subject-predicate asymmetries in his *Subjects and Predicables.* So far as the predicate side goes, Heintz early on suggested that identity conditions for predicables require that the expressions for these must mutually satisfy, with coincident truth-values, the modifiers that attach to them.

8. This use of 'mundane' in the context of "world-theory" is due to Robert Binkley. More important, the form as well as the underlying ideas of world-theory as characterized here owe much to Binkley.

9. This isn't quite as clean, nor as clear-cut, as one would like. For [s][G]M(G cop s), in which the modifier governs the sentential clause, has transparent occurrences of 's' and 'G' quite as much as has the targeted occurrence of the cop-mod [s][G](G M(cop) s). Scope alone is insufficiently fine-grained to distinguish between them. There is, however, a difference. If the latter is

the form of, say, a sentence like "John is possibly a candidate," then the former must run something like this: "With respect to John and with respect to candidacy (or being a candidate,) it is possible that he is one." The former achieves transparency, unlike the latter, at the price of a prefixed nominalized specification of the general term.

10. One might suppose that these differently positioned adverbs take their shared lexical significance from the adjective; that on the one hand, whoever gestures in a certain way ("flips the finger," say) is a rude person. But also, on the other hand, whoever gestures on a certain occasion (at a presentation ceremony, say) is a rude person as well. But this is not in general true. Consider, "James Bond initially cleverly spoke stupidly to his interrogators. Later, when fatigued, he stupidly spoke cleverly to them." It does not follow from the narrative that he was on either occasion at once both clever and stupid. And from the fact he spoke stupidly to his interrogators it does not of course follow that he was stupid. We are told he was clever to do so. The upshot is that capturing the common lexical core of paronymous adverbs is a more complicated (and so more interesting) semantical task than one might initially think. (For examples like this and a general discussion of the topic, see the reference to Ernst, footnote 6, as well as further citations in his thesis.)

Why Did Russell Think 'E!a' Was Meaningless?

Nicholas Griffin

It is a well-known but puzzling fact that Russell thought expressions of the form 'E!a', where 'a' is a logically proper name, were meaningless. That is, he thought it was meaningless to ascribe existence (or non-existence) to items referred to by a logically proper name. The very simplest explanation of this would seem to be that he took over the position directly from Frege without thinking too much about it.[1] Another simple explanation is that the existential expression 'E!' is defined only for descriptions, by

PM *14.02 E!(ιx) (ϕx) = ($\exists b$) ($\forall x$) ($\phi x \equiv x = b$) Df.

But now we need to know why the definition of 'E!' is so restricted. Russell plainly intended the restriction to capture some philosophical requirement on a logically perspicuous notation. The problem is to identify the requirement. It is compounded (rather than alleviated) by the fact that just about every explanation that has occurred to anyone can be given some basis in the various texts in which Russell deals with the matter.

It seems to me that Russell came to hold his view about 'E!a' primarily for two reasons, neither widely recognized. The first derived directly from Frege, but was reinforced by Russell's own type theory. The second argument, based on Russell's theory of judgment, has not, to my knowledge, been previously recognized in the secondary literature. Of the two arguments, the one from the theory of judgment strikes me as much the more powerful, making Russell's conclusion about 'E!a' all but inescapable. By contrast, the type-theoretic argument seems to me to beg the question. In addition to these two arguments, however, Russell put forward a number of others — all much weaker than the original two.

These weaker arguments appeared for the most part in works written during or after 1918. By this time Russell had come to doubt the validity of the theory of judgment upon which his earlier arguments depended. Russell never gave up his thesis that 'E!a' was meaningless,[2] though he never afterwards espoused the theory of judgment that had originally made it necessary. It must be supposed, therefore, unless there is some further argument for the thesis that has so far escaped detection, that he considered his later arguments sufficient to establish the thesis. The second section of this paper will argue that they are not. First, however, I shall consider some general features of Russell's account of the logic of 'exists'. In the third section I shall explain the type-theoretic argument, and in the fourth section the argument from the theory of judgment which originally led Russell to adopt the thesis. In the final section I shall consider some important loose ends which are not tied up on my account, nor, so far as I know, on any other.

It must be admitted, however, that it will not be possible to form an interpretation of Russell's position that consistently combines all texts. Some of the tensions which can be found between Russell's various statements on the topic are due to changes in his philosophical position, particularly the changes in his theory of judgment referred to above. But not all discrepancies can be cleared up this way. Thus in 1912 Russell admits as a judgment of perception a judgment such as 'there is that' 'which simply asserts the *existence* of the sense-datum, without in any way analysing it'.[3] This passage was written between the publication of the first volume of *Principia* and the writing of *Theory of Knowledge*, with both of which it seems directly inconsistent. Barring some subtlety of interpretation which escapes me, the passage from *Problems* must be put down to simple inadvertence.

I

For Russell, as for Frege, existence was a higher order property, 'a property of a propositional function', as Russell put it.[4] What this means is that talk about existence amounts to talk about the satisfaction of propositional functions. Thus, as he goes on to explain, to say that 'Unicorns exist' is to say that the function '$\hat{x}$ is a unicorn' is possible, that is, for some assignment to x, 'x is a unicorn' is true, or '$(\exists x)$ (x is a unicorn)'. Similarly, to say that 'Unicorns don't exist' is to say that the function '$\hat{x}$ is a unicorn' is impossible, that 'x is a unicorn' is false for every value of x, or '$-(\exists x)$ (x is a unicorn)'. This, of course, is straight classical semantics where variables range only over existents (though Russell's own terminology, which talks of the necessity, possibility or impossibility of propositional functions, now appears quaint).[5] In short, the business of asserting existence or nonexistence gets taken over by the quantifiers.

When it is desired to assert the existence of some particular thing it becomes necessary, according to Russell, to do so by means of definite descriptions. These contain the propositional functions which are necessary if assertions of existence or non-existence are to be expressed entirely by means of quantifiers. How this is done is revealed by *14.02, which also allows the introduction of 'E!', which may be regarded as a grammatical, but not as a logical, predicate. Russell puts the point this way:

> To say 'My present sense-datum exists' is to say (roughly): 'There is an object of which "my present sense-datum" is a description.' But we cannot say: 'There is an object of which "x" is a description', because "x" is (in the case we are supposing) a name, not a description.[6]

Now this obviously gives us part of the explanation we want. For it explains how, in a great many cases, assertions of existence can be handled by quantification without the need for a special existence predicate. But it does explain *only part* of what we want explained. For there are in English two devices which are typically used to assert existence, the quantifier 'there is' and the predicate 'exists'. What Russell has shown (following Frege's lead) is that quantification is sufficient to handle many existential claims, including many which, in natural language, are more naturally expressed by means of the existence predicate. When Frege writes in 'On Concept and Object' (*op.cit.*, p. 50) that 'There is Julius Caesar' is senseless he is avoiding the issue which here concerns us. For the existence of Julius Caesar is not asserted in natural language by the quantifier expression, but by the existence predicate. Nothing has been done to show that 'Julius Caesar exists' is meaningless. Russell, with the help of the theory of descriptions, is able to push the account further by showing how 'The conqueror of Gaul exists' can be handled by quantifiers; and even, with the help of his description theory of names, how 'Julius Caesar exists' can be so handled, by construing the name as a description. But this has done nothing to show that quantifiers can handle all ascriptions of existence. For to do that along the lines sketched would require the elimination of all names in favour of descriptions, and this Russell explicitly denies in the case of logically proper names. Moreover, even if this were done (as it is by Quine's proposals for the elimination of singular terms, e.g.) it would only have been shown that a special existence predicate was unnecessary. It would not have been shown that the use of such a predicate resulted in meaninglessness. Russell's theory of quantification, therefore, even when supplemented by the theory of descriptions and the description theory of names, does not explain why he thought that 'a exists' was meaningless when 'a' was a logically proper name.

II

In introducing 'E!' in *Principia Mathematica* Russell apparently appeals to ordinary language for support: 'When, in ordinary language or in philosophy, something is said to "exist", it is always something *described*, i.e. it is not something immediately presented ... but something ... which is known by description as "the so-and- so".'[7] Since logically proper names can apply only to items immediately presented ('PLA', p. 178), it would follow that 'a exists, where 'a' is a logically proper name, never occurs in ordinary language. It is hard to see why such sentences should never occur, though it is not difficult to see why they should be at least rare. For if *a* is immediately presented, its existence is obvious and thus not worth asserting. Similarly, to deny that *a* exists will be false. Thus 'E!*a*' will be trivial, while '−E!*a*' will be contextually self-refuting.

It has commonly been assumed that this was all Russell meant when he said that 'E!*a*' was meaningless.[8] Indeed, Russell himself does give this account:

> There is no sort of point in a predicate which could not conceivably be false. I mean, it is perfectly clear that, if there were such a thing as this existence of individuals that we talk of,[9] it would be absolutely impossible for it not to apply, and that is the characteristic of a mistake. ('PLA', p. 211)

But this cannot have been all he meant by saying that 'E!*a*' was meaningless. For it is one thing to say that an expression is trivial and quite another to say that it is meaningless.[10] In fact Russell's type theory ensures that whatever is trivially true cannot be meaningless. Nor was Russell inclined to confuse triviality with meaninglessness. On occasion, it is true, it may seem as though he does, as, for example, when he writes, in denying that facts have truth-values, 'you could only say of a thing that it was true, if it was the sort of thing that *might* be false' ('PLA', p. 165). But this remark is ambiguous, depending upon whether it is read as a modal claim or as a significance claim. It can hardly be that Russell is saying that nothing can be true unless it were *possible* for it to be false; what he is saying is that nothing could significantly be said to be true unless it were also the sort of thing that could significantly be said to be false. Propositional functions which are satisfied for all values of their variables, in fact, are essential both to his logic and his metaphysics.[11] Our conclusion is reinforced by Russell's remarks about judgments of perception (*PM*, I, p. 43) in which a judgment is derived from a perception of a complex by mere attention. Such a judgment might be '*a* is red', where *a* is a red sense-datum present to a subject who is aware of its colour. Russell admits that we might err in thinking a given judgment was a judgment of perception when in fact it was not, but if we have a genuine judgment of perception we cannot be mistaken as to its truth. Judgments of perception must be true, but for all that it doesn't follow that they are meaningless, indeed it follows precisely that they are significant. What is there to prevent our construing 'a exists' as a judgment of perception?[12] The answer, on present showing, must be, nothing.

Another argument of Russell's, this time from the *Introduction to Mathematical Philosophy*, at least takes us from triviality to genuine meaninglessness. According to Russell, if 'a' is a logically proper name, 'a' means a ('PLA', p. 173), and the meaning of any sentence in which 'a' occurs will be a function of the meaning of 'a'. Thus the sentence 'a exists' will be meaningless if a does not exist. So, too, will be 'a does not exist'.[13] Russell puts the argument this way:

> It is only of descriptions — definite or indefinite — that existence can be significantly asserted; for if 'a' is a name, it *must* name something: what does not name anything is not a name, and therefore, if intended to be a name, is a symbol devoid of meaning, whereas a description, like 'the present King of France', does not become incapable of occurring significantly merely on the ground that it describes nothing, the reason being that it is a *complex* symbol, of which the meaning is derived from that of its constituents.[14]

Orenstein[15] presents this as the following argument from significant negation: If 'a exists' is meaningful, then so is '_a exists'. But '_a exists' is not meaningful, therefore neither is 'a exists'. This may well be an accurate reconstruction of the argument Russell intended, but it is not a very good argument. For the meaninglessness of '_a exists' has not been established. What has been established is that if 'a' does not name anything then '_a exists' and 'a exists' are both meaningless. Thus, in the case where 'a' does not name anything, there is no need to proceed via the principle of significant negation; while in the case where 'a' does name something nothing has been done to establish that either 'a exists' or its negation is meaningless. Another thing to be noted about Russell's argument is that its application is not restricted to ascriptions of existence. For if 'a' is a name which does not name anything then 'ϕa' will be meaningless for *any* function '$\phi \hat{x}$'. This is an extension which Russell is prepared explicitly to countenance.[16] Put in different terms, it is an immediate consequence of the fact that names which do not name anything are not logically proper that they do not occur in a logically perfect language. In a logically perfect language, therefore, there will be no such well-formed expression as 'ϕa' where 'a' does not name anything.

This being so, however, it is difficult to see why Russell thought his argument in *Introduction to Mathematical Philosophy* would show that 'E!*a*' was meaningless. Moreover, it is difficult to imagine any principle which would get him from what has been established, namely that 'E!*a*' and every expression of the form '*φa*' is meaningless when *a* does not exist, to what he wants to establish, that 'E!*a*' is meaningless whether or not *a* exists, *without* also yielding the general conclusion that '*φa*' is meaningless whether or not *a* exists. And the chances of such a principle's being true are very much slimmer!

Sainsbury construes the same argument rather differently:

> Any meaningful sentence has a meaningful negation. So any meaningful sentence is one which, if it were false, would be meaningful. So if '*a* exists' is meaningful, it would be meaningful even if it were false. But it would not be meaningful if false, for '*a*' would be bearerless. Therefore, '*a* exists' is meaningless, whether we envisage it to be true or whether we envisage it to be false. (Sainsbury, *op.cit.*, p. 80)

The argument is invalid, as Sainsbury goes on to point out, because from the fact that every meaningful sentence has a meaningful negation it does not follow that any meaningful sentence is such that it would be meaningful if it were false. Sainsbury gives 'Some sentences are meaningful' as an obvious example for which the inference fails. Now there would certainly be no reason for Russell to be impressed by this counter-example of Sainsbury's, nor by any of his others. For type theory would rule out as meaningless 'Some sentences are meaningful' on the only interpretation of the range of its quantifier which would make it work as a counter-example. But even if Russell did intend the argument that Sainsbury puts forward on his behalf, there are good Russellian grounds for rejecting it. It relies on the distinctly non-Russellian principle that 'E!*a*', if it were false, would be meaningless. But what is false is never meaningless. Thus either 'E!*a*' is not false or it is meaningful. Since 'E!*a*' is never false, we can infer nothing from this argument as to whether it is meaningful or not. Sainsbury's version of the argument, therefore, does not get us any further than Orenstein's.

Russell's case for the meaninglessness of 'E!*a*' so far looks surprisingly weak. Yet strong justification is exactly what the thesis desperately needs, for it has hardly any initial plausibility of its own, as Russell is prepared to acknowledge ('PLA', p. 205). Moreover, strong arguments can be mounted against it, as Moore has shown (*op. cit.*, pp. 124-5). Moore argues that for any named, individual object of acquaintance, *a*, it is always meaningful to say of *a* that it might not have existed, and this implies that the proposition '*a* does not exist' might have been true, and this in turn implies that it is significant and not true. But if it is significant and not true, it must be false. But if '*a* does not exist' is false, '*a* exists' is true, and, if true, then significant. Ayer (*op.cit.*, pp. 36-7) takes this to show (as does Moore), not that Russell is wrong, but that there is a sense of 'exists' which is not touched by Russell's analysis. Ayer maintains that this new sense is that which is operative in philosophical ontology. Unfortunately, Russell does not allow himself any such easy way out. Russell clearly thought his analysis of 'exists' applied to all senses of the word, and he is emphatic (*PM*, I, p. 175) that it is applicable to the senses used in philosophical ontology. It is clear therefore that Russell must have some reply to Moore's argument. It seems to me most likely, especially in view of his suspicion of propositional modalities,[17] that Russell would deny Moore's premise, that it is significant to say of *a* that it might not have existed. Quite apart from his rejection of '*a* exists', it is difficult to see how Russell could have expressed '*a* might not have existed' in his canonical language.

III

Russell's first really important argument for the claim that '*a* exists' is meaningless is best known in the following form:

> You can consider the proposition 'Unicorns exist' and can see that it is false. It is not nonsense. Of course, if the proposition went through the general conception of the unicorn to the individual, it could not be even significant unless there were unicorns. Therefore when you say 'Unicorns exist', you are not saying anything about any individual things, and the same applies when you say 'Men exist'. If you say that 'Men exist, and Socrates is a man, therefore Socrates exists', that is exactly the same sort of fallacy as it would be if you said 'Men are numerous, Socrates is a man, therefore Socrates is numerous'. ('PLA', pp. 204-5)[18]

Unfortunately, in this form, it looks as if Russell's point is a mere corollary of what was earlier called the argument from significant negation. In fact, the argument Russell is presenting is quite different. Russell states the new argument more clearly elsewhere:

We may correctly say 'men exist', meaning that '*x* is a man' is sometimes true. But if we make a pseudo-syllogism: 'Men exist, Socrates is a man, therefore Socrates exists', we are talking nonsense, since 'Socrates is not, like 'men', merely an undetermined argument to a given propositional function. The fallacy is closely analogous to that of the argument: 'Men are numerous, Socrates is a man, therefore Socrates is numerous.' In this case it is obvious that the conclusion is nonsensical, but in the case of existence it is not obvious .... (*IMP*, pp. 164-5).

Perhaps because the *Introduction to Mathematical Philosophy* is little read nowadays, while the more popular version in 'The Philosophy of Logical Atomism' doesn't clearly distinguish the argument from the argument from significant negation, Russell's new argument is not now widely recognized (an exception is Orenstein, *op. cit.*, pp. 16-17).

The new argument is type-theoretic in nature and derives from the central claim of Russell's theory of existence, that 'exists' applies primarily to propositional functions. Consider Russell's pseudo-syllogism:

	(i)	Men exist
	(ii)	Socrates is a man
Therefore	(iii)	Socrates exists

If we formalize (i) as Russell prescribes, as '$(\exists x)$ (*x* is a man)', it is immediately clear that we have no corresponding way of formulating the required conclusion. Moreover (and here's where type theory comes in), if we did provide ourselves with some means of formulating the required conclusion, e.g. by introducing a primitive first-order predicate 'exists', it would not make the argument valid. For 'exists' as it occurs in the first premise is a function of functions — the first premise asserts that the function ' $\hat{x}$ is a man' is possible — while 'exists' as it occurs in the conclusion is a function of individuals. Thus 'exists' is used ambiguously in the argument. Accordingly, even with a device for expressing the existence of individuals, the argument would be invalid.

Even so, Russell's argument is hardly compelling. For if we allow ourselves an existence predicate applicable to individuals, then we can use it to formulate (i) in a non-Russellian way. It would be quite natural for those not initiated in classical quantification theory (as for those who've seen its defects) to formulate (i) as

(i') $(\forall x)$ (*x* is a man $\supset$ *x* exists).

Indeed, it might be objected to the Russellian formulation of (i) that it did not capture what was plainly intended by (i), namely that *all* men exist. With (i) construed as (i′) the argument goes through to the conclusion 'Socrates exists' without any ambiguity. Of course, we haven't done enough yet to show that our formulation of the argument is preferable to Russell's. But we have done enough to show that Russell's use of the argument to prove that existence cannot be meaningfully ascribed to individuals begs the question. Russell would have to show that there was something wrong with our construing (i) as (i′), but his only ground for objection is that '*x* exists' is meaningless, which it was the purpose of his argument to demonstrate.

IV

There is, however, a further argument of Russell's against '*a* exists', one which to my knowledge has never previously been recognized. It is, moreover, an argument which has certain important advantages over all the arguments previously considered. For one thing, it is an argument directly and unambiguously to the conclusion that '*a* exists' is *meaningless*, rather than to claims that such expressions can be avoided or are trivial. For another, it is valid. For a third, it enables us to explain why so many commentators have assumed that Russell was arguing that '*a* exists' was vacuous (as well as why some of Russell's own remarks suggest that interpretation). For it will turn out that on Russell's theory of judgment '*a* exists' is vacuous, but in a different and more radical sense than that usually supposed.

Russell himself puts the crucial argument so briefly and obscurely (maintaining, quite falsely, that it is 'fully explained' in *PM*) that it is little wonder it has been neglected. He writes:

> Words that go in pairs, such as 'real' and 'unreal', 'existent' and 'non-existent', 'valid' and 'invalid', etc., are all derived from one fundamental pair, 'true' and 'false'. Now 'true' and 'false' are applicable only — except in derivative significations — to *propositions*. Thus whenever the above pairs can be significantly applied, we must be dealing either with propositions or such incomplete phrases as only acquire meaning when put into a context which, with them, forms a proposition. Thus such pairs of words can be applied to *descriptions,* but not to proper names: in other words, they have no application whatever to data, but only to entities or non-entities described in terms of data. ('RSDP', p. 23)

Russell does not explain how the various pairs are to be derived from 'true' and 'false', nor does he attempt to justify his claim that members of the pairs can only be applied to propositions or (other) incomplete symbols — on this last point he refers, rather optimistically, to *Principia* for clarification. Nonetheless, his general motivation is readily explained. Like all classical logicians, Russell found it necessary to do semantics within an ontologically constrained framework, that is without ineliminable reference to non-existent items of any kind. In the case of the paired terms this is hard, for a (referential) semantical interpretation has to be given to both members of the pair, yet if one member of the pair holds, the other does not. This suggests a natural semantic interpretation in terms of non-existent objects or nonfactual situations, etc. One member of the pair is semantically assigned an existent item, the other a non-existent one. In the fundamental case of 'true' and 'false' Russell thought he had, in the multiple relation theory of judgment,[19] a way to do the semantics without reference to non-existent items, in particular without reference to false propositions or non-actual complexes. To see how this applied to existence and non-existence it is necessary to explain the multiple relation theory in a little more detail, and to switch our attention to judgments as to the existence or non-existence of individuals.

As is well-known, Russell had a two-tier epistemology, based upon acquaintance, a two-place relation between a subject and a presented object. One has to be acquainted with an object in order to name it ('PLA', p. 201). At the level of acquaintance questions of truth and falsity do not arise, they belong exclusively to the second tier of Russell's epistemology. Since Russell was unwilling to countenance propositions as objects of belief (for, under the terms of Russell's realism, that would require the existence or subsistence of false propositions), he adopted the view that belief was a 'multiple relation', relating the believing mind to a variety of objects of belief. Thus, famously, 'Othello believes that Desdemona loves Cassio' does not relate Othello to the proposition that Desdemona loves Cassio (for there is no such thing), but severally to the object terms of the judgment, namely, to Desdemona, Cassio and the universal *loves*. Truth and falsehood apply primarily to beliefs: a belief is true if the objects of the belief are related together as the believer supposes them to be related, and false otherwise. Propositions strictly drop out of the picture entirely, but Russell keeps the term to apply to incomplete symbols which are in themselves meaningless outside the context of so-called propositional attitudes, such as belief or understanding. A proposition may be said to result from the occurrence of a (psychological) complex united by a multiple relation such as belief or understanding. The key point, for present purposes, is that truth and falsity only arise in connection with multiple relations. The object of a dyadic relation, such as acquaintance, *cannot* be true or false. For truth or falsity one requires a multiple relation, relating the epistemic subject to two or more object terms.

These considerations can be applied fairly directly to the case of '*a* exists'. If '*a* exists' is meaningful, it expresses some proposition, true or false. But there can only be such a proposition if someone entertains it by adopting an appropriate propositional attitude, for example if someone makes a judgment to the effect that *a* exists. This would seem not to be difficult, since anyone who was acquainted with *a* might be thought in a position to do so. In fact, however, it turns out to be absolutely impossible. For in order to make a judgment to the effect that ϕa it is necessary to be acquainted with the subject *a* and with the universal ϕ that appears in the predicate. But in the case of '*a* exists' there is no such universal. In order for a judgment to be possible there must be at least two object terms, but in the case of '*a* exists' there is only one, *a* itself. As Russell puts it, 'Socrates himself does not render any statement true or false. You might be inclined to suppose that all by himself he would give truth to the statement "Socrates existed", but as a matter of fact that is a mistake.' ('PLA', p. 164). The point is the familiar one that saying of a presented object that it exists makes, as the saying goes, 'no addition to it'.[20] Existence is not a universal, not because everything exemplifies it, but because it's empty of content. A universal, to be an object of cognition, must have some content, existence has none.[21] Hume had already used this point in an argument designed to show that beliefs involving only a single idea were possible, for, he claimed, it was possible to believe that *a* exists even though the only idea involved in this belief was that of *a* itself (*Treatise*, I, iii, 7; Selby-Bigge edn., p. 96n). Russell quotes the argument (*TK*, pp. 137-8), but draws a quite different conclusion from it. Russell accepts Hume's claim that saying of a presented object that it exists adds nothing to the presentation: 'We seem to judge that objects of sense exist, and to add nothing, in so judging, to what is already given in sense' (*TK*, p. 138). However, since Russell is committed to a multiplicity of object terms in a belief, he draws from this the opposite conclusion to Hume's: namely, that a judgment that *a* exists, where *a* is an object of acquaintance, is impossible. From this it follows that there can be no proposition which '*a* exists' expresses and no question can arise as to whether '*a* exists' is true or false. Accordingly, '*a* exists' must be meaningless.

By 1918 Russell had abandoned the multiple relation theory, and was searching for a new theory of judgment and belief (which he now distinguished for the first time) along behaviourist lines. In his prison writings on the topic, he reconsiders Hume's argument, this time accepting it without demur:

[B]elief does not seem to involve *necessarily* any complexity of ideas. A single idea, felt in a certain way, and operative in a certain way, may be a belief, namely what we call the belief that such-and-such a thing 'exists' ....[22]

On the face of it, this remark would seem to indicate a reversal of his position. Admitting that we may believe in the existence of presented particulars would seem to undermine Russell's claim that '*a* exists' is meaningless. In fact, however, this consequence is blocked because Russell now wishes to distinguish between beliefs, judgments and propositions in ways in which he didn't while he held the multiple relation theory. Russell is attempting to explain belief in terms of an idea coupled with a certain type of feeling and a certain kind of causal efficacy. But the judgment is different, for the 'logical content' of the judgment corresponding to this belief is 'the object of this idea exists' (*ibid.*). Propositions are different again, though more closely related to judgments than beliefs.[23] In fact, in his developed neutral monist theory of propositions, as it emerged in 'On Propositions: What they Are and How they Mean', a proposition is defined as '[w]hat we believe when we believe truly or falsely' (*Collected Papers*, vol. 8, p. 279). But Russell is at pains to point out (*ibid.*, p. 296) that he is neither asserting nor denying that 'what is believed must always be the sort of thing which we express by a proposition', on the grounds that 'a single simple image may be believed'. Thus Russell's willingness, as an embryonic neutral monist, to countenance beliefs that presented particulars exist, does not entail a revision of his view that propositions which use logically proper names to assert that they do are meaningless.

V

We have seen that Russell was forced to regard '*a* exists' as meaningless because there was no such universal as existence. These considerations take care of at least one potentially puzzling feature of Russell's position.[24] Russell on many occasions ('RSDP', p. 23; *PM*. I. p. 67) admits that an item denoted by a logically proper name may also be denoted by a definite description. Now suppose we have '$a = (\iota x) (\phi x)$' and '$E!(\iota x) (\phi x)$', by substitutivity '$E!a$' follows. In fact, however, this argument is blocked for Russell because 'existence' is not a universal, and thus '$E!$' is not a predicate and so cannot be instantiated in substitutivity arguments. It is as well that this is so, because otherwise '$E!a$' would be *provable* within *Principia*. For we have *14.2, $\vdash (\iota x \ (x=a) = a$, and $E!(\iota x) \ (x=a) = (\exists b) (\forall y)(y = a \equiv y = b)$ Df.

But one further point needs to be considered. We have not so far seen why Russell was unable to extend the definition of 'E!' to apply to logically proper names. As is now well-known, '*a* exists' can be classically replaced by '($\exists x$) ($x =$ *a*).[25] So that to say that '*a* exists' is to say that the function '$\hat{x} = a$' *is satisfied by some value of* its variable. Thus there would seem to be no objection, so far, to extending exists' is to say that the function '$\hat{x} = a$' is satisfied by some value of the definition of 'E!' by adding to *14.02

$$*14.02a \quad E!a = (\exists x) (x = a) \; Df.^{26}$$

Russell never, to my knowledge, used this, now standard, device for expressing existence. It is possible that he never thought of it, even though he has its analogue for descriptions:

$$PM *14.204 \quad E!(\iota x) \; \phi x) = (\exists b) (\iota x) (\phi x) = b).$$

He came closer later when he considered representing 'There is at least one thing in the world' by '($\exists x$)($x = x$)', or, as he puts it, '$\hat{x} = \hat{x}$' is possible ('PLA', p. 210). In fact, Russell had had this notational device from Wittgenstein as early as 1913, if he had not previously thought of it himself. In a letter of 29th October 1913, Wittgenstein signs himself, 'Yours as long as E!L.W.'[27] The valediction of his next letter is more correct formally: 'Yours as long as ($\exists x$).$x =$ L.W.' (*ibid*, R20, p. 34). Unless this notation occurs in one of Russell's many unpublished logic manuscripts, this joke of Wittgenstein's would seem to be its first occurrence anywhere.

Wittgenstein, however, was far from proposing the notation for use. On its first occurrence, he appended a footnote to it which reads: 'This prop[osition] will probably turn out to have no meaning.' (*ibid.*) He did not arrive at this conclusion immediately, however, for in another letter later the same year, Wittgenstein refers to '($\exists x$)($x = x$)', reasonably enough, as 'a proposition of *physics*', in contrast to '($\forall x$)(($x = x$) $\supset$ ($\exists y$)($y = y$)', *i.e.*, ($\exists x$)($x = x$)$\supset$ ($\exists y$)($y = y$), which is genuinely logical (*ibid.*, R23, p. 42). Wittgenstein's subsequent thought on the matter is to be found in his notebooks. Thus on 11th November 1914 he describes using '($\exists x$ ($x = a$)' to express '*a* exists' as a 'swindle'.[28] Indeed, it seems rather worse than a swindle, for elsewhere in the *Notebooks* '($\forall x$) ($x = a$)', 'or the like', are said to be pseudo-propositions (*ibid.*, p. 34; see also, p. 47). The reason is not hard to find, for as Wittgenstein put it: 'To say of two classes that they are identical means something. To say it of two things means nothing.' (*ibid.*, p. 4). Wittgenstein's early thinking on identity culminates with its abolition in the *Tractatus* 5.53ff.

In this, as in much else, the early Wittgenstein is pushing to its logical conclusion a doctrine only hinted at by Russell. It is true that Wittgenstein in the *Tractatus* criticizes Russell's theory of identity (PM*13), but Russell had pointed out that the chief use of identity was in connection with descriptions (PM, I, p. 23), and later he notes that the use of identity in connection with proper names results in triviality (*ibid*, p. 6-7; also 'PLA', p. 215). Now if Russell has grounds for dismissing (as meaningless) propositions of the form '$a = b$', where 'a' and 'b' are names, then he has grounds for dismissing '$(\exists x)(x = a)$' as a canonical notation for 'a exists'. Wittgenstein obviously thought there were such grounds and Russell, later on, may have accepted Wittgenstein's position. But even before Wittgenstein's position emerged, Russell, I believe, would still have had some grounds for holding that '$a = b$' is meaningless, namely that there is no more an identity universal holding between particulars than there is an existence universal which they instantiate. On Russell's account of higher-order judgments (PM, I, pp. 41-7), a judgment to the effect that $(\exists x)(x = a)$ amounts to the judgment that some judgment of the form $x = a$ has first-order truth. Plainly definite descriptions will be inadmissible as substitutions for 'x' in such an elementary judgment. Accordingly, the requisite elementary judgment may be represented by '$b = a$', where 'b' is a logically proper name. Clearly a judgment of this form will be true only when 'a' and 'b' are two logically proper names for the same item. In order to make such a judgment, on Russell's theory, one would have to be acquainted with the item they both name, and with some universal. But here the universal seems every bit as elusive as it was in the case of 'a exists' and it is tempting to conclude that Russell held that no judgment to the effect that $a = b$ was possible where 'a' and 'b' are both logically proper names, and thus that '$a = b$' was meaningless. If this is so, it is immediately clear why he could not accept '$(\exists x)(x = a)$' as any improvement on 'a exists'.

Against this we must note that when, in *Principia*, he notes that identity is mainly useful in conjunction with descriptions, Russell *implies* that propositions of the form '$a = b$' are merely trivial, not meaningless. If this is what he intends to claim and if he is not just simply inconsistent on the point then he must have some independent ground for rejecting '$(\exists x)(x = a)$' as a reading for 'a exists'. Otherwise, his logically perfect language would translate a meaningless natural language sentence into a trivial canonical language proposition. It could be, of course, that Russell simply didn't think of reading 'a exists' as '$(\exists x)(x = a)$' in which case the discrepancy would be simply an oversight, which would require some modification to the text of *PM*, I, pp. 23, 67 to correct. Wittgenstein's own objection to reading 'a exists' as '$(\exists x)(x = a)$' is implied by *Tractatus* 5.5352. There he argues that 'There are *no* things' cannot be read as '$\neg(\exists x)(x = x)$' because, even if the latter were a proposition, it would be consistent with 'there are things but they are not identical with themselves'. Similarly, we could distinguish between 'a exists' and '$(\exists x)(x = a)$', on the grounds that a might exist but not be identical with itself (and *a fortiori* not identical with anything else) and thus that there was nothing such that it was identical with *a*. This would certainly provide an argument against reading '*a* exists' as '$(\exists x)(x = a)$' which was quite independent of the arguments that both were meaningless. Yet one can be reasonably sure that it is not an argument that would appeal very strongly to Russell given Russell's strong inclination, from his earliest analytic days, to associate being or existence with self-identity.[29]

There is, therefore, some doubt as to what Russell's actual position on identity was, and how it changed as a result of Wittgenstein's influence. But this much at least is clear: he could not consistently hold (i) that '*a* exists' could be represented by '$(\exists x)(x = a)$', (ii) that '*a* exists' was meaningless and (iii) that '*a = b*' was meaningful but trivial. It seems to me altogether most likely that he would have rejected (iii). Certainly, in lieu of any argument against (i), it seems to me that (iii) is what he ought to have rejected.

Notes

1. See Frege, *The Foundation of Arithmetic,* transl. J.L. Austin. (Oxford: Blackwell, 1953), p. 65; 'On Concept and Object' in P. Geach and M. Black (eds.), *Translations from the Philosophical Writings of Gottlob Frege* (Oxford: Blackwell, 1977), p. 50. Perhaps the very latest wisdom is a variant of this, namely that Russell took the doctrine over from Frege without understanding it.

2. He appeals to it in his 1948 debate with Copleston on the existence of God in *Why I am Not a Christian,* ed. by Paul Edwards, (London: Allen and Unwin, 1967; 1st edn. 1957), pp. 141-2. He also had the thesis early, in fact immediately after the theory of descriptions. It is stated clearly in a letter to P.E.B. Jourdain on 13 January 1906. The letter contains an excellent, concise account of the theory of descriptions, much clearer than the one published in 'On Denoting' in *Mind* (1905). See I. Grattan-Guinness, *Dear Russell — Dear Jourdain* (London: Duckworth, 1977), p. 70.

3. *The Problems of Philosophy* (Oxford: Oxford University Press, 1974; 1st edn. 1912), p. 66.

4. 'The Philosophy of Logical Atomism', in *The Collected Papers of Bertrand Russell,* Volume 8, ed. by J.G. Slater, (London: Allen and Unwin, 1986), p. 204. Henceforth cited as 'PLA'. A good general account of Russell's theory of existence, bringing together the various published sources, is to be found in C.E. Cassin, *The Origin and Development of Bertrand Russell's Theory of Descriptions* (Ph.D. Thesis, Florida State University, 1969), pp. 116-125.

5. In this, I think classical semantics is fundamentally mistaken. But I shall make no further reference to its defects. For the rest of this paper my framework will be resolutely classical.

6. 'The Relation of Sense-Data to Physics', in *Collected Papers,* Vol. 8, p. 23. Henceforth cited as 'RSDP'.

7. A.N. Whitehead and B. Russell, *Principia Mathematica* (Cambridge: Cambridge University Press; 2nd edn. 1925-7; 1st edn. 1910-13), Vol. I, pp. 174-5. Henceforth cited as 'PM'.

8. Cf., e.g., A.J. Ayer, *Russell and Moore: The Analytical Heritage* (London: Macmillan, 1971), pp. 35-6; D.F. Pears, *Bertrand Russell and the British Tradition in Philosophy* (London: Fontana, 1967), p 57n; Ronald Jager, *The Development of Bertrand Russell's Philosophy* (London:

Allen and Unwin, 1972), p. 257; Herbert Hochberg, *Thought, Fact and Reference. The Origins and Ontology of Logical Atomism* (Minneapolis: University of Minnesota Press, 1978), p. 242; R.M. Sainsbury, *Russell* (London: Routledge and Kegan Paul, 1979), pp. 80-2.

9. In this admission Russell would seem to undermine his own ordinary language argument in *Principia.*

10. As G.E. Moore pointed out in an important discussion of Russell's views 'Is Existence a Predicate?' in Moore's *Philosophical Papers* (London: Allen and Unwin, 1959), p. 124.

11. Rejection of such functions as meaningless has traditionally been a key feature of various projects for the elimination of rational metaphysics. See, e.g., Wittgenstein's treatment of formal concepts, *Tractatus Logico-Philosophicus,* (London: Routledge and Kegan Paul, 1966), 4.126ff; and Carnap, *Logical Syntax of Language,* (London: Routledge and Kegan Paul, 1967), pp. 292ff. For criticism relevant to our present concerns see Quine, *Ontological Relativity and Other Essays* (New York: Columbia University Press, 1969), p. 93.

12. As Russell on one occasion did, in the passage cited above from *The Problems of Philosophy* (p. 66).

13. It is not in fact a mistake to say '*a* does not exist' is meaningless if *a* does not exist, for I am discussing Russell's logically perfect language in a different metalanguage. However, it may seem to beg the question. In fact, the point can be expressed in a more Russellian metalanguage as follows: '*a* does not exist' is meaningless if _E! (ιx)(x = a). (The meaning of a sentence in which a description occurs, of course, is not a function of the meaning of the description — for descriptions are meaningless — though it is a function of the propositional functions which occur in the description.)

14. *Introduction to Mathematical Philosophy* (New York): Simon and Schuster, n.d.; 1st edn., 1919), pp. 178-9. Henceforth cited as '*IMP*' (See also 'PLA' pp. 212-3.) The last clause of the quoted passage does not violate Russell's claim that descriptions are meaningless, for a few pages earlier (p. 174) Russell has introduced a special sense of 'meaning' (marked with scare quotes) in which the 'meaning' of a definite description results from the meanings of its constituent words.

15. Alex Orenstein, *Existence and the Particular Quantifier* (Philadelphia: Temple University Press, 1978), p. 17.

16. Cf *My Philosophical Development* (London: Allen and Unwin, 1959), p. 84.

17. For Russell's dislike of modalities see Nicholas Rescher's over-stated case in 'Bertrand Russell and Modal Logic', in Rescher's *Studies in Modality, American Philosophical Quarterly* Monograph No. 8 (Oxford: Blackwell, 1974), pp. 85-96. That for Russell modalities are applicable only to propositional functions, not to propositions as Moore's argument requires, is emphasized in *IMP*, p. 165.

18. This parallel between cardinality and existence comes from Frege, for whom both are second-level concepts. See *Grundlagen*, p. 65 for existence and the introduction to the *Grundgesetze* for cardinality.

19. Russell held this theory from 1910 to 1913 or 1914, abandoning it for good sometime after Wittgenstein's attack on it in May 1913. For details, see 'On the Nature of Truth and Falsehood', *Philosophical Essays* (New York: Simon and Schuster, n.d.; 1st edn. 1910); *The Problems of Philosophy (op.cit.),* Chapt. 12; 'Knowledge by Acquaintance and Knowledge by Description', *Mysticism and Logic,* (London: Allen and Unwin, 1963; 1st edn. 1917); *Theory of Knowledge, The 1913 Manuscript,* ed. by E.R. Eames and K.M. Blackwell, *The Collected Papers of Bertrand Russell,* vol. 7, (London: Allen and Unwin, 1984), Pt. II, Chapt. 1-5 (henceforth cited as *TK*). For Commentary see Nicholas Griffin, 'Russell's Multiple Relation Theory of Judgment', *Philosophical Studies, 47 (1985), pp. 213-47.*

20. The saying is Hume's (*Treatise,* I, ii, 6; Selby-Biggs edn. p. 67), but is endlessly repeated

by others.

21. The point can be made in terms of the Bradleian distinction between thatness and whatness, whatness being characteristically expressed by predicates. 'Exists' fails as a predicate because it expresses no whatness, it (allegedly) merely reduplicates the thatness of the subject. This distinction, though terminologically antiquated, was presumably not so far from Russell's mind circa 1913.

22. 'Views as to Judgment, Discarding the Subject', in *Collected Papers*, vol. 8, p. 263.

23. See 'Belief and Judgment', in *Collected Papers*, vol. 8, p. 265.

24. It puzzled me when reviewing Routley's *Exploring Meinong's Jungle and Beyond:* see 'Russell's Desert and Meinong's Jungle', *Russell: The Journal of the Bertrand Russell Archives*, N.S. Vol. 2, No. 2, (1982), p. 58. My criticisms there of Routley's position, incidentally, now seem to me to be based on a misunderstanding.

25. Fortunately, we don't have to worry about other possible representations of 'E!a'. For it can be shown that, without identity, there is no formula which can replace 'E!a' and preserve the following two postulates: $(\forall x(A \,\&\, E!a) \supset A \,[a/x]$ and $(\forall x)\, E!x$. See R.K. Meyer, E. Bencivenga and K. Lambert, 'The Ineliminability of E! in Free Quantification Theory without Identity', *Journal of Philosophical Logic*, 11 (1932), pp. 229-31.

26. Alternatively, by replacing the logically proper name 'a' by the description '$(\iota x)(x=a)$', thus bringing 'E!a' within the scope of *14.02 itself.

27. L. Wittgenstein, *Letters to Russell, Keynes and Moore*, ed. by G.H. von Wright, (Oxford: Blackwell, 1974), R19, p. 31.

28. L. Wittgenstein, *Notebooks, 1914-1916*, ed. by G.H. von Wright and G.E.M. Anscombe, (Oxford: Blackwell, 2nd edn. 1979), p. 29.

29. See *The Principles of Mathematics* (London: Allen and Unwin; 2nd edn.: 1964; 1st edn.: (1903), pp. 43, 96; and 'The Classification of Relations' (1899) in *The Collected Papers of Bertrand Russell*, vol. 2, ed. by Nicholas Griffin, (London: Allen and Unwin, forthcoming).

Individuals: A Prolegomenon to Future Metaphysics

John W. Heintz

Thirty years ago, in "Space, Time and Individuals," N.L. Wilson set out to answer the question: What is an individual?[1] Although much has been written in the intervening years under the heading of "identity," the issue remains unresolved, partly because the question which Wilson identified as central has become obscured.[2] In this paper I outline the problem as Wilson posed it, his solution, and some important subsequent developments. I conclude by drawing some morals and suggesting the direction a true solution must take.

Wilson put the question this way:

> If we ask what it is to be an individual in the domain of a given language, we shall be told that we know the answer when we know the identity conditions for individuals. We immediately ask: When are two individuals identical? We are now told that two individuals are identical if and only if they have all their properties in common. The difficulty with this answer is that it merely states the syntactical properties of the identity sign but gives us no help in deciding in a given case whether to declare two individuals identical. What we want is an operational definition. I suggest tentatively that two individuals are identical if they have their essence in common, and that essence depends, not on the particular designation of an entity (the received doctrine), but rather on the total language.[3]

The difficulty here can best be disclosed in terms of a specific example involving substance-individuals. In theosophical circles, I believe, it is held that Leonardo da Vinci is the reincarnation of Judas Iscariot, that is, that Leonardo is identical with Judas. It *follows from* this identification that the individuals have all their properties in common. Leonardo betrayed Christ in the first century and Judas painted *The Last Supper* in the fifteenth. The example is intended to show how useless the all-properties-in-common criterion is in helping us to decide whether two individuals are identical, whether, that is, they do in fact have all their properties in common. Presumably in a theosophist's language some property of these two men is essential and its common possession justifies theosophists in treating the two men as identical. If we, on the other hand, wish to treat them as distinct, then it is incumbent upon us to state the principle of individuation. This is the major problem arising in connection with a substance-language.[4]

Wilson often emphasized the emptiness of Leibniz's law in its strong form. Although not circular, it is not informative, for it neither supplies nor provides the theoretical basis for supplying a method of individuation. Wilson has similar objections to Davidson's criterion of event-identity: events are the same if all their causes and effects (which are themselves other events) are the same. His criticism was vindicated last year at Rutgers during the *Götterdämmerungsfeuer der analytischen Philosophie* when Quine reiterated his (and Wilson's) complaint and Davidson, in a hushed moment, declared "I recant."[5]

Wilson's goal was to elucidate the essence of individuals. His means to that end was to specify a principle of individuation for such individuals. Although, as I shall claim, his axioms are not wholly adequate, the project was correctly defined: the nature of things mutually determines their principles of individuation, which are governed in the first instance by the character of the language as a whole.

Why must we pay attention to the language as a whole? Wilson's target in this paper is what he calls a "space-time language." The entities in a space-time language occupy positions in, or chunks of, four-dimensional space-time.[6] They are the "river-stages" and "planet-stages" of Quine's "Identity, Ostension, and Hypostasis."[7] For Quine, the River Caÿster is "a process through time and the river-stages are its momentary parts." Wilson elaborates:

> In particular, the planet Venus will be regarded as a four-dimensional spiral segment of space-time — or rather, as something *having* this spiral segment as a property. Parts of Venus will fall into temporal spans during which it is visible in the evening and the individual sum of these parts will be referred to by the expression, "the evening star," which functions as a definite description. Similarly for "the morning star." Then the individual, Venus, will be the sum of the individuals, the morning star, the evening star, together with those parts of Venus during whose temporal span the planet is not visible from the earth.[8]

Space-time individuals do not move, nor do they literally change.

> An individual is a four-dimensional entity and it "changes" if a later part has properties different from those of an earlier part (rather like a building at Yale which "changes" from Georgian on the east to Gothic on the west and is nevertheless the same building).[9]

By contrast, individuals in a substance-language *do* literally change and move. If Wilson was right in believing that the character of a language as a whole determines the essence of its individuals, then working out the principles of individuation for a space-time language, and contrasting them with the principles of individuation in a substance-language, will reveal major differences in the kinds of individuals referred to in the two types of language.

What do these two languages look like? In a space-time language, positions are designated by quadruples of real numbers, for example, '<u1, u2, u3, t1>'. and 'P', 'Pi', 'Pj' are variables ranging over positions. 'Q', 'Qi', 'Qj' are variables ranging over non-positional qualities. Wilson's axioms for a space-time language are:[10]

Ax.A1. $(x) (\exists P)(Px)$

("Every individual has at least one position.")

Ax.A2. $(Pix \,\&\, Pjx) \supset (Pi = Pj)$

("Every individual has at most one position.")

Ax.A3. $(P)(\exists x)(Px)$

("For every position there is at least one individual which has it.")

Ax.A4. $(Px \,\&\, Py) \supset (x = y)$

("For every position there is at most one individual which has it.")

We can derive two theorems which give the principle of individuation for a space-time language:

Th.A1. $x = y \supset (\exists P)(Px \ \& \ Py)$

Th.A2. $[(\iota x)(Qix) = (\iota x)(Qjx)] \equiv \quad (\exists P)[P(\iota x)(Qix) \ \& \ P(\iota x)(Qjx)]$

The essence of an individual in a space-time language is its *position*. Individuals which are the same occupy the same position. The evening star, as described in this language, is not identical with the morning star, although they are kindred in being parts of Venus. To state how the individuals combine into "planets" or their histories, we must supplement the language with an account of the kinship relations. Recently, Robert Nozick has provided that supplementation.[11]

A substance-language, by contrast with a space-time language, contains triples (not quadruples) of real numbers, referring to places in space (not positions in space-time). Accordingly, 'P' will be a variable ranging over places, 'Q' a variable ranging over non-spatial qualities, and an expression such as 'P-t(x)' will mean that x is at place P at time t. The axioms for a substance-language are:[12]

Ax.B1. $(x) \ (\exists P)(\exists t)P\text{-}t(x)$

("For every individual, there is at least one place and a time such that the individual is at that place at that time.")

Ax.B2. $(x) \ \{[Pi\text{-}t(x) \ \& \ Pj\text{-}t(x)] \supset (Pi = Pj)\}$

("Every individual occupies at most one place at a time.")

Ax.B3. $(x)(y) \ \{[P\text{-}t(x) \ \& \ P\text{-}t(y)] \supset (x = y)\}$

("Two individuals occupying the same place at the same time are identical.")

Ax.B4. $(x)[P\text{-}t(x) \supset (\exists Q)Q\text{-}t(x)]$

Ax.B5. $(x)[Q\text{-}t(x) \supset (\exists P)P\text{-}t(x)]$

Axioms B4 and B5 together state that if an individual occupies a place at a time, then it must manifest a non-spatial quality at that time, and *vice versa*.

Ax.B6. $(\imath x)([Pi\text{-}ti(x)] = (\imath x)[Pj\text{-}tj(x)] \equiv$ there is a continuous series of places including Pi and Pj and a continuous series of times including ti and tj such that for any time t of the time series between ti and tj there is a place P of the place series between (series-between, not spatially between) Pi and Pj such that there is an individual at P at t; and for any two places Pm and Pn series-between Pi and Pj, if Pm is series-prior to Pn then there is a time tm and a time tn both between ti and tj such that tm is earlier than tn and there is an individual at Pn at tn.

The following are derivable as theorems by ordinary logic:

Th.B1. $P\text{-}t(\imath x)[Q\text{-}t(x)] \equiv \{Q\text{-}t(\imath x)[P\text{-}t(x)] \,\&$
$(y)[Q\text{-}t(y) \supset P\text{-}t(y)]\}$

Th.B2. $Pj\text{-}tj(\imath x)[Q\text{-}ti(x)] \equiv$
$\{(\exists Pi) \{Pi\text{-}ti(\imath x)[Q\text{-}ti(x)] \,\&\, (\imath x)[Pi\text{-}ti(x)] = (\imath x)[Pj\text{-}tj(x)]\}$

Th.B3. $\{(\imath x)[Qi\text{-}ti(x)] = (\imath x)[Qj\text{-}tj(x)]\} \equiv$
$\{(\exists P)(\exists t) \{P\text{-}t(\imath x)[Qi\text{-}ti(x)] \,\&\, P\text{-}t(\imath x)[Qj\text{-}tj(x)]\}$

"Th.B3 is the sought analogue in substance-language of Th.A2. Given appropriate factual information, then Th.B3 would enable us to identify the author of *Waverly* and the author of *Marmion* and differentiate the betrayer of Christ from the painter of *The Last Supper*."[13]

It is, however, Ax.B6 which gives the principle of individuation peculiar to a substance-language, for it is that axiom which guides the various methods we employ to determine whether an individual which occupies a certain place at a given time is identical to an individual which occupies a different place at a later time. We try to find out about the history of the individual identified at the later time to determine whether or not it followed a continuous path from that earlier time and place. We may trace it through fingerprints or serial numbers; we may employ other inferences ("You're not sunburned enough to have spent last week in Arizona"); we may consult witnesses ("Did you sit next to this person throughout the trip?"); or we may ask the individual to consult its memory. Whichever we do, we are seeking evidence for the satisfaction of Ax.B6.

The essence of an individual in a substance-language is not its *place*, for an individual occupies many places at different times. The essence of an individual in a substance-language is not its *position*, for it has no position. It makes no sense within a substance-language to say that an individual has a position.

The most important thing that happens when we pass from a S-T language to a substance-language is this: *in general,* the individuals lose part of their essence. *In particular,* the time determinant is shifted across the copula of empirical sentences from subject to predicate.[14]

In our S-T language we might record a simple matter of fact in a sentence like the following:

(ιx) (x occupies (u1, u1, u1, t1)) is blue.

In substance-language we might say:

a is blue at (time) *t1*.

where the copula "is" is used tenselessly. (These sentences cannot be synonymous.) Notice that the time symbol 't1' has been shifted across the copula from subject to predicate.[15]

The essence of a substance-individual, given Ax.B6, is that throughout its existence, at each moment it occupies *some* place, and the series of places is continuous.

The argument goes one step further: since ordinary language is (and must be) a substance-language, the true nature of things in our world will be given by the principles of individuation for a substance-language. The evening star is not a discontinuous *part* of Venus, it *is* Venus. In general, whatever we say about principles of individuation for things will be subject to the constraints of a substance-language. This is really the punch-line of Wilson's paper. We return to it below.

Meanwhile, there are two embarrassments in Wilson's account. The first is that neither the individuals of a space-time language nor those of a substance-language occupy point-positions or point-spaces. They typically occupy spans of space-time or volumes in space. Wilson, aware of this second point, wrote

> Thus the variable 'P' in Ax.B3 has to be taken as ranging over volumes.... Now, the value expressions of the variable 'P' are not simply triples of real number expressions, but expressions considerably more complicated, and Ax.B6 has to be replaced by an axiom much more elaborate. It is more than likely, however, that we have reached the point where further technical elaboration would not provide greater illumination.[16]

Like Wilson, I will not elaborate further on this technical problem, but turn to the second, more serious embarrassment:

> ... if we were to see a pumpkin change into a coach, would we say it was the same individual or not? Again, suppose the Eiffel Tower were to vanish from Paris and an exact replica were to appear in Central Park, New York. Would we say that it was the same individual or not? Perhaps all that can be said is that it is a very good thing that this sort of change does not occur outside of quantum mechanics .... Even if we could get some kind of replacement for Ax.B6 there would still be cases where identification and differentiation would be a matter of ad hoc decision and not a matter of principle (e.g., the fission of an amoeba).[17]

With the 20-20 hindsight of 30 years we know that cases of radical transformation and splitting, rather than being easily dismissed as only occurring in quantum mechanics, or matters of ad hoc decision, have dominated discussions of identity. Lacking the means to deal with such cases, Wilson's axioms for a substance-language are inadequate. This is not true in the same way of his axioms for a space-time language. Two things are identical in a space-time language if and only if they have the same position. That is all there is to it. Definitions of 'kinship' are added only to construct those mereological sums of space-time individuals which correspond to the histories of familiar objects. The principles of individuation for the basic objects in a space-time language are secure.

The problems for Ax.B6 are total. The axiom by itself only requires for the identity of $(x)[Pi\text{-}ti(x)]$ and $(x)[Pj\text{-}tj(x)]$ that *something* exist at every point in time between ti and tj somewhere along the place series between Pi and Pj. The axiom would thus be satisfied by an egg and the hen who laid it, a car and its detached muffler, a marble and what's left after it's been smashed with a hammer, a man and the hair on the barbershop floor. Worse, everything (as we should say) is identical with anything its historical path intersects. Given enough intersections, there is only one object. Ax.B6, as an unadorned continuity principle, simply does not distinguish what we would consider one substance from another. The principle of individuation for a substance-language requires supplementation to individuate anything at all.

The inadequacy is not fatal. It has been repaired by David Wiggins in *Sameness and Substance*. Wiggins says:

> If the man reports that the thing that runs is the same as the thing that is white, then his judgment has no chance of being true unless at least two preconditions are satisfied: (a) there exists some known or unknown

answer to the question *'same what?'*; and (b) this answer affords some principle by which entities of this particular kind — some kind containing things that are such as to run or be white — may be traced through space and time and reidentified as one and the same.[18]

Suppose I ask: Is *a*, the man sitting on the left at the back of the restaurant, the same person as *b*, the boy who won the drawing prize at the school I was a pupil at in the year 1951? To answer this sort of question is surprisingly straightforward in practice, although it would be a complicated business to spell out the full justification of the method we employ. Roughly though, what organizes our actual method is the idea of a particular kind of continuous path in space and time which the man would have had to have followed in order to end up here in the restaurant; and the extraordinary unlikelihood (if the man himself were questioned and these dispositions investigated) of certain sorts of memory-dispositions existing in anyone or anything that had not pursued that path .... Once we have dispelled ... any doubt that there is a path in space and time along which we could have traced that schoolboy and found him to coincide in the fashion of human being with the person at the back of the restaurant, the identity is settled. And *then* we can say that, no matter what Ø is (provided it stands for a genuine property), and no matter whether the entity's satisfying or not satisfying Ø figured into our inquiry into the spatio-temporal paths of *a* and *b*, Ø*a* if and only if Ø*b*. The continuity in question here is not bare continuity, however. It is the kind of continuity that is brought into consideration by what it is to be a human being. (If *mutatis mutandis* we had been speaking of democracies or republics for instance, or of proper spatio-temporal continuants less tolerant of intermittent manifestation than these but more tolerant of it than men, then a different conception of tracing and a different allowance of gappiness would have operated.)

In so far as the notion of continuity is imported at all, it is always some kind-specific continuity, and this is brought into consideration by some sortally specific relation (such as *x* is the *same donkey* as *y*, the *same house* as *y*) appropriate for the particular terms of the identity. As Leibniz points out: 'By itself continuity no more constitutes substance than does multitude or number .... *Something* is necessary to be numbered, repeated and continued' (Gerhardt II, 169).[19]

Wiggins formalizes this notion in a set of principles, two of which are:

D(iii): *a* is identical with *b* if and only if there is some concept F such that (1) f is a substance concept under which an object that is an f can be singled out, traced, and distinguished from other f entities and other entities; (2) *a* coincides under f with *b*; (3) 'coincides under f' stands for a congruence relation: i.e. all pairs <x, y> that are members of the relation satisfy the Leibnizian schema Øx Øy.

D(iv): f is a substance concept only if f determines (with or without the help of further empirical information about the class of fs) what can and cannot befall an *x* in the extension of f, and what changes *x* tolerates without there ceasing to exist such a thing as *x*; *and only if f determines (with or without the help of further* empirical information about the class of fs) the relative importance or unimportance to the survival of *x* of various classes of changes befalling its compliants (e.g. how close they may bring *x* to actual extinction).[20]

The principle of individuation in a substance-language is empty in the absence of predicates which stand for substance concepts. The "abstract nature" of a substance, as defined by Wilson's axioms, is too thin to individuate anything. Thus it is not the form of the language alone, but the presence of predicates of a certain sort, and the laws governing the workings of the references of those predicates, which together determine principles of individuation in a substance-language.

Detailed discussion of fission cases is not to the point here. It is, however, necessary to emphasize the strength and plausibility of D(iii) and D(iv). Wiggins supposes, correctly, that when there is a biological kind such as the amoebas or hydras, which reproduce by splitting, the normal function of reproduction determines a principle of individuation. In amoeba-like cases, neither offspring counts as the original. In hydra-like cases, where the offspring is a tiny fellow, produced by budding, the original parent continues to exist. Neither result is affected by the early demise of any offspring.

A main competitor to the substance-language account of individuation is Nozick's "closest continuer" theory.

> The closest continuer view holds that y at t2 is the same person as x at ti only if, first, y's properties at t2 stem from, grow out of, are causally dependent on x's properties at ti and, second, there is no other z at t2 that stands in a closer (or as close) relationship to x at t1 than y at t2 does.

> Closeness, here, represents not merely the degree of causal connection, but also the qualitative closeness of what is connected, as this is judged by some weighting of dimensions and features in a similarity metric.[21]

It may appear that Nozick's account is neutral, that it could supplement equally well a space-time or a substance-language. That appearance is encouraged by his examples: the Vienna Circle, where the members (what continues) are paradigm substances, namely, people; the ship of Theseus, where the parts are planks which get taken off, moved around and stored. This appearance is deceptive. When Nozick begins to discuss the difficult cases, such as splitting and overlap, the drawings make it clear that the predecessors and successors are person-stages: occupants of four-dimensional positions in space-time. 'Overlap' means overlapping in the temporal dimension. Individuals referred to in a substance-language have only spatial dimensions.[22] Discussing whether identity statements are necessary Nozick refers explicitly and necessarily to person-stages.[23] So the first, and most important contrast between Nozick's theory and Wiggins's is that they are embedded in different language types; they are not rival supplements to a common linguistic framework.

There are other significant differences between the accounts. The central cases for Wiggins are members of natural kinds, governed in their growth and development by lawlike statements that hold in the real world, which we may or may not know. In this he follows Putnam's familiar account of the semantics of natural kind terms.[24] A natural kind term is defined by reference to a set of things and will denote all the entities which are most closely related to the objects in the set by the most explanatory and comprehensive true theory. Wiggins's account of artifacts is grafted onto this account of the central cases.

Nozick, by contrast, begins his analysis with collections (The Vienna Circle) and artifacts (the ship of Theseus). The "closeness measures" which give substance to his analysis are not governed by laws involving the things themselves, but by the weighted sum of various dimensions within our concepts of the things.

> Our concepts may not be sharp enough to order all possible combinations of properties according to the closeness of continuation. For complicated cases, we may feel that which is closest is a matter to decide, that we must sharpen our concept to settle which is (identical with) the original entity.[25]

On personal identity he says

> I do not believe there is some one metric space in which to measure closeness for each of our identities. The content of the measure of closeness, and so the content of a person's identity through time, can vary (somewhat) from person to person.[26]

Nozick can afford this approach precisely because the fundamental ingredients of his ontology — the four-dimensional occupants of space-time positions — have a clear principle of individuation. Operating within a space-time language, where the ultimate individuals are just the things with the smallest spans, it becomes natural to find a degree of arbitrariness in grouping them together into larger individuals. So Nozick says

> This quandary about temporal overlap is intrinsic, I believe, to any notion of identity applicable to more than atomic-point-instants. Any such notion trades off depth to gain breadth; in order to encompass larger entities, it sacrifices some similarity among what it groups together ....[27]

Wiggins, working within a substance-language, does not have the luxury of atomic-point-instants with their fixed principle of individuation. To get *any principle of individuation going in a substance-language,* as we have seen, it is necessary to have predicates which stand for natural kinds, and with these come the non-arbitrary laws which underlie individuation. Similarity does not enter into the identity conditions in a substance-language except as a mark of some already assumed regularity. The underlying language types, as Wilson claimed, determine what is possible for the individuation of objects.

Which underlying language type is ours?

Nozick cites an experiment in support of his account, and so, by implication, in support of the thesis that our language is a space-time language.[28]

If it governs our judgments about identity over time, it seems plausible that the closest continuer schema also should fit our perception of things continuing through times; it should fit what we see as (a later stage of) what. In parallel to Piaget's famous experiments with objects disappearing behind a screen, we should be able to devise experiments to uncover the closest continuer schema and reveal aspects of the metric of closeness. Show a film of an object x going behind a screen followed by something y coming out at a different angle (Figure 1.1); with color and shape held constant and velocity suitably maintained, a person should see this as the same object emerging, deflected by a collision with something behind the screen. Similarly, with a suitably chosen delay followed by emergence with increased velocity, it should be seen as the same object popping out after being somewhat stuck. Yet if along with y an even closer continuer z also is presented, for example, something emerging straight out at the same velocity, that thing z, rather than y, would be seen as the earlier x emerging, even though in z's absence, y would be seen so, since it then would be x's closest continuer (Figure 1.2) ... Though the research seemed plausible, no one I spoke to knew of any, until I met an Israeli psychologist, Shimon Ullman, who had just completed his doctoral dissertation where he had done these experiments. His results fit the closest continuer theory ....

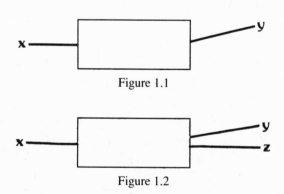

Figure 1.1

Figure 1.2

We may wonder whether Ullman's experiments actually provide evidence for Nozick's view. The closest continuer theory is supposed to be an account of *what identity consists in*. It must be framed, I have argued, in a space-time language. But Nozick describes the experiments in apparent substance-language terms: the object "pops out" after being "somewhat stuck." That is, the theory the subjects employed would seem to be one framed in a substance-language. Their judgments are just what we would expect if their conceptions of an object's identity were to require that it follow a continuous path behind the screen (Wilson's Ax.B6), and if their conception of the object included some fairly natural assumptions about the sort of changes it might undergo (see Wiggin's D(iii) and D(iv). The best explanation of what the subjects observe in Figure 1.1 cases would be just the one Nozick gave: it's simpler to suppose that the object continued behind the screen, and was deflected, than that it vanished and another object was produced (or indeed than any of the other mechanisms which could *really* produce the same effect. In the case of Figure 1.2 it is simpler to suppose that the original object kept right on going (emerging as z) and a second one was shot out, that the original object split, or that it was deflected and another sent along its original path, or so on.

What is important to note (in favor of the substance-language account) is that these explanations are only simpler or more natural given a certain conception of the object, what kind of three-dimensional thing it is. For a different kind of thing, a different explanation would be a better one. If the police chase a man into one door of a store and see two people running out another door, one wearing skirts and the other trousers, they are likely to pursue the one with the trousers (if their hearts are in their work). They may be wrong. What will make them wrong, or right, is determined by whether the principle of individuation for humans is satisfied by the fugitive running in and the person with the trousers running out. For certain, the one coming out must be a "continuer;" that is, he must be spatio-temporally continuous, in the sense of Ax.B6, under the concept human, with the one who went in. "Closeness" under a similarity metric is just a mark of this continuity; it does not supplement it to yield identity, for the continuity, so described, needs no supplementation. The closest continuer theory describes the techniques we use in attempting to determine identity, not what identity consists in.

Neil Wilson identified two types of answer to the question: When is a thing *a* identical to something *b*? One is Leibniz's Law in its strong form: two things are identical if they have all their properties in common. This may be true, but it certainly is inadequate, for the reasons we saw at the outset.

The second type of answer is what Wilson called "an operational definition," a Principle of Individuation. A Principle of Individuation, the sort of thing given by his Ax.B6 supplemented by Wiggins's D(iii) and D(iv), may not be very "operational;" it may not enable us to determine whether *a* is in fact identical to *b*. Ullman's experiment is a case in point. The subjects do not see behind the screen. They do not see which object, if any, follows a continuous path; nor do they see what happens to the object(s) along the path.

So we require a third type of answer, some *methods* we use to determine whether the Principle of Individuation has been satisfied in a given case. The Principle of Individuation, together with empirical fact and theory, will often provide a basis for some method we can apply to determine identity in a set of cases. The subjects in Ullman's experiment extracted such a method from the Principle of Individuation they supposed to apply to the object they were viewing. The Closest Continuer Theory may be a way of describing the method the subjects used, assuming some physics, assuming that the "object" was a persisting substance of a familiar kind, and employing the Principle of Individuation for substances of that apparent kind. The Closest Continuer Theory is not a theory of identity but a method for coming to a reasonable answer to an identity question, given an already-assumed Principle of Individuation.

There is a difference between a creature's development being subject to certain laws, on the one hand, and our deciding that a certain change (say from tadpole to frog) is to count as the development of a creature. From the outside, say, to an anthropologist of knowledge, the claim that there are certain laws might seem to be nothing more than just such a decision. From within the framework, however, the claim that there are laws amounts to a commitment not to decide but to try to find out what the laws are. Nozick's description of the Closest Continuer Theory seems to come from the outside. None of us can get outside of our language, and Nozick's vacillation between the idioms of a space-time language and those of a substance language reflects that impossibility.

.   .   .

Following Wilson, I have been claiming that the two keenest competitors for an adequate account of the nature of things are embedded in two different language types. What is to be said for his claim that the correct account is to be given within a substance-language? There is a revealing passage in "Space, Time, and Individuals."

> If the River Caÿster (to return to Quine's example) is a "process through time and the river-stages are its momentary parts," then I myself must be a sort of four-dimensional worm. The trouble is that I do not *feel* like a four-dimensional worm. Moreover, swimming is an activity, and since a S-T individual cannot significantly be said to move or engage in activity, I do not see how Quine can say that I *swim* in the River Caÿster

(except possibly in an odd sense of the word "swim"). Again, on Quine's view it is only *part* of me that is in *part of a part* of the river, whereas I should want to say that *all* of me went swimming. I left no parts of me on the bank with my clothes .... Might I not be content with interpreting what I want to say as meaning that *all* of a temporal slice of me is totally surrounded by the contemporaneous temporal slice of the Caÿster? This is one of those seductive invitations to think with the learned and speak with the vulgar. In general I think we ought to disapprove of this gambit, because speaking one way and "construing" it another represents a subtle form of philosophical dishonesty.

In this case the construction is very odd. Worse, if the notion of a S-T individual were fully worked out in terms of the corresponding language, then it would turn out that we could not use such a language for saying the things we want to say — even though, in principle at least, the angels could use such a language for framing a complete state-description of the world .... Ordinary language is a substance-language, and, whether we like it or not, we have not the slightest intention of abandoning this language *type*.[29]

I am sympathetic to this point of view, but as an argument it is not compelling. Nor do I know of a compelling argument at this point.[30] Still, all natural languages are substance-languages. So the burden of proof is clearly upon the shoulders of those who would have us "think with the learned and speak with the vulgar" to show us how they can articulate, in their thoughts, in a space-time language, what we *seem* to say in ordinary substance-language. Until that challenge is met, we can safely ignore the details of views such as Nozick's and perhaps Parfit's, which only make sense within a space-time language. If we are unsatisfied with Wiggins's supplementation of Wilson's account of identity, we at least know that one is needed, and it's up to us to find it.

. . .

It is time to draw some morals.

The first moral is that no decision concerning the nature of individuals can be found in the absence of decisive arguments for the correctness of one of the basic language types. This is part of the point of my subtitle. Future metaphysics must, in this area, focus on the question whether a substance-language is fundamental. We may then ask which accounts of identity are compatible with the correct language type.

The second moral is more of a caution. What if there is no best representation of (our picture of) the world? What if a number of different language types will all work, or, more likely, different types will work for different (but important) parts (or pictures) of the world? The unity of science — hoped for by those empiricists such as Carnap whom Wilson acknowledges to be an inspiration[31] — is not guaranteed *a priori*. Unity of science requires unity of language type. If there is no (single) correct language type, then there is no (single) nature of things, no way the world is.[32] This thesis is the route to anti-realism from philosophy of language, well trod these days on both sides of the Atlantic. Or perhaps it is another step towards the Absolute Idealism Wilson often teased us with in class. As Michael Stack said yesterday, "Neil Wilson was never hesitant. He was clearly a philosopher in the realist tradition of Plato and Kant,[33] and Bradley and McTaggart and ...."

There is a third possibility. About a hundred years ago Frege began the project of formalizing folk semantics — our pre-scientific understanding of how language relates to the world. Thirty years ago, Wilson's paper was a contribution to that ongoing project. (The project was known, for a while then, as "descriptive metaphysics.")[34] If Wilson was right, then this picture of our language requires that the world of individuals is a world of substances. Let us grant for a moment that he was right. Must we also grant that this picture of language — the formalization of folk semantics — is correct?

Compare folk science — our pre-scientific way of organizing the way things work in the world.[35] Modern science, though an outgrowth of folk science, replaces it. Its categories are not the same, and there is no one mapping of current physical theory, say, onto the best formalization of folk science. It seems likely that similar changes will occur as folk psychology is refined and replaced by new discoveries relating neuro-physiology and behavior. The categories and principles of folk psychology — some of which Frege employed even as he criticized the psychologism of his day — may be replaced by new and incommensurable ones.[36] I see no reason to believe that folk semantics is immune to such revision. As we begin to investigate the relationships among human speech, communication, understanding, community and action, the categories of folk semantics may be altered or abandoned. The familiar distinctions, even the subject-predicate analysis which we (I, anyway) know and love so well, may also yield to new and incommensurable distinctions and categories; the distinction between a substance-language and a space-time language may prove to be as real as phlogiston. In that case, the question with which we began will vanish, to be replaced, no doubt, by another whose form we can not now, literally, imagine.

Notes

1. *Journal of Philosophy* LII (1955), 589-98, hereinafter STI.
2. See John Perry, ed., *Personal Identity* (Berkeley: University of California Press, 1975) and Amelie Oksenberg Rorty, ed., *The Identities of Persons* (Berkeley: University of California Press, 1976) for selections and further bibliography.
3. Compare S. Kripke: "In general our reference depends not just on what we think ourselves, but on other people in the community, the history of how the name reached one, and things like that." *Naming and Necessity* (Cambridge: Harvard, 1980), 95.
4. STI, 592-3.
5. Reference to Davidson conference volume, if available.
6. For 'occupy' read 'exemplify': "By 'occupies,' I mean 'has' or 'exemplifies.' That is, positions are to be regarded as properties exemplified in individuals. The alternative would be to observe a distinction between the position P and the property of occupying P, and such a distinction seems to me useless." STI, 589.
7. *The Journal of Philosophy,* XLVII (1950), 621-33.
8. STI, 590.
9. STI, 591.
10. STI, 593-4.
11. In *Philosophical Explanations,* (Cambridge: Harvard, 1981), ch. 1.
12. STI, 595-6.
13. STI, 596
14. STI, 592.
15. STI, 594-5.
16. STI, 597
17. STI, 595, 597.
18. (Cambridge: Harvard, 1980), hereinafter SAS, p. 15.
19. SAS, 49-50, 52.
20. SAS, 68-9
21. PE, 36-7.
22. PE, 44-5.
23. PE, 656-9.
24. SAS, ch. 3. Hilary Putnam, "Is Semantics Possible?", *Metaphilosophy,* 3 (1970).
25. PE, 34.
26. PE, 69.
27. PE, 46.
28. PE, 36. Nozick might not agree that his account requires that our background language be a space-time language. I have already mentioned why it must be, and reflections on this experiment will further bring out the tension in his account.
29. STI, 591-2.
30. Rarely are philosophical prayers so quickly answered as on the occasion of my reading this paper. Robert W. Binkley, in his paper "Particular Actions," which followed this one at the conference and is reproduced in this volume, supplied a decisive argument from another of Wilson's papers, "Notes on the Form of Certain Elementary Facts," in Paul Welsh, ed., *Fact, Value and Perception: Essays in Honor of Charles A. Baylis* (Durham: 1975), 43-51. Time and place are not

symmetrical in unambiguously reporting facts: time is essential; place is not. To see this consider the answer to the question "Where was Philip drunk?" regimented as "Where was Philip when (at the time(s)) he was drunk." The answer will specify one or more places at all of which Philip was drunk at some time. The answer to the question "When was Philip drunk?" regimented as "When was Philip at the place(s) he was drunk at?" will specify one or more times, but Philip may not have been drunk at all those times. He might have been in the agora at noon and at midnight, but drunk only at midnight. Substance-languages reflect this asymmetry, space-time languages cannot.

31. STI, 594.

32. Something like this is envisioned by Nelson Goodman in *Ways of Worldmaking* (Indianapolis: 1978). Wilson's analysis provides the major premise for the argument.

33. 'Rationality and Realism,' this volume.

34. P.F. Strawson so described it in *Individuals* (London: Methuen, 1959). I use the phrase 'folk semantics' by analogy with 'folk psychology', used by P.M. and P.S. Churchland, Stephen Stich, and others for the manifest image in the area of human experience and action.

35. For 'folk science' Sellars uses the phrase 'manifest image'.

36. See *Neurophilosophy: Toward a Unified Science of Mind/Brain*, by Patricia Smith Churchland (Cambridge: MIT, 1986)

Intensional Logic and the Pragmatics of Belief

Francois LePage

The first aim of this paper is to propose a new strategy to deal with the problem of belief, a strategy which could be called pragmatic. Secondly, I will try to show how to apply this strategy within the framework of intensional logic, with some instances to be given.

My starting point will be what is currently known as Kripke's puzzle.[1] It is not my intention to discuss at length the ins and outs of the question but only to give attention to a specific point.

Roughly, the puzzle is as follows. Under very general and hardly contestable assumptions, Kripke described a situation in which a given person could be said to have inconsistent beliefs. Pierre, who is a French speaking native and does not speak English, is said to believe that London is pretty because he gives his assent to the statement 'Londres est jolie'. Moving to London and learning English by the direct method, he is brought to give his assent to 'London is not pretty' and so can be said to believe that London is not pretty, although he continues to give his assent to 'Londres est jolie' (not knowing that 'Londres' is the French name for 'London').

Among the principles Kripke appeals to in setting up his puzzle, the following one is used as a criterion for evidence of belief.

> Disquotation Principle: *If a normal English speaker, on reflection sincerely asserts 'p' then he believes that p.*

No doubt that this principle possesses a very strong intuitive content, because it describes a very familiar way of expressing our beliefs. But if we consider this principle as an effective empirical criterion, it is surely not applicable. Its logical form is the following: "For any x, if x is an English speaker and x is reflective and x is normal and x is sincere and x asserts 'p', then x believes that p" and thus, its applicability relies on the effectiveness of our capacity to determine that, for a given x, the premises are true. Two of the conditions deserve special attention: to be *normal* and to be *reflective*. By no means I would let it be understood that it is not an interesting problem to examine what it is to be sincere or to be an English speaker; I just think that these notions are not specially related to the problem of belief.

What is it to be normal and reflective? Let us quote Kripke:

> When we suppose that we are dealing with a normal speaker of English, we mean that he uses all the words in the sentence in a standard way, combines them according to the appropriate syntax, etc.: in short, he uses the sentence to mean what a normal speaker should mean by *it*.[2]

And concerning reflection:

> The qualification "on reflection" guards against the possibility that a speaker may, through careless inattention to the meaning of his words or other momentary conceptual or linguistic confusion, assert something that he does not really mean, or assent to a sentence in linguistic error.[3]

These formulations require some explanations. First, the characterization of a normal speaker is flatly circular. I think that we must interpret the second occurrence of the expression 'normal' in the sense of 'ideal' or 'competent'. But what is it to use all words in a *standard way*? What is it to use a sentence to *mean* what a normal speaker *should* mean by it? I propose to interpret what a normal speaker is by the following criterion:

> NS: *A normal speaker is a speaker who gives to words their genuine semantic value.*

This criterion seems to satisfy Kripke's requisite. A normal speaker should use 'London' as a name for London and not, for example, as a name for Paris, he should use the expression 'dogs' to refer to dogs and not to cats, and so on.

Before going further with the notion of normality, let us examine the second notion, that of reflection.

Kripke's explanation of what he means by a reflective speaker is not very clear. Two different notions are implicitly used. The first, that reflection guards against the possibility that a speaker through careless inattention may mean something he does not really mean, seems to me redundant with normality. The second notion concerns momentary conceptual or linguistic confusion. Although there is no absolute evidence, it seems that Kripke wants a reflective speaker to be able to derive straightforward logical consequences from what he asserts. I propose to interpret this criterion in the following way:

> RS: *A reflective speaker uses logical words and the associated deriva-tion rules as they ought to be used.*

These criteria of normality and reflection seem very plausible but will be of little help for solving Kripke's puzzle: Pierre cannot be normal and reflective in our sense and yet give his assent to both 'London is not pretty' and 'Londres est jolie' because these two statements are flatly contradictory beliefs.

Let us return to the notion of normality. NS is, in my opinion, the source of the puzzle as well as of most of the problems concerning belief: the requirement that speakers use words to mean what they mean appears to be too strong.

What do we expect from Pierre? We expect him to give to the words 'London', 'Londres', 'pretty', etc., semantic values such that when he uses them in semantic calculations, these semantic values do not mislead him. Let us be slightly more precise. One of the sources of the puzzle, maybe the only one, is that we allow Pierre to be normal and yet not to see that 'London' and 'Londres' have exactly the same semantic value. It appears that a possible solution to the puzzle could be based on a slightly more liberal characterization of normality. The problem is: in what direction should we liberalize?

Let us consider a very simple example using the word 'cat'. I suppose that every one in this room can be said to be normal in as much as this word is concerned. But if we try to apply Kripke's criterion, nobody here would pass the test for a very good reason: there are quite a number of things about cats we do not know, and thus many sentences of which we cannot reach the truth value because the semantic values each of us uses in association with the word 'cat' *do not cover entirely* the genuine semantic value of the word 'cat'.

These considerations show that we need a criterion of normality authorizing a normal speaker to have only "partial knowledge" of the semantic value of the words he uses. In turn, this move suggests replacing NS by the following:

> NS*: *A normal speaker is a speaker who gives to words values such that when these semantic values are used in the process of calculating the truth value of a sentence, they contribute **correctly** to this attribu-tion.*

What is intended here by the word 'correctly' is that the utilization of these semantic values instead of the genuine ones should not change the truth value of the sentence from true to false or from false to true.

Is this criterion really less restrictive than the former? The answer is yes, and the possible semantic values satisfying it can be characterized in a very general way.

A formalization of the NS* criterion

We will restrict our attention to a language **L** whose interpretations satisfy the following property. First, **L** is a categorically based language with grammatical rules G_i. I give to the expression 'grammatical rules' a specific content: those are construction rules based exclusively on grammatical categories. The most elementary of these rules is concatenation and all other rules are used for introducing logical constants. Second, a finite number of expressions of **L**, the basic expressions, receive arbitrary semantic values taken from a set **M**. To each grammatical rule G_i, i.e., a rule used to construct complex expressions, corresponds a semantic rule S_i. For example, the rule corresponding to the introduction of negation will be that rule which transforms **true** into **false** and **false** into **true**. Concatenation will be interpreted as functional application, etc. This implies that logical constants will have no semantic value, although they contribute to the semantic value of expressions in which they occur. The function **f**, the interpretation function, which gives each expression its semantic value is such that

$$f(G_i(<x_1,...,x_n>)) = S_i(<f(x_1),...,f(x_n)>)$$

i.e., **f** is an homomorphism. We will refer to this property as the property of *compositionality of meaning*. Further, we will suppose that there are two special semantic values, namely the **true** and the **false**. Can we, for this language, express a criterion playing the role of NS*?

Let **a** be a speaker of the language **L**, f_a the interpretation function **a** is using, S_{ai} the semantic rule **a** is attaching to G_i and M_a the set of all semantic values used by **a**.

We will suppose that the property of compositionality of meaning holds for f_a, i.e.:

$$f_a(G_i(<x_1,...,x_n>)) = S_{ai}(<f_a(x_i),...,f_a(x_n)>)$$

We can now express that **a** is a normal speaker by the following condition:

NS**: *A speaker* **a** *is normal if there is a morphism* **g** *from* **M**$_a$ *into* **M** *such that:*

$g(\textbf{true}_a) = \textbf{true}$

$g(\textbf{false}_a) = \textbf{false}$

$g(S_{ai}(<f_a(x_i),...,f_a(x_n)>)) = S_i(<g(f(_a(x_i)),...,g(f_a(x_n))>)$ *whenever* $S_{ai}(<f_a(x_i),...,f_a(x_n)>))$ *is defined*

This condition ensures us that **M**$_a$ will satisfy the NS* criterion because if a sentence **p** is true (resp. false) then all the expressions x_i occurring in **p** must receive from **a** a semantic value $f_a(x_i)$ such that if **a** attributes a truth value to **p** then this truth value will be the value **true** (resp. **false**).

According to the NS** condition, it is quite natural to use the expression knowledge for the relation between normal speakers, expressions and the semantic values these speakers attribute to expressions since the NS** condition can be interpreted as expressing what a speaker knows about the semantic values of expressions.

What now about belief? First, for purely practical reasons, I will use a notion of belief excluding knowledge (in the sense just introduced). So, if **p** is a sentence and **a** a speaker, to say that **a** believes that **p** will imply that fa(p) is undefined. Belief can then be interpreted as a relation between **a, p** and the value **true**; explicitly, **a** believes that **p** if and only if **a** is committed to the truth of **p**.

Well, a big step for humanity, would you say? No more problem with belief, just a little problem with the notion of "to be committed to the truth of". The step is that this notion gives rise to a very simple pragmatic treatment of belief: no *normal* and *reflective* speaker should be convicted of commitment to false sentences, i.e., to believe something false.

Let us return to our example. What is the problem with Pierre? He expresses commitment to the truth of mutually incompatible sentences. If he is normal and reflective, this gives us clues to convict him for believing something false. To do so, we will have to enrich the semantic values he is attaching to expressions until he will know that "Londres" and "London" are two names for the same city.

It is in fact possible to express these notions in a very elegant framework, that of intensional logic. But before, let me give a formal characterization of what I have called the RS criterion.

This criterion specifies that a reflective speaker must use logical words as they ought to be. As said earlier, for the languages considered here, logical constants have no semantic value; they correspond to semantic rules. So, a natural interpretation of the criterion would be that the semantic rules should be applied every time they are appealed to. More precisely, this can be expressed in the following manner.

RS*: *A reflective speaker is a speaker for whom semantic rules are maximally defined, without violating the normality criterion.*

It is not possible to give a more precise characterization of reflection without a formal framework, but it can be done within the framework of intensional logic.

Normality, reflection and intensional logic

It is not the place here to give a detailed exposition of the framework of intensional logic. I will only pay attention to the structure of the set of semantic values.[4]

The starting point is the definition of the set T of types. T is the smallest set such that

i) $e \in T$ (e is the type of individuals)
ii) $t \in T$ (t is the type of truth values.)
iii)   if $\sigma, \tau \in T$ then $<\sigma, \tau> \in T$
        ($<\sigma, \tau>$ is the type of functions from entities of type σ into entities of type τ.)
iv)   if $\tau \in T$ then $<s, \tau> \in T$
        ($<s, \tau>$ is the type of sense of entities of type τ).

In order to construct the set of semantic values, which I will from now on call the set of *intensions*, let us start with two sets I and E respectively called the set of *possible worlds* and the set of *individuals*. We then define the sets of *possible denotations* of each type:

$D_e = E$
$D_t = [\textbf{true, false}]$
$D_{<\sigma\tau>} = D_\tau D_\sigma$
$D_{<s,\tau>} = D_\tau^I$

An interpretation for a language L is given by a function f which associates to each expression of that language an *intension*, i.e., a function from I into D_τ, τ depending on the grammatical category of the expression. Such a function defines a space of semantic values, explicitly the set of all the intensions which are images of expressions by f.

We have now to define sets that could be said to be sets of semantic values used by normal (and reflective) speakers. In order to do that, let me introduce the following recursive definition of a *good-representation* (gr) of a denotation.

i)   if $a \in D_e$ or $a \in D_t$, x is a *gr* of a if $x = a$.

ii)   if $h \in D_\tau D_\sigma$, then h' is a *gr* of **h** iff for any a' which is a *gr* of **a**, $h'(a')$ is a *gr* of **h(a)**, if $h'(a')$ is defined.

iii)   if $h \in D_\tau I$), then h' is a *gr* of **h** iff for any $i \in I$, $h'(i)$ is a *gr* of **h(i)**, when $h'(i)$ is defined.

It is very useful to introduce an ideal element, ψ which is to be interpreted as an undefined entity: instead of writing, for instance, that $h'(a')$ is undefined we will write that $h'(a) = \psi$.

Part (iii) of the definition is to be considered as a definition of a *gr* of an intension.

It can be proved that the set of all the *gr*'s of a given intension (as well as the set of all the *gr*'s of a given denotation) is a *complete lattice*[5]

My task will be now to define a set M_a (in fact a family of sets) satisfying the condition NS**. In order to do that, I must explicitly define the semantic rules S_{ia}.

Let S_F be the functional application and let

$S_F(<f(x),f(y)>))_a(i) = (S_{Fa}(<f(x)_a,f(y)_a>))(i) = f(x)_a(i)(f(y)_a(i))$

if this last entity is defined and ψ otherwise.

For negation, the following condition expresses exactly what we want:

$S_t f(p))_a(i) = S_{tA} f(p)_a)(i)$

where S_{ta} is such that $S_{ta}(z)(i) = $ **false** if $(z)(i) = $ **true**

$S_{ta}(z)(i) = $ **true** if $(z)(i) = $ **false**

$S_{ta}(z)(i) = \psi$ if $(z)(i) = \psi$

For conjunction, I propose the following condition:

$S_\&(<f(p),f(q)>))_a(i) = S_{\&a}(<(f(p))_a,(f(q))_a>)(i)$

where $S_{\&a}$ is such that

$S_{\&a}(<z,w>)(i) = $ **true** if $z(i) = $ **true** and $w(i) = $ **true**

$S_{\&a}(<z,w>)(i) = $ **false** if $z(i) = $ **true** and $w(i) = $ **false**

$S_{\&a}(<z,w>)(i) = $ **false** if $z(i) = $ **false** and $w(i) = $ **true**

$S_{\&a}(<z,w>)(i) = $ **false** if $z(i) = $ **false** and $w(i) = \psi$

$S_{\&a}(<z,w>)(i) = $ **false** if $z(i) = \psi$ and $w(i) = $ **false**.

$S_{\&a}(<z,w>)(i) = $ **false** if $z(i) = $ **false** and $w(i) = $ **false**

and ψ for all other arguments.

For the λ abstractor, the situation is not really more complex. We will suppose, for simplicity, that the assignation function for variables is one of the components of **i**. $S\lambda(<f(x_\sigma),f(F)>))(i)$ will be that function on $D\sigma$ such that

$S\lambda(<f(x_\sigma),f(F)>)))(i)(b) = f(F)(i')$

where **i** is like **i'** except that $f(x)(i') = b$.

We can now define

$S_\lambda(<f(x_\sigma),f(F)>))_a(i) = S_{\lambda a}(<f(x_\sigma)_a,f(F)_a>))(i)$

where $(S_{\lambda a}(<f(x_\sigma)_a,f(F)_a>))(i))$ is that function of gr's of elements of D_σ such that $(S_{\lambda a}(<f(x_\sigma)_a,f(F)_a>))(i)(b')) = (f(F)_a(i')$ where i' is as above and $f(x_\sigma)_a(i') = b'$.

For $S\wedge$ and $S\vee$ i.e., respectively the rules for passage to intension and to extension, the definitions are straightforward.

For quantifiers (or for identity, since quantifiers are definable in terms of λ-abstractor, identity and negation), the situation is a little bit more complex. Let me put emphasis on the existential quantifier. Let

$(S_\exists(f(x_\sigma),f(P))))_a$

be that function belonging to $\{true,false\}^1$ such that:

$(S_\exists(f(x_\sigma),f(P)))_a(i) = true$ if there is some b_a gr of any $b \in D_\sigma$ such that $f(P)_a(i)(b_a) = true$

$(S_\exists(f(x_\sigma),f(P)))_a(i) = false$ if there is no b_x gr of any $b \in D_\sigma$ such that $f(P)_a(i)(b_x) = true$

$(S_\exists(f(x_\sigma),f(P)))_a(i) = \psi$ otherwise.

One can easily verify that for all the S_i introduced here $S_i(<f(x_1),...f(x_n)>)_a$ is a gr of $S_i(<f(x_1),...,f(x_n)>)$.

Let us consider now a set M_a' of gr's of intensions of basic expressions of L. The idea now is to define a closure of M_a' for all the semantic rules. This can be done in the following manner. Let M_a be the smallest set such that $M_a' \subset M_a$ and if $x_1,...,x_n$ are two expressions of L and $f(x_1)_a \in M_a$,..., $f(x_n)_a \in M_a$ then $S_F(<f(x_1),...,f(x_n)>)_a) \in M_a)$ when $S_F(<f(x_1),...,f(x_n)>)_a)$ is defined.

Proposition m_a satisfies the criterion NS[**].

In order to show that, let us define the following equivalence relation R_a on L: $R_a = \{<x,y>/ f(x)_a = f(y)_a\}$ and let us call L/R_a the quotient set and $x_{/Ra}$ the equivalence class of x. Clearly there is a function $g' : M_a \to L/R_a$ which maps every element of M_a on the set of expressions of which this element is the gr in M_a

Furthermore, we can define operations S_i in such a way that

$S_i'(<g'(f(x_1)_a),...,g'(f(x_n)_a)>) = g'(S_{ia}<f(x_1)_a,...,f(x_n)_a>)$

These operations exist because the argument $S_{ia}<f(x_1)_a,...,f(x_n)_a>$ does not depend on the particular x_i's chosen but only on the value of the $f(x_i)_a$'s i.e., on the equivalence classes to which the x_i's belong.

So, $g' : M_a \to L/R_a$ is a morphism.

Let us now define $g'' : L/R_a \to M$ such that, if x is a basic expression $g''(x_{/Ra}) = f(y)$ where y is any expression such that $f(y)_a = f(x)_a$ and $g''(S_i'(<\beta_1,...,\beta_n>)) = S_i(<g''(\beta_1),...,g''(\beta_n)>)$. Clearly, there are many such g''. Let us define $g = g'' \circ g'$.

$\mathbf{g} : \mathbf{M_a} \rightarrow \mathbf{M}$ is a morphism needed in order to satisfy the NS** criterion.

Let us return now to Kripke's puzzle.

I will consider that the semantic values of proper names are of type <s,<<s,<e,t>>,t>>. More specifically, 'London' and 'Londres' will have the same semantic value, namely $\wedge\lambda(\vee P(\angle))$, where $\angle$ is the individual city of London.

Now, although $\mathbf{f(London)} = \mathbf{f(Londres)}$[6] it is not necessarily the case that $\mathbf{f_{Pierre}(London)} = \mathbf{f_{Pierre}(Londres)}$. The only restriction on these, Pierre being normal and reflective, is that they both have to be *gr* of $\mathbf{f(London)}$. But this does not mean that Pierre does not know anything about London. In fact he may know many things about London, things he could express in English using the word 'London', and many other things he could express in French using the word 'Londres'. But he could meanwhile fail to know that 'London' and 'Londres' are two names of the same city without ceasing to be normal and reflective.

In conclusion, let me come back to my global approach. One of the consequences of my treatment of belief is that all the logic of belief relies on knowledge: there is no restriction on belief other than to preserve normality and reflection. Independently of my particular proposal in intensional logic, this approach has some plausibility, expressing exactly under which circumstances we are forced to give up beliefs. And this is exactly what we should expect from a theory about belief.

Notes

1. See Kripke S., "A Puzzle About Belief", in Margalit A. (ed.), *Meaning and Use*, Dordrecht: Reidel, 1979, 239-283.

2. "A Puzzle About Belief", p. 249.

3. "A Puzzle About Belief", p. 249.

4. In my presentation of intensional logic, I follow Montague R., "Universal Grammar", in Thomason R.H. (ed.), *Formal Philosophy*, New Haven and London: Yale University Press, 1974, 222-246.

5. For a demonstration see Lepage F., "The Object of Belief", in *Logique et Analyse*, 27, 106, (1984), 193-206.

6. Strictly speaking, it is not the same function $\mathbf{f'}$ for the French dialect as the function $\mathbf{f}$ for the English dialect. But the problem is the same: we must have

$\mathbf{f'(Londres)} = \mathbf{f(London)}$

and we can have

$\mathbf{f'_{Pierre}(Londres)} \neq \mathbf{f_{Pierre}(London)}$.

Sensation Deconstructed

Evan Simpson

Locke's theory of ideas led him to entertain the possibility that "the same object should produce in several men's minds different ideas at the same time". The idea that a violet produces in one person's mind might be the same that a marigold produces in another person's, and vice versa. Nevertheless, one would be able to "understand and signify those distinctions marked by the names 'blue' and 'yellow,' as if the appearance or ideas in his mind received from those two flowers were exactly the same with the ideas in other men's minds."[1]

Neil Wilson developed an interesting argument for rejecting Locke's conjecture. Following suggestions of C.I. Lewis, Wilson proposed that "proper names of properties are really variables" and that the cognitive content of a corpus of utterances including the word "green," for example, is exhausted by the proposition that there is precisely one color quality exemplified in the individuals referred to in those utterances. "The color sentences of a corpus describe simply the *structure* of the color facts."[2] There being no residual content, we can quickly dismiss questions of that sort: what would the world be like if everything yellow were purple and everything purple were yellow and, more generally, if everything had the color complementary to that which it actually has? Since the question describes no change in the structure of the color facts, the answer is that a color-inverted world would be exactly the same. As for Locke's "fantasy" that "there is something about the facts which eludes description," it can be explained as "the result of the initial, mistaken separation of the quality yellow from its anchorage to its actual extension."[3] I want to take this case a step further and maintain that it is mistaken to suppose, in the absence of evidence to the contrary, that different animals which make the same discriminations experience different sensations.

I

As a repudiation of Locke's view, Wilson's proposal is not quite convincing. The cognitive content of color claims, as he characterizes it, is distinct from the significance or designation of color terms. To suppose that a complete "green"- corpus implies that there is precisely one color quality exemplified in the individuals named exhausts what can be communicated, but it does not convey this quality to anyone who is unacquainted with the color. This takes us perilously close to a distinction between color-impressions and color-qualities, hence to the possibility that our private, visual worlds may differ even though the real world and its color complement are the same. The emptiness of the inverted-world hypothesis leaves open the possibility of deeply subjective spectrum-inversion.

As if in answer Wilson insists that a purely semantical doctrine should apply to any domain of objects, and even if we represent "color talk" as about sense-data, color words are variables, a color is tethered to its extension, and no communicable content is left out. "The puzzle dissolves once we recognize that there is not and cannot be any such incommunicable or unreportable content."[4] This seems to be an heroic stand. We can suppose that color talk might be "about a private visual sense field" and insist that no content escapes description as long as we mean cognitive or structural content, but Locke's issue concerns sensuous content or significance. How is this distinction to be made in the case of our own visual field? What clear meaning can we attach to the notion of sense data as the extension of color words? Sensation does not seem to involve a domain of objects of relevance to semantics.

Even so, Wilson's attack on ineffability is philosophy of a high order. Sensation has been generally regarded as a simple and indisputable autophenomenological fact, but in philosophy obviousness is usually the sign of *a priori* assumptions operating undisclosed. Wilson sees common convictions about sensations as consequences of supposing that colors exist independently of their pattern of exemplification, and he challenges claims of indubitability, saying in effect that what seems necessary may not be so. His arguments show that we must take seriously the proposition that the hypothesis of systematic intersubjective differences is untenable.

In exploring this hypothesis, it is not necessary to adopt Wilson's strategy. Semantic analysis, I have already suggested, is a problematic tool. Color words are variables only under a certain regimentation, and no one who continues to view qualia as existing independently of objects can be compelled to submit to the regime — especially one so severe as to require that "red," "orange," "yellow," "green," "blue," and "purple" signify specific shades and the only shades there are. One might reasonably suppose that the concepts of significance and designation cannot do justice to a reality of millions of discriminable shades. My own strategy, therefore, will be more epistemological than semantical. (There will be some semantical consequences, but they will support an historical rather than a referential semantics.) I will try to show that Wilson was right to say that when it comes to discriminating hot and cold or blue and yellow we function as crude (albeit self-reading) thermometers or spectroscopes and that he should have been able to "shake the conviction that when I look at the blue sky, I am immediately aware that something possesses a simple, unclustered property, and I am aware of it in a peculiarly personal way."[5]

The distinction between cognitive content and significance which helps to sustain this conviction appears in various forms throughout the discussion of mental acts. It resembles Peter Geach's idea, for example, that the content of judgement is always general and conceptual and includes no acquaintance with particular sensible things. Judgements are tied down to objects only in a particular sensory context.[6] One result of this contrast is the kind of uneasiness expressed by Wilson. Another is a problem about the identity of judgements. Whereas Geach identifies the conceptual content of "the cat is on the mat" and "a cat is on a mat," Romane Clark finds it "quite evident" that the intelligible content of the two sentences is different.[7] No doubt he would say the same of Wilson's view that the cognitive content of color claims is exhausted by formal relationships and is independent of their significance. The point is indeed evident if one accepts a conceptualist account of sensation, as Clark does, and the plausibility of such an account is clear when tested against views of sensuous judgments, like that of Wilfrid Sellars, which stress causal mechanisms as well as the content of experience.

In the course of commenting on Locke and his empiricist successors, Sellars argues that " all awareness ... is a linguistic affair."[8] An "obvious objection" to this doctrine appears to be "the existence of raw feels — pains, whatever feelings babies have when looking at colored objects, etc."[9] Sellars's response includes a distinction between awareness as discriminative behavior and awareness as "being able to justify what one says." The former is simply the ability to respond to stimuli, and it is shared by photo-electric cells, sunflowers, and human beings. The latter requires conceptual capacities, the ability to identify sorts of things. But what about the experience of pre-linguistic children when they know, or are acquainted with, the color red in whatever sense photoelectric cells are not? The sense-impression can be an object of consciousness rather than an act of conceptual awareness, in which case infants can know what the color is like in a way which does not include knowing what sort of thing it is — namely, in the sense of having a color-sensation.[10] This account thus preserves the notion that awareness is a linguistic affair. In doing so, however, it raises other questions.

The confidence which many repose in thought experiments involving infants violates my earlier criterion for good philosophical reasoning. These experiments repeatedly demonstrate that there are raw data, a sensory core, non-epistemic experience, etc.[11] How do we reach these conclusions? Why not suppose instead that infants are behaving only as discriminators? Since neither memory nor any unambiguous evidence serves us here, we must be employing a conception of what sense-impressions are necessarily like. This is not a mode of thinking in which philosophers should place any confidence. It certainly should not lead us to accept sense-impressions as non-cognitive constituents or objects of perceptions in the absence of other relevant information, and we do not have such information. Nor does Sellars suppose we do. On the contrary, as Clark points out, he seems to accept the puzzling idea that there may be impressions of color without any awareness of colour.[12] Clark's own account of sensuous judgements follows Everett Hall in abandoning the connection between language and awareness in favor of an analogy between "overt, communal acts of assertion" and "covert, personal acts of thought."[13] Since the comparison permits speaking of a "natural language of sensory perception,"[14] it appears that conceptual and sensuous phenomena originally occur inextricably combined. The point is evident in the details of the account: In making a simple assertion we do two things, refer to something and ascribe something to it. Of course counting mental actions is subject to serious difficulties, but so long as we regard Clark's point as heuristic rather than analytical, we can say that seeing how something is also consists in two acts, one of demonstrative reference to the object of sensuous judgment and one ascribing the sensible content of a sense impression to what is before us. Sense impressions are like predicates of declarative sentences; having sense impressions in the natural order is analogous to using quality predicates in the conventional order of linguistic assertion. In short, occurrences of sense impressions constitute natural vehicles by which reference and ascription are carried in sensuous judgments, and they thus include acts of acquaintance which establish "a natural ... relation linking the mind with objects of thought in a relation of primitive awareness."[15]

Understood in this way, sensations are judgments and sense impressions are conceptual constituents of these perceptual judgments. Awareness is not only a (conventionally) linguistic affair, and there is no apparent danger of sense-impressions receding below consciousness. When we come to phenomena, as Maurice Merleau-Ponty says, "we find ... a whole already pregnant with an irreducible meaning."[16] Since meanings are communicable, this implication of the idea of a natural language suggests a use for the account in criticism of Locke's conjecture.

In ascribing qualities to objects, sensuous judgments make cognitive claims which cannot be separated from their sensible content. If it can be shown that this connection rules out cognitively identical sensations having different sensible aspects — if, that is, these inseparable aspects are also indistinguishable — then the conjecture can be rejected.

Clark does not attempt this further task, and his references to the "sensible content" of a sense impression leave a crucial question open. Is sensible content the overtly exhibited color quality of the object before one or is it a covert quality experienced while perceiving colored things but detachable from them? In the former case Locke's question does not arise, but in the latter it remains. The natural way to secure the first option is to treat "secondary qualities" in the way that Locke treats "primary qualities." Thus, the shape of which one has an impression when viewing a red disk from the side is round, and one attributes roundness to the thing; and the color of which one has an impression when viewing the disk in dim light is red, and we ascribe that color to the thing. Here the question of subjective differences in insensible content does not seriously arise. The illusion of subjectivity can hardly be combatted, though, by depending upon the controversial doctrine of primary qualities.

The subjectivity of sensible qualities comes seriously into question when we see that agents may be unaware of their sensings and that the natural link between the mind and objects of thought does not have to be one of which we are even conscious. Patricia Churchland describes a case of "blind-sight" which undermines part of the set of assumptions behind Locke's conjecture by questioning his (and Clark's) notion that "to imprint anything on the mind without the mind's perceiving it seems to me hardly intelligible."[17] After the removal of part of a man's primary visual cortex he reported having no perception in his left visual field. When tested for visual discrimination he could nevertheless "guess" whether he was being presented with a picture of horizontal bars or vertical bars, with X's or O's, with red lights or green lights. Clearly he was using visual information which was not consciously accessible to him.[18] Clearly, too we can say of this case either that he made visual reports on his environment without having perceived it or that his reports were based on a special, non-conscious form of perception. Whichever we choose, a Lockeian prejudice is confounded, for we cannot accept both the idea that making an observational report about something in the perceivable world requires having perceived it and the idea that to perceive something is to be conscious of it.

In order to regain a coherent concept of perception, some more comfortable accommodation has to be found between conceptualist views like Clark's and materialist views like Sellars's. The idea of a natural language can play an important role here, but it needs to be extended first. We will then be able to say of sensory experience, as Wittgenstein says of systems of belief, "light dawns gradually over the whole."[19] Our conscious ability to sense and feel depends upon experience and learning, and there is nothing "raw" in the perception of the qualities of things. Only discriminatory and behavioral capacities should be ascribed to us initially, and sensations, therefore, are not original facts of psychology.

II

Rousseau noted that "Whether there was a language natural and common to all men has long been a subject of research. Doubtless there is such a language, and it is the one children speak before knowing how to speak... When children begin to speak, they cry less. This is a natural progress. One language is substituted for the other. As soon as they can say with words that they are in pain, why would they say it with cries, except when the pain is too intense for speech to express it?"[20] Approaching the question of sensuous content through Rousseau rather than through Locke presents an entirely different picture. It permits us to move eventually from the undetachability of aspects of sensations to the impossibility of differentiating them. The basic move is an assimilation of the structural features of sensations to those of emotions. The communicability of the affective aspects of emotion then serves as an argument for the complete communicability of sensations.

It is a notable feature of Rousseau's conception of a natural language that he characterizes it in terms of affect and behavior rather than sense impressions and demonstrative reference. His account belongs to a tradition which holds that "an object looks attractive or repulsive before it looks black or blue, circular or square."[21] A second point of interest in Rousseau's idea is an important dilemma which it suggests. We may say that, since crying is a kind of speech, responsive behavior expresses a conceptual state; or we may say that, since infant behavior is pre-conceptual, language is not inherently conceptual. Neither option seems desirable, but we are not forced to choose between them if the alternatives presuppose an untenable distinction, that is, if we often operate with a narrower sense of "conceptual states" than is necessary. Given new knowledge of the brain, the appropriate interpretation of our natural language includes recognition that we cannot clearly differentiate pre-linguistic experience from conceptual knowledge. As a result, separately identifiable feelings (or the so-called content of experience) drop out as fictions. Raw feelings do not enter as an essential part of this picture.

The ideas I have just described constitute a weak form of conceptualism, the view that "the possession of concepts is a necessary condition of all perceptual experience."[22] Any such view will entail a form of innatism. If perception depends upon concepts in some sense, then the origin of these concepts needs explanation. The conceptualism hypothesis rules out ascribing them to acts of perception however primitive, so that we have no alternative than to regard some of them as innate. Any innatist view of intelligence, though, will assign a peculiarly abstract character to such concepts. They will refer to no particular, singular reference requiring that a concept which is originally general has become attached to an individual object or property. Such attachment requires experience, sometimes singular — as in the phenomenon of imprinting in birds — but, in the case of beings less governed by rigid instincts, plural.[23]

This attachment, once secured, can be modified but it cannot be reversed. The resulting property of non-detachability is exemplified by what I shall call "complexes". Some elements of complexes are, as Frege might say, incomplete. Propositional attitudes, such as belief and fear, are complexes in that they only occur when embedding certain claims. It is widely accepted that to feel fear is to entertain the proposition that danger is present, as well as to experience affective arousal, and we will not ordinarily ascribe the emotion to persons who do not identify something as a threat. The full complexity of the relationship is evident, though, only from a further reflection: the concept of danger does not arise separately from fear. Danger is a bad thing. It conflicts with the desire for security which is also part of fear, and its "repulsiveness" thus results from the emotional state which is in turn partly constituted by a proposition about danger. In consequence, danger is meaningless to one who cannot be afraid, so that even if we may upon occasion believe fearlessly that danger is present the judgment depends upon a structure of experience which includes fear.[24]

There are, to be sure, certain elementary affective states which arise prior to and independently of real fear, pity, and love and appear to lack cognitive attachments. We can observe behavioral and intellectual features which differentiate fright and fear, sympathy and compassion, sexual desire and love. But this possibility does not warrant saying that the first term of each pair — a partly unlearned response to certain stimuli — is best understood as a simple aversion or attraction, whereas the second includes a conception of the object which occasions it. While we speak of the displeasure of fear, pity, anger, and guilt, there is nothing recognizably the same in these feelings. Isolated affects cannot be identified in reality and should be regarded as analytical postulates. Moreover, the arousal of elementary attitudes by events in the environment is best understood in terms of a disposition to respond to, or be "completed" by, particular types of information. Even primitive attitudes are complex. Their affectivity and receptivity to information are aspects of experiences which cannot be bifurcated into feelings and thoughts.

My thoughts in making these suggestions are transparent. If sensations are complex in this sense — having sensitive and cognitive aspects — then, just as isolated affects cannot be identified, there are no identifiable isolated sensations. Sensory experience is best understood as a physical capacity to make discriminations and an undifferentiatable sensitive-cognitive state. Any account of perception as sensuous awareness in which the sensation has potentially separate existence misrepresents the nature of the constituents of a complex. It is to strengthen this case and enable it to work against Locke that I propose to assimilate two types of experience and judgment that are generally kept apart. But, philosophical motivations apart, what could be more natural than to treat all propositional attitudes as members of the same class rather than assigning emotions to ethics and sensations to epistemology?

Turning now to argument, an obvious problem for any nativist defense of these claims is that it will imply, or appear to imply, the occurrence of mental events prior to learning. It is one thing to make an assertion in a natural language and another to have evidence for it. Since the first may be possible while the latter is not, affects and sensations should be understood as primitive psychological states whose unsullied feeling-content must be acknowledged. Elementary experiences of fear, for example, include a concept of danger which is the abstract content of fear as it occurs prior to learning. It is not bound by the standards of evidence which result when experience permits distinguishing between real and apparent harm and leads to a particular interpretation being placed upon the original idea. Once such distinctions are made we are sensitive to standards of evidence which occasion judgments of validity and truth, but until that time the natural language of fear expresses an untutored feeling associated with indiscriminate response to certain natural causes of fright. Fear is educated fright in which the abstract conceptual structure of the latter has taken on a settled significance.

This account binds cognitive and affective content inseparably together without seriously challenging the idea of raw experience in one respect: in spite of including intelligible content, some feelings remain primitive experiences. Because aspects of the content are complexly related, however, the account leaves no clear room for the possibility of differences in affective content among individuals who express fear. On the contrary, in virtue of the fact that the meaning or expressible content of the state is constitutive of the emotion, the affective quality of the experience can also be taken to be expressible. It is for this reason, I think, that no one seriously proposes that the subjective feeling of fear might differ in the manner often supposed possible for sensations of color. Since the constituent parts of fear presuppose one another, there is no seam between them where the one could be pried apart into a realm of subjectivity where the qualitative character of the affective aspect of fear resides ineffably.

In order to extend this account to sensible qualities, one further point needs to be made about Rousseau's hypothesis. It only appears to imply the occurrence of conscious events, including feelings, prior to learning. To identify the abstract content of emotions may involve no more than reference to an innate capacity; the abstract idea need not be a constituent of a covert mental state. Speaking of the abstract content of fear implies only that to be afraid of something is to regard it as dangerous; and, since different individuals may fear very different sorts of things, their respective conceptions of danger may vary considerably. To have no such conception, however, is to have no particular experience; in other words, to have only the abstract concept of danger is not yet to be aware of one's circumstances. Any such particular conception of danger, though, will be based upon a history of experience. It follows that occurrences of the discriminative responses to certain events in the environment which we call fright are sufficient for the occurrence of the abstract of danger, whereas the feeling of fear in all its affective richness depends upon the particular content of concepts which arises only through familiarity with a family of cases. Rousseau's natural language, in short, does not express intentional or even conscious states and requires the presence of concepts only in a particularly restricted sense. It is a sense which shows a clear compatibility between Rousseau's view and Churchland's. Both accept concepts which cannot be sharply distinguished from physical capacities.

This argument recognizes the inherent limitation of innate ideas. They cannot refer to particulars and therefore cannot be included in the phenomenology of consciousness, however much they may guide and constrain perception. Awareness arises only with interpretation of the conceptual contents of propositional attitudes. There can then be no conscious state until this interpretation occurs, and because interpretation entails communicable meanings the possibility of intersubjective discrepancies is excluded. The primary role of comparisons in consciousness precludes regarding assertions made in the natural language as support for more than instinctual discriminations.

The severe tests for this general proposition are the sensations of pain and color. Even if fear and other examples of affective perception are fully expressible, sensuous perceptions of color do not appear as tightly bound to communicable meanings. Pain is an ostensibly intermediate case which we are inclined at different times to represent according to the affective or the sensuous model — a fact which, along with Berkeley's arguments linking pain with sensory experience, should make us cautious about the initial division into categories of awareness. While there are undeniable differences between the cases, the sense of their importance is arguably an artifact of modern philosophical paradigms. Once these presuppositions are dismantled or decay, little of interest remains to differentiate affective and sensuous perception.

Sensation, we have noted, is, like emotion, a conceptual act, or has many features in common with what we ordinarily think of as conceptual acts. Sensation and emotion are so much alike, I will try to show, that the conceptual content of sensations may be understood partly in terms of innate discriminatory capacities. It is plausible to speak of an abstract concept of the color blue which constitutes a human capacity to distinguish objects of certain sorts from others. Like the corresponding concept of danger, this innate idea requires interpretation of the kind made possible by a history of experience. Only as this occurs does visual perception gain its sensuous content, and at no point in the process is it plausible to regard this content as an element of experience in addition to a capacity for discrimination and the gradual completion of the abstract concept through comparisons.

The justification for saying this can be drawn from the answer to a problem about pain. Pain, too, has a conceptual structure. For something to seem painful is for it to be experienced pityingly, just as for something to seem dangerous is to experience it fearfully. Pity is not only a reflection upon suffering but also a conceptually constitutive factor in it. When we do not feel sorry for ourselves, I suggest, we are not in distress, though there are many instances in which this self-pity is tempered with the knowledge that the suffering must be borne without complaint. The abstract idea of suffering needs interpretation before what we call pain reaches awareness, so that pain can be understood as a form of discrimination which permits such concrete conceptualization.

By viewing awareness as consisting in propositional attitudes, feelings and sensations can only be represented as products rather than data of experience. To identify danger is to identify something which is fearful if the danger is significant, and for a threat to be seen as trivial is for the emotion to evaporate. So also for pain. To identify it is to identify something pitiable. Even in one's own case this is a matter of judgement, and as one's expectations change so do one's identifications. Pain viewed as trivial lacks its normal affective character. If this is so, then the ostensible detachability of pain from conceptual judgement is specious. That it is so is well-known from studies of cognitive contributions to the perception of pain, and little remains to sustain contrary philosophical views of the matter.

As for the perception of color, self-reading spectroscopes have to learn how to read. The data they collect come alive when we learn how to interpret the discrimination made possible by the relevant abstract conceptual structures. Far from displaying a peculiar independence from the cognitive content of judgments, color-perception includes concepts in such a way that sensations cannot be viewed as providing any naive knowledge of reality.

It is all too easy to suppose that judgement is less important in the perception of color than in the experience of fear and pain. We well know, however, that our attention is drawn to certain colors, such as the blue of the sky on a fine day and the pure colors as refracted by a prism. Such colors impress us as worthy of attention, as do some pale and mixed colors once we have developed a little sophistication. Judgments of interest-worthiness might seem less closely bound to perceptions of color than judgments of pitiability are to perceptions of pain, since the perception of color remains even in uninteresting cases — unlike pain judged as trivial. But this line of thought is dubious: pain which lacks its normal affective character can still be identified, in the sense that one knows how to answer the question, "Where does it hurt?" Similarly, we can answer the question, "What color is it," in cases where the color is without interest or attraction for us — cases in which it never occurs to us that an impression is peculiarly ours. Far from suggesting the possibility of primitive acts of acquaintance, such identification depend upon complex cognitive-affective capacities rather than representing primary abilities. Interpretation is essential, and the conceptual content of feelings and sensations ensures that they can be described without subjective remainder.

Ultimately, the strength of this case is a function of the extent to which the assimilation of sensation to emotion succeeds. The nature of the interdependency of affective and cognitive aspects of emotion is such that they are not only undetachable but also intersubjectively comparable. The same claim can be made for the sensitive and cognitive aspects of sensation. Insofar as the claim rests upon similarities between the two cases, the argument is analogical rather than deductively tight. In describing sensation in a way which precludes Locke's conjecture, though, it deprives that conjecture of its obviousness, reinforces Neil Wilson's doubts about the ineffability of sensation, and protects us from the temptation to slide back into the notion that our perception of sensible qualities might be peculiarly personal.

Notes

1. John Locke, *An Essay Concerning Human Understanding* (New York: New American Library, 1974), II.xxxii.15. Compare Plato, *Theatetus.* 154.

2. N.L. WIlson, "Color Qualities and Reference to Them," *Canadian Journal of Philosophy,* 2 (1972), 145-169, pp.148 and 154. Compare C.I. Lewis, *Mind and The World Order* (New York: Dover, 1956), pp. 75-82.

3. Wilson, p. 155

4. *Ibid.,* p. 157.

5. *Ibid.,* p. 169. Contrast Ludwig Wittgenstein, *Philosophical Investigations* (Oxford: Blackwell, 1953), sec. 275, with which Wilson was familiar.

6. P.T. Geach, *Mental Acts* (London: Routledge & Kegan Paul, 1957), pp. 64-65. A related distinction is drawn by Sydney Shoemaker, "Functionalism and Qualia," *Philosophical Studies,* 27 (1975), 291-315, p. 308.

7. Romane Clark, "Sensous Judgements," *Nous,* 7 (1973), 45-56, p. 50. Compare Christopher Peacocke, *Sense and Content. Experience, Thought and their Relations* (Oxford: Clarendon Press, 1983), p. 184.

8. Wilfrid Sellars, *Science, Perception and Reality* (London: Routledge & Kegan Paul, 1963), pp. 160-161.

9. For this characterization of the objection see Richard Rorty *Philosophy and the Mirror of Nature* (Princeton: Princeton Univ. Press, 1980), p. 182.

10. See *ibid.,* pp. 183-184. See also Romane Clark, "Sensibility and Understanding: The Given of Wilfrid Sellars," *The Monist,* 65 (1982), 350-64. p. 352

11. See, for example, Edmond Wright, "Recent Work in Perception," *American Philosophical Quarterly,* 21 (1984), 17-30, pp. 18 and 25; Alan H. Goldman, "Appearing as Irreducible in Perception," *Philosophy and Phenomenological Research,* 37 (1976-77), 147-64; Fred I. Dretske, *Seeing and Knowing* (London: Routledge & Kegan Paul, 1969), p. 75; C.I. Lewis, *Mind and the World Order,* p. 50

12. Clark, "Sensibility and Understanding," p. 355.

13. Clark, "Sensous Judgments," p. 51.

14. Everett W. Hall, *Our Knowledge of Fact and Value* (Chapel Hill: University of North Carolina Press, 1961), pp. 30, 38-63.

15. Romane Clark, "Acquaintance," *Synthese,* 43 (1981), 231-246, pp. 244-45.

16. M. Merleau-Ponty, *Phenomenology of Perception* (New York: Humanities Press, 1962), pp. 21-22.

17. Locke, *Essay,* I.xx.5

18. Patricia Smith Churchland, "A Perspective on Mind-Brain Research," *Journal of Philosophy,* 77 (1980), 185-207. p. 192.

19. Ludwig Wittgenstein, *On Certainty* (Oxford: Blackwell, 1969), sec. 141.

20. Jean-Jacques Rousseau, *Emile or On Education* (New York: Basic Books, 1979), pp. 65, 77.

21. K. Koffka, *The Growth of the Mind,* quoted by Merleau-Ponty, p. 24

22. Joseph Runzo, "The Radical Conceptualization of Perceptual Experience," *American Philosophical Quarterly,* 19 (1982), 205-217, p. 205.

23. On imprinting see N. Tinbergen, *The Study of Instinct* (Oxford: Clarendon Press, 1951). This type of attachment need not be regarded as a form of singular reference, of course.

24. See my *Reason over Passion* (Waterloo, Ontario: Wilfrid Laurier University Press, 1979), pp. 33-34.

Ontic Antics Diagnosed

Elmer Sprague

Two Case Studies

Looked at in one way, philosophy can be taken to be a discipline in search of a subject matter. Philosophy is a kind of science like physics or logic or history. So the practitioners of philosophy introduce us to entities that only they can find out about, and we can find out about too, if we follow their methods. Yet there is the curious consequence that when philosophical entities are examined philosophically, they fade away to nothing. In this paper, I want to take a close look at some examples of this fading away. What gives philosophical entities their insubstantiality? What are the props that first support, and then fail to support, them?

What I mean by the philosophical examination of philosophical entities is something that I hope will be made clear as we proceed. There does not seem to be any general recipe for it beyond the conviction that philosophical entities are suspect, but the cast of mind that invents them must be taken seriously. In this paper, the philosophical entities that I shall consider are Russell's sense-data and physical objects and Professor Donald Davidson's mental and physical events.

Russell's Problems

Russell tells us about sense-data and physical objects in *The Problems of Philosophy*[1]. Let us start with sense-data. To give a little context to their story, let me say that Russell brings sense-data on stage, because he wants to tell us something remarkable about tables and other everyday objects of that kind. What he wants to tell us is that these things are not what we take them to be; and this despite the paradox that before we began reading Russell, we feel perfectly sound on the subject of tables. We shall have to return to this paradox before we are finished with sense-data.

At the very beginning of our consideration of Russellian sense-data, we must note an important point. One might think that one can ask "What are sense-data?" and answer it as one asks and answers such questions as "What are zebras?" or "What are unicorns?" But the question "What are sense-data?" is not like those. For sense-data have what might be called *occasions:* That is, they are invoked to meet a philosopher's need. In what follows, we must take care to keep sense-data and their occasions marching together.

Russell's immediate starting point on the way to sense-data is the question, "What can we know (know, and not be in doubt) about his writing table?" Without apology or warning, the *know* here slides into *perceive.* So Russell says that when we "concentrate attention on the table", "To the eye it is oblong, brown and shiny, to the touch it is smooth and cool and hard, when I tap it, it gives out a wooden sound." (8) Russell's starting point then is what might be called the table's perceptible or sensible characteristics. Russell's next step is to pick out one of these characteristics and to squeeze it in a certain way for a certain end. Let me try to make this clear.

The table's characteristic that he picks is its color, and he squeezes it to show "that there is no colour which preeminently appears to be *the* colour of the table, or even of any one particular part of it" (9). The squeezing (9/10) consists of pointing out that the parts of the table that reflect the light look much brighter than the other parts. Some parts even look white because of reflected light. What is more, the apparent distribution of colors "on the table" can be changed by changing one's point of view so that there is a change in the parts of the table that reflect the light. Again no two viewers will look at the table from exactly the same point of view; so no two viewers still see exactly the same distribution of colors. "And we know that even from a given point of view the colour will seem different by artificial light, or to a colour-blind man, or to a man wearing blue spectacles, while in the dark there will be no colour at all..." (9) Taking these considerations together, Russell then feels entitled to say that "...colour is not something which is inherent in the table, but something depending upon the table and the spectator and the way the light falls on the table." (9)

We can say at this point that Russell has succeeded in scraping the color off the table. Or less dramatically, we can say that Russell is persuading us to regard color as an independent phenomenon. Then given the great variability in that phenomenon, Russell can say that "...we are compelled to deny that, in itself, the table has any one particular colour." (10)

Notice what Russell has accomplished here. Where we formerly supposed that there was one thing, namely a brown table, we must now say that there are two, the table and the highly varied color phenomena. Having made this split, Russell goes on to say that of these two kinds of things, it is only the color that we immediately experience. So we can now formally introduce the term 'sense-datum'. A given instance of color, "immediately known in sensation", is a sense-datum. (11) The other half of the split, the table, "...is not *immediately* known to us at all, but must be an inference from what is immediately known." (11) In Russell's terminology, the table is an instance of *a physical object*. "The collection of all physical objects is called 'matter'." (12) It is important to notice that sense-data, the immediately known in experience or sensation, are to be understood in contrast with physical objects or matter. We have a conceptual package deal here.

To continue with sense-data, color phenomena are, of course, only one kind of sense-data. Other kinds, in Russell's phrase, are "...sounds, smells, hardnesses, roughnesses, and so on." (12) So far as his writing table goes, the sense-data that Russell particularly notices are texture, shape, hardness and sounds. (10/11) For each of these characteristics, he notes that when we attend to it exclusively — and we do not usually do that, *we* might add — we find great variability in each characteristic. For Russell, that variability implies separability from the table, and independence from it. With sense-data well in hand then, it is time to see how they got there.

My first point is that Russell wants to make it look as though he has discovered sense-data by an examination of what there is. But against that, I want to show that he has really taken advantage of what we can say, by emphasizing one of our ways of discoursing over another. Let us take talking about color and talking about a table as our example. Suppose that I go to a furniture store to buy a table. I might say to the clerk, "I don't like the color of that table; but the shape is right. Do you have one like that in a blue instead of a red?" In that speech, color — I want to say "the table's color" — is my subject. But I might equally well have said, "I like that table; but I'd prefer a blue one." Here the subject of my speech is a table, or tables.

So talk about tables is as possible for us as talk about color. I ask here for no more emphasis than *as possible*. But Russell would have us forget what we can say about tables, and concentrate on what we can say about colors. That we can and do talk about colors as distinguishable subjects in our discourse certainly paves the way for Russell's talk of color sense-data. We get a start on color sense-data by thinking, of course, that Russell is just talking about colors; and we certainly know how to do that. But Russell's aim is to get something more than that.

Just as we know how to talk about the brown color of the table as well as the brown table, we also know how to talk about the rectangular shape of the table as well as the rectangular table. This gives Russell his opening for the sense-datum of shape. Again we know how to talk about the smooth feel of the table top as well as the smooth table top. This gives Russell his opening for the sense-datum of texture. But if we keep our heads, these openings need not be seen as very wide.

But the hardness of the table and "the sounds which can be elicited by rapping the table" (11) do have advantages in them, however, that I should like to keep from Russell. He presents hardness as a deliverance of the sense of touch, so he can speak of it as a sensation "that the table always gives us". (11) But we must remember that this is not the only possible way of thinking about hardness. There are plenty of occasions, when not my sensation, but the property of a table is at issue. I am the manager of a cafeteria, and I need dining tables with hard tops. I am a meat-cutter, and I need hard-topped butcher blocks. I am a joiner, and I need a hard-topped work bench. These tables do not give sensations of hardness; they are hard.

In thinking of hardness as a sensation given by a table top, Russell has indeed been thinking of an analogy with sound. For he finishes his remarks about hardness by saying, "And the same applies still more obviously to the sounds which can be elicited by rapping the table." (11) This is his only remark about sound, and his last remark about the detachableness of the table's qualities. It is surely strategically placed to leave a strong picture in the reader's mind. Sound is just the sort of thing we say a table can "give off"; and we have no easily available form of words for noting a table's capacity to sound. So we have nothing to put up against our willingness to think of sound as an unattached entity. It is this bit of our vulnerability that Russell exploits here; and our only counter move is to remember sound's exceptional independence in contrast with a table's color, shape and hardness.

At the end of his consideration of what he calls our "troubles" (8) with the table, Russell sums up by saying, "Thus it becomes evident that the real table, if there is one, is not the same as what we immediately experience by sight or touch or hearing." (11) The real table is an instance of what Russell calls *a physical object*; and before we are finished with this bit of Russell, we shall have to take a close look at physical objects. But for the moment, notice where Russell has taken us. According to him, the proper object of perceptions are the sense-data. That means that properly speaking, I can only say that I see colors and shapes. What I cannot say is that I see or touch a table. For seeing and touching are "immediate"; and, for Russell, whatever it is, the table is not immediate.

Now the point that I want to make here is so simple that it might be thought to be simple-minded. How can the table — whatever it is — that melted into elusivity on page 11 have been the subject of certain confident remarks on page 8? There Russell says "I believe that, if any other normal person comes into my room, he will see the same chairs and tables and books and papers as I see..." Russell sounds pretty sure of seeing a table there. Lest you be tempted to say that his initial "I believe..." gives room for illusion, notice the invitation he gives at the beginning of the very next paragraph: "...let us concentrate attention on the table." Russell seems pretty confident that no one is going to say, "What table are we talking about? I only see a lot of browns and grays and shininess broken into rect-angles and half circles." Can you imagine Russell's saying, "Yes. That's what I mean." Surely the fun of being a philosophical discoverer is that people cannot find a philosophical entity until you tell them how. But to tell us how to find sense-data, Russell is in the peculiar position of supposing that we know how to find things like tables, that he will later tell us that we cannot find.

There is another curious point about Russell's method here. He emphasizes our perceptual acquaintance with things. So he proceeds as though the meaning of the word "table" were fully explicated in what we see. Only a passing notice is given to tables as things that have uses.

Perhaps somewhere among the various considerations that I have been advancing, I have said enough to make some people see how Russell could think that he had got to sense-data, and see that he has really not got anywhere. But still someone might object that I have not yet come to appreciate the relation that Russell found between sense-data and physical objects, and that to see the point of sense-data, I must see how they go along with physical objects. So on to physical objects. I want first to pay attention to a point that Russell is quite casual about, namely the relation between physical objects and sense-data. Then I want to consider how Russell says that we might know about the existence of physical objects.

Russell characterizes the relation between physical objects and sense-data in several different forms of words which share some degree of interchangeability. The channel for Russell's thought here is probably marked out by the sentence, "The real table, if there is one, is not immediately known to us all, but must be an inference from what is immediately known." (11) That is we can infer physical objects from sense-data. But of what is the inferential bridge made? Consider these passages:

(a) In speaking of the sensation of hardness, Russell says that the sensations

"...cannot be supposed to reveal *directly* any definite property of the table, but at most to be *signs* of some property which *causes* all the sensations, but is not actually apparent in any of them." (11)

Even when we respect Russell's immediately following and careful distinction between sensations ("the experience of being immediately aware") (12) and sense-data ("things immediately known in sensation") (12), we can see that his thought about physical objects and sense-data is running along causal lines here.
(b) But Russell is very slow to push the causal connection between sense-data and physical objects. What he repeats more than once is the assertion that sense-data may be the sign of something:

"...what we directly see and feel is merely 'appearance', which we believe to be a sign of some 'reality' behind." (16)

"The problem we have to consider is this: Granted that we are certain of our own sense-data, have we any reason for regarding them as signs of the existence of something else, which we can call the physical objects?" (19/20)

Having posed that problem, Russell advances several considerations to convince us that there must be physical objects. The strongest of these considerations, in Russell's own judgement, is that it is simpler to suppose "...that there really are objects independent of us, whose action on us causes our sensations." (23) He both illustrates and supports the appeal to simplicity with his example of the moving cat. First I see the cat in one corner of the room; and a little later while the cat has been outside of my notice, I see it again in another corner of the room. Two interpretations are then open to me. I could regard the cat as "merely a set of sense-data", in which case"...it cannot have ever been in any place where I did not see it; thus we shall have to suppose that it did not exist at all while I was not looking, but suddenly sprang into being in a new place." (23) Russell means to imply that this interpretation of the cat's existence is absurd; and I had better go to a second interpretation, namely that between my separate perceptions of cat sense-data, the real cat passed from one corner of the room to the other. This would be according to Russell, "...to adopt the natural view, that there really are objects other than ourselves and our sense-data which have an existence not dependent upon our perceiving them." (24)

We can, I think, take the example of the moving cat as a story that gives the sense of Russell's claim that sense-data are a sign of something beyond themselves. The sense-data accompany something else. It would seem that what Russell wants is a parity of occurrences, without a hint of a causal connection. Something like a royal salute's being a sign of the Queen's arrival; but she does not fire the cannon herself; and that example is to be distinguished from a bump in the rug, the bump being both a sign that there is something under the rug, and the effect of whatever is there. But Russell is not a phenomenalist; and the impetus for a slide from sense-data's being a sign to their being an effect is present. So, as we have noticed, we have first of all admission of the "the common sense hypothesis"; "There really are objects independent of us, whose action on us causes our sensations." (23) A few pages later, we get the concession "...that physical objects cannot be quite like our sense-data, but may be regarded as *causing* our sensations." (30) Though Russell calls this only a provisional agreement, he has indeed edged up to the claim that physical objects cause sense-data. He must, for he wants to make physical objects more than a conclusion dictated by a canon of simplicity. He holds out the hope that we can have knowledge of them; and he is led to make the causal claim direct.

The kind of knowledge that we may have of physical objects is what Russell calls "knowledge by description". That kind of knowledge is to be understood in contrast with what he calls "knowledge by acquaintance". Russell characterizes the contrast in the following ways. What we know by acquaintance we know directly, immediately and noninferentially. When we know something by acquaintance, its existence cannot be questioned. Russell's point is that we could not be acquainted with whatever it is we are acquainted with, if it were not there. For Russell, sense-data are preeminent examples of what we can know by acquaintance. In contrast with acquaintance, what we know by description, we know indirectly, mediately and inferentially. To know by description, we must put together something we know by acquaintance with a truth, or maybe truths, to reach a conclusion. Before we look at Russell's claim that we may know physical objects by description, we must look at Russell's best non-controversial example of knowledge by description. We need not only to understand what it is to have knowledge by description, we must also ask if and how knowledge by description can assure us of the existence of something. After all, one of Russell's big questions here is 'Do physical objects exist?'

I think we may say that Russell's promise is that knowledge by description may yield a knowledge of existence; but how and why needs to be made clear. In the first place, Russell is careful to limit himself to definite descriptions, instances of *the* so-and-so, where one and only one thing can fit a description. Given this limitation, Russell is prepared to say "...we may know that the so-and-so exists when we are not acquainted with any object which we know to be the so-and-so, and even when we are not acquainted with any object which, in fact is the so-and-so." (54)

The most illuminating case that Russell offers is that of an election contest for a seat in Parliament. His presentation of the case is sketchy; and I shall take the liberty of filling it out. The election is, as I said, contested; so we shall say that there are two candidates, A and B. Now, before the election, a voter may very well be acquainted with A and B; but until the election is held, the voter does not know which candidate will obtain the seat. Yet the voter knows "... that the candidate who gets the most votes will be elected..." (53) When the voter puts that truth together with his acquaintance with A and B, he knows that there is someone, though he does not know whether it is A or B, who is the next holder of the seat.

This story is meant to fulfill Russell's claim that even when we are not acquainted with any object which, in fact, is the so-and-so, we may nonetheless know that the so-and-so exists. But the story may look too much like a rule-governed set-up. 'The candidate who gets the most votes is the winner' is only one rule among the many that make the conduct of the election possible. The rules say that there will be a winner; so before the election, the winner is a curious entity. On the one hand, it looks as though we have something that has been defined into existence. On the other, since voters can be acquainted with A and B, they seem both to know and yet not know the winner. If this is to be our example of knowing by description that something exists, we really do not know whether we do or don't.

But there is a point that we may now draw from this example. While we may say that before the election, we only know "the winner" by the description, there is a day when the votes are counted; and then, if we are so inclined, we may shake hands with the winner. So while knowledge by description may not in and of itself be a knowledge of something that exists, in Russell's Parliamentary election example at least, the description does come to be cashable for acquaintance. If existence claims may be made "by description", that consequence seems just. But whether there can be an existence payoff in Russell's claim to know physical objects by description remains to be seen. Here is the essential passage.

> My knowledge of the table as a physical object... is not direct knowl-
> edge... My knowledge of the table is of the kind which we shall call
> 'knowledge by description'. The table is 'the physical object which
> causes such-and-such sense-data'. This *describes* the table by means of
> the sense-data. In order to know anything at all about the table, we must
> know truths connecting it with things with which we have acquaintance:
> we must know that 'such-and-such sense-data are caused by a physical

object'. There is no state of mind in which we are directly aware of the table; all our knowledge of the table is really knowledge of *truths,* and the actual thing which is the table is not, strictly speaking, known to us at all. We know a description, and we know that there is just one object to which this description applies, though the object itself is not directly known to us. In such a case, we say that our knowledge of the object is knowledge by description. (47/48)

How are we to get at what Russell is up to here? How are we both to understand what he wants to do but not to be so mesmerized by his effort that we fail to test his way of proceeding? Let me say first of all what I think Russell wants to accomplish here. What he is most interested in establishing is that physical objects exist. He seems to accept as the criterion for the existence of physical objects, that to exist is to be knowable. But then he says of our knowledge of his exemplary physical object, the table, that

Our knowledge of the table is not direct knowledge.

There is no state of mind in which we are directly aware of the table.

The actual thing which is the table is not, strictly speaking, known to us at all.

The object itself is not directly known to us.

In short, Russell rules out our having knowledge by acquaintance of the physical-object table. If knowability is to remain his criterion of existence, he must provide some kind of knowledge other than knowledge by acquaintance. He turns then to knowledge by description. To understand Russell, we must balance both the way he characterizes that knowledge, and what it is that we are supposed to know. First his characterization of our knowledge:

All our knowledge of the table is really knowledge of *truths.*

What truths, we ask?

We must know truths connecting the table with things with which we have acquaintance: we must know that such-and-such sense-data are caused by a physical object.

But surely we are now at a sensitive point, not to say the shrieking nerve of Russell's proceedings here: How are we to know that the 'table' physical object causes the 'table' sense-data, when we can only be acquainted with the sense-data? How are we to discover a causal connection that crosses over from what we can never be acquainted with? This 'connection' between physical objects and sense-data calls for scrutiny. Here are the relevant bits:

> The table is 'the physical object which causes such-and-such sense-data'. This *describes* the table by means of the sense-data.

> We know a description, and we know that there is just one object to which this description applies... In such a case, we say that our knowledge of the object is knowledge by description.

Given these bits, I think we must say that Russell wavers between two different connections: The physical object causes sense-data; and the sense-data describe the physical object. I suppose that these "connections" are to Russell something like the slippery stones that a man must jump on to cross a stream. If he does not put too much weight on any one stone, and jumps quickly to the next, he will make it to the far bank dry shod. I have already hinted at the difficulties in the claim for a causal connection between physical objects and sense-data. Let us see how much weight *description* will bear.

When I first began to think of what Russell might mean by "description" here, I thought of descriptions given in words; and Russell has an inclination to think that way too. Hence his attention to the difference between definite and indefinite descriptions. But verbal descriptions will not do for Russell here, because, as we all know, fictions can be described in words as easily as facts. So when Russell backs his verbal description — The table is 'the physical object which causes such-and-such sense-data' — with "This *describes* the table by means of the sense-data", he appears to be sliding toward non-verbal describing. Try these cases of non-verbal describing:
a) Charlie described his girlfriend's shapeliness with a wave of his hand. (But of course, in order to read that wave, we have to know about human bodies.)
b) *The Oxford English Dictionary* tells us that William Lambarde says of the river Stour, that it divides itself two ways and describes the Isle of Thanet. (But that was in 1576. We might now say something like "marks off".)
What I get out of these cases is that when Charlie's wave describes his girl friend, and when the Stour describes the Isle of Thanet, it is outlining that is going on. That reminds me that Russell is a mathematician, and calls up these additional

cases:

c) Two (or more) points describe a line.

d) The numbered dots in a child's drawing puzzle describe a rabbit. (You will see it, if you connect the dots.)

e) The pinholes in the quilting pattern describe the double-wedding-ring stitches to be transferred to the quilt.

If these cases help, then I think we can see the picture that informs Russell's use of "describe", when he says that the sense-data describe the physical object. "Describe" here means "outline" or "pick out". So the sense-data outline the physical object. Or the sense-data pick out the physical object. These uses will let us bring in two more cases.

f) The runway lights pick out the runway.

And perhaps

g) The Christmas tree lights show up the tree.

But if these cases help, we are now in a position to see that sense-data fail to describe physical objects. That the mathematician's points describe a line means that the line can be drawn. That the pinholes pick out a pattern means that the pattern can be stitched into the quilt. That the runway lights show the runway means that there is indeed a runway for the pilot to find. But the sense-data's describing a physical object is not like that. The sense-data describe, pick out, show the location of nothing that we can find. So the sense-data's describing is a describing with no follow through — a very odd kind of describing.

I want to say that Russell misses his footing on the stepping stone of description, well, non-verbal description any way. But how about his shifting back to verbal description, as in his

> The table is 'the physical object which causes such-and-such sense-data'.

This verbal description of the table requires us to make something of causation here. But as I have already remarked, how are we to establish such a causal claim about the physical table, when we are only allowed to be acquainted with the sense-data? So, for starters the causal claim here is an odd one. To offer that causal claim as a piece of knowledge by description is odder still. For as we pointed out in the parliamentary election example, there comes a time when a voter can be acquainted with the winner. But no one could ever be acquainted with the physical object table. Can it then be a proper candidate for being known by description?

But yet Russell concludes this crucial passage by saying, "We know a description...In such a case, we say that our knowledge of the object is knowledge by description." Suppose we took up a last ditch position, and said that at the very least Russell is telling us that we have to think that there are physical objects. Or we have to think that physical objects cause sense-data. There may be a "have to think" hovering over what Russell says here, the "have to think" of the mathematician who is accustomed to working from the descriptions of mathematical subjects — I hesitate to say "objects". Of course in mathematics there are no lift-up-the-stone-and-look questions about existence. Questions of that kind simply have no place. Beyond mathematics, we come to metaphysics; and we shall have to say that Russell's insistence that physical objects cause sense-data begins to look like an effect-to-cause argument that bears an embarrassing resemblance to the Prime Mover Argument. A little pushing and we shall end up with a Saint Bertrand of natural hylology.

If I am allowed to make a major claim here, it is that Russell gets on this track of having to think of physical objects and of sense-data, by his supposition that we can see colors and shapes, but we cannot see tables. Or to put it another way, our talk of 'the brown color [of the table]' is ruled in; but our talk of the 'the brown table' is ruled out. What is more Russell is inclined initially to equate knowledge with perception. He overlooks the importance of knowledge by use. If I were a Marxist critic, presumably I would point out that Russell spent too many afternoons watching the butler wheel in the tea trolley, and see to all those other arrangements that make tea time possible. Without attending to knowledge by use, Russell can have no qualms about the table's fading away into the nebulousness of appearance. It is his susceptibility to that cast of mind that sets Russell on his way to sense-data and their metaphysical counter weight, the physical object. But we cannot leave our subject without speculating a bit about Russell's motives.

There are hints in these early pages of *The Problems of Philosophy* that Russell aims at solving larger problems than he states. The hint at one of these problems comes in the remark that "sober science" tells us that "our familiar table" is "a vast collection of electric charges in violent motion". (16) Or again, Russell says, "Physical science... has drifted into the view that all natural phenomena ought to be reduced to motions... That which has the wave-motion is either aether or 'gross matter', but in either case is what the philosopher would call matter." (28) As a physical object, and therefore an instance of matter, a real table must somehow come under these sentences about wave-motion. But Russell leaves the how unexplained. The problem that I take these sentences to hint at is a gap between what ordinary people can know about and what physicists can know about, a gap that Russell feels obliged to close. His plans for closing the gap amount to a scheme whose elements are already familiar to us. First of all what ordinary people are supposed to know are sense-data. Then what physicists can know about are physical objects. But ordinary people, while knowing about sense-data, can never know physical objects. There is the gap. It is closed through Russell's claim that we can know that physical objects are the cause of sense-data.

There are two issues here expressible by the questions: Has Russell closed the gap? and Is there a gap to be closed? Let us begin with the first question. Russell's claim that physical objects cause sense-data closes the gap in a very odd way. Ordinary people can only know the cause of their sense-data by inferring it from its effects. So for ordinary people, the claim takes on the status of a kind of scientific 'natural theology'. Then physicists who are the ones who know about physical objects must be in the position of mystics, or perhaps Platonic seers. That is, it must be that physicists are somehow in touch with something that ordinary people do not and *cannot* know about. This picture is a compelling one until we remember that unlike the Guardians in Plato's *Republic,* physicists have their ordinary side. They do have their tea breaks; and they get the tea into their cups by picking up the tea pot and pouring, just the way ordinary people do. So there is no gap to be closed, once we demystify the status of physicists, and once we see through Russell's notion of sense-data.

But even supposing that Russell's means fail him, is it still not the case that there is a gap to be closed between what can be ordinarily known and what a physicist can know. I should like to do what I can to persuade you that there is no gap; so no bridging operation need be instituted. There is no gap, but a difference. Because of laboratories and because of physicists' experience therein, physicists do know about things that ordinary people know nothing about. But the difference here is like the difference between what the theater-goer knows about a play and the stay-at-home does not, or what a husband knows about marriage and a bachelor does not, or what someone who plays a game knows and a spectator does not. But stay-at-homes can become theatergoers; and ordinary people can put on lab coats.

It might be said, however, that I am missing something. I can hear someone saying, "Look! All we want here is for ordinary people to acknowledge that physicists know about the ultimate nature of 'every day objects'; and we want ordinary people to make that acknowledgement without knowing about what physicists know about". If that is the issue, then I think I know what to say. Whether or not physicists know about the ultimate nature of "every day objects" is a metaphysical issue that will have to be subjected to the kind of examination that metaphysics allows. But what is really important here is the issue of what ordinary people can understand. Physics is surely understandable by any person of good will who is ready to make the effort. So in principle there is no obstacle to an ordinary person's putting on a lab coat. When we see the gap between ordinary people and physicists as a difference in what they know, rather than as a difference created by what physicists know and ordinary people cannot and never could know, then the pressure to see the difference as a gap will be relieved.

I said that there are hints in these pages that Russell aims at solving larger problems than he states. Another of these problems is hinted at in the title of his first chapter: "Appearance and Reality". Russell has to be aware of F. H. Bradley's great book of that name; and he is surely engaged in a bit of tongue-in-cheek concept-napping here. You think that philosophy ought to be about appearance and reality. Very well. The appearances are our sense-data, and the reality is matter, or "the collection of all physical objects". Russell comes on then in the role of counter-metaphysician, playing Mephistopheles to Bradley's Gabriel. But to take up that pose is to accept the metaphysical distinction between appearance and reality without examination. The metaphysical prospect of appearance and reality is approached by many roads; and we have only considered Russell's here. The aim of these remarks on 'sense-data' and 'physical object' has been to show that they provide not even the possibility of a track for the metaphysical wayfarer.

Mental Events?

I turn now to Professor Donald Davidson's diaphanous essay, "Mental Events".[2] Just as sense-data were the hot item in the philosophy shops at the beginning of this century, so mental events look to be best sellers in our century's later half. As with any philosophical entity, the nature of the product depends on the supplier; so I cannot lay too much stress on the limitations of an enquiry in which mental events are to be considered solely from the point of view of Davidson's interests and aims. If mental events are to be anything here, indeed if they are to be, they must be in a context that Davidson supplies.

The outermost skin of the onion would seem to be Davidson' allegiance to mind-body dualism. Hanging out in the better philosophy shops, you might have heard of mind-body dualism; and you might see a gap between mind and body, an unbridgeable gap maybe; and you might think that gap ought to be closed. These thoughts are fairly common to philosophy students; and Davidson seems to have shared them. But his response to the gap turns out to be an oblique one. While it may look as though there is a gap, there really isn't any. Properly considered, mental events turn out really to be physical events. You do not need a bridge to get from one island to another, because there is really only a single piece of solid ground. Two different map makers' different symbols marking the same terrain are just that, and not different symbols for two different terrains. This would seem to be Davidson's large scheme for escaping the difference between the mental and the physical. Making something of it turns on making something of Davidson's notion of 'mental events'.

Let us look at what Davidson has to say. His attention is caught by an apparent contradiction that he finds with respect to mental events. Mental events which by definition are non-physical are nonetheless said to cause physical events. To put the point more in Davidson's way: Given that mental events are anomalous — that is, we know of no laws of mental events, is there not a contradiction here, since causation requires that "...events related as cause and effect fall under strict deterministic laws"? (208) Davidson's resolution of the apparent contradiction is simple. He just invokes the Principle of the Nomological Character of Causality, which "...says that when events are related as cause and effect, they have descriptions that instantiate a law". (215) Hence, whenever we can say that a mental event caused a physical event, the mental event must have a description that permits it to be a part of the instantiation of a law, that is, a physical description. Some events can wear two hats. So what we used to take to be an event just wearing a mental hat, we now see, under Davidson's instruction, to be an event that also wears a physical hat; and under that physical cover, or lid, laws of causal necessity obtain. But when we just see one of these events in its mental hat, it is not surprising that we find it in a lawless, non-physical realm. That is just where it would wear its mental hat.

Davidson begins his paper with the sequence, "Mental events such as perceivings, rememberings, decisions, and actions resist capture in the nomological net of physical theory". (207) The casual reader might say, "Of course physicists can't talk about the mental. They are not supposed to". But readers who persist to the end of Davidson's essay find its opening sentence is a joke. When a Davidsonian mental event wears its physical hat, it lines up under physical laws right along with the most amenable objects a physicist ever had to study. I do not like to spoil a party by explaining a joke; but I would like to be sure about whom the joke has been played on.

I have summarized Davidson's views to show that he is more interested in the scrapes he thinks that mental events can get into than he is in mental events *per se*. In fact, Davidson uses "mental event" in a loose way, when the pursuit of his interests requires a careful consideration of its meaning. In what follows, I aim to show that Davidson does not give us clear direction for the use of his term "mental event"; and I want to give some hint of the consequences of that failure for Davidson's interests.

For clues to what Davidson means by "mental event" we have a mixture of (1) lists, (2) something that may, or may not, be a definition, and (3) an example.

(1.1) The first list clearly identified as "mental events" contains

> perceivings
>
> rememberings
>
> decisions
>
> actions. (207)

(1.2) The second list occurs in a sentence about "mental events": "We may call those verbs mental that express propositional attitudes like

> believing,
>
> intending,
>
> desiring,
>
> hoping,
>
> knowing,
>
> perceiving,
>
> noticing,
>
> remembering, and so on." (210)

What we can derive from these lists is that in characterizing mental events, Davidson favors gerunds. (In the first list, since Davidson offers "rememberings" for "memories", we may transmute "decisions" to "decidings", and "actions" to "actings".)

(2) The possible definition of "mental events" follows from the list at (1.2), and is perhaps captured in these words: "...the distinguishing feature of the mental is... that it exhibits what Brentano called intentionality. Thus intentional actions are clearly included in the realm of the mental along with thoughts, hopes, and regrets (or the events tied to these)." (211) What I want to reserve for future use is the notion that exhibiting intentionality is a distinguishing feature of the mental.

(3) Davidson offers one extended example to illustrate what he means by "mental event". It comes in the context of his introducing the Principle Of Causal Interaction: "...that at least some mental events interact causally with physical events."

> "Thus for example if someone sank the *Bismarck* then various mental events such as perceivings, notings, calculations, judgements, decisions, intentional actions and changes of belief played a causal role in the sinking of the *Bismarck*. In particular, I would urge that the fact that someone sank the *Bismarck* entails that he moved his body in a way that was caused by mental events of certain sorts, and that this bodily movement in turn caused the *Bismarck* to sink." (208)

In effect, the example gives another list of mental events:

> perceivings
>
> notings
>
> calculations
>
> judgements
>
> decisions
>
> intentional actions
>
> changes of belief

The added point of interest here is that these mental events are contrasted with something else, presumably physical events:

> "he moved his body in a way that was caused by mental events of certain sorts"
>
> "bodily movement"
>
> the *Bismarck's* going down

Given the lists, the attempt at definition, and the example, we can see that Davidson has difficulty in specifying what he means by "mental event". I think that there are honorable reasons for these difficulties well beyond Davidson's immediate interests. For instance, there is the pervasive metaphysical arbitrariness inherent in the philosophy of mind. But let us see what we can do with what Davidson has to offer us.

The example is meant to show us events that are causing a physical event. Let us consider first the physical events at the end of the mental chain. We have "...he moved his body in a way that was caused by mental events of a certain sort and ...this bodily movement in turn caused the *Bismarck* to sink." What are these words supposed to capture?

Let us suppose that the *Bismarck* was sunk by Senior Lieutenant Chomondeley; and let us suppose that we may question the lieutenant. "Sir, when you sank the *Bismarck,* what was the last thing that *you* did?"

Chomondeley replies: "I moved the triggering lever to the FIRE position. That's how we let off the 'pedoes', you know."

Then we say, "Yes; but what did you actually do?"

Chomondeley replies: "Well, actually I said, 'That'll scrap the bugger!' But the Admiral doesn't like us to admit that, when we're on the telly. So I usually say what the Press Office advises, that I said, 'God save the King' or 'the Queen', depending on the monarch, you know."

Clearly Chomondeley is not playing the game; so we shall have to help him a little. "Yes, yes", we say. "But didn't you move your body right there at the end?"

Chomondeley replies: "Well, you might say that; but wouldn't you be missing the point like? Of course, I moved my hand. But that's a poor description of what I was doing, if it can even be called a description. Surely you wouldn't stick to that, unless you were wedded to a point of view. Look here, I wasn't just moving my hand. Not at all. I was firing the 'pedoes'."

Chomondeley may be wedded to a point of view too, of course. Neither "There was a bit of bodily movement" nor even "Chomondeley moved his hand" catches what was going on, in the way that "Chomondeley moved the lever to the FIRE position" does. Could we understand what was going on without the last sentence? And isn't that decisive? Indeed that the last sentence is at the center of a vortex that carries in its whirl Chomondeley's nationality, his social class and education, his naval training, his rank in the Royal Navy, his being in a submarine, and Britain's being at war. Chomondeley was not just firing torpedoes. He was fighting a war. By now we should be able to see, of course, that making sense of what Chomondeley was doing requires us to see him buoyant in a sea of intention.

But perhaps there is another chance for a physical event in Davidson's example. Let us consider the *Bismarck,* struck by the torpedoes and sinking to the bottom of the ocean. Surely the *Bismarck* is a good material object, and its sinking is a physical event. Well, yes; but then again, no. The *Bismarck* was after all a weapon of war, an intentional object. That was not just a mass of metal that went to the bottom. To take a first step toward the light: the *Bismarck* was a system of sophisticatedly organized hardware. The next step is to note that a lot of purposes, plans and uses went to the bottom of the ocean, when the *Bismarck* sank. In Berlin, the high command registered the loss of a major weapon in the conduct of the war. In London, the war cabinet registered a victory in the significant reduction of the enemy's war-making capacity. These considerations would be enough to assure an old-time British Idealist that in the sinking of the *Bismarck,* we have a mental event. If we hold back, our restraint can only be explained by metaphysical predilection. At the very least, I hope that I have said enough to show that Davidson's example is not of much help in providing a clearcut instance of a physical event, when intentionality figures in our criteria for the mental.

But in the end, the usefulness of "physical event" to Davidson depends on whether "mental event" can be made to stand up. Mental events are hard to find, not because they slide into the physical, but just because they are hard to find. Let us go back to Lieutenant Chomondeley before he fires the torpedoes. Davidson tells us that "...various mental events such as perceivings, notings, calculations, judgements, decisions, intentional actions and changes of belief" played a causal role in the sinking of the *Bismarck*. Thus we are offered seven kinds of mental events. What we want to do is to pick out at least one instance of one kind.

Let us try perceivings. Suppose that cashes for "Chomondeley sees the *Bismarck* in his scopes". First question: What about those philosophers who think of seeing as an achievement and not an occurrence? Pass over that one. What about "Chomondeley is looking for the *Bismarck*"? There is occurrence for you. After he finds the ship, what about "Chomondeley is holding the *Bismarck* in his field of view"? Those are to count as perceivings. But notice that our result hardly fits the Davidsonian promise. What we get is *Chomondeley* doing this or that. Mental events attach to persons. Where Chomondeley is concerned, mental events are simply a selected set of his doings. Given this intimacy between persons and mental events, can we make a cut in the doings themselves, to distinguish mental events from physical events? Then have we a scalpel fine enough to divide Chomondeley from his doings? The Davidsonian notion of "mental event" requires these cuts. Can they be made?

Let us try first distinguishing mental events from physical events in Chomondeley's story. It looks as though all the way from Chomondeley's looking for the *Bismarck* to his moving the lever to the FIRE position we shall find nothing but mental events. Here we are saying nothing more than that Chomondeley's doings cannot be understood as doings, unless they are looked at in the context of his life. But that is a very powerful consideration, for it sweeps even the *Bismarck's* sinking to the bottom of the ocean into the context of Chomondeley's life. We then run out of candidates to be contrast cases with mental events. It seems highly doubtful that Davidson has given us an example of a mental event's causing a physical event. The very notions have melted away. What is more, if Chomondeley's doings cannot be understood as doings, unless they are looked at in the context of his life, how can we produce mental events by, so to speak, cutting the doings away from Chomondeley? What are the doings without him? Yet the image of separating mental events from Chomondeley is one that enlivens the thinking of those who are on the lookout for mental events. I shall comment below on where I think that image has its source.

We are left with some questions. Why might someone want to go from "Chomondeley sank the *Bismarck*" to "Mental events cause physical events"? Having got there, why should someone want to see that mental events are catchable by the nomological net of physical science? The remarks that follow must be taken as sheer speculation, the persisting hallmark of philosophy.

Many who frequent the campfires of philosophy have thought that there should be a single, all-encompassing conceptual scheme, in which the explanation for anything and everything could be found. In our own age, with our loss of faith in the Design Argument, some of us have found physics to be the most persuasive candidate for our comprehensive explanatory scheme. Hence the drive to be forever extending the compass of physics. One of the things that physics is good at is events, incredibly minute, short-lived events, on which all else seems to rest. If one is then moved to assimilate the category of the mental to the physical, one way to go would be to look for mental events. There is one possible drawback, in that mental events as here conceived are not within the ken of ordinary people. Sporting events, social events, the event of the season, historical events — all are within the ken of ordinary folks. But not mental events. When were you last invited to a mental event? When did someone last offer to sell you a ticket to a mental event? I'll bet you'd buy the Brooklyn Bridge first. But, of course, mental events being outside the ken of ordinary people is just the thing to make them a prospective staple for philosophy. Philosophers like it when they can claim to know something which ordinary folks do not. In being unknown to ordinary folks, mental events would be like atoms and sub-atomic particles — an attractive consideration to some thinkers.

By itself, an analogy with the subject matter of physics is not enough to help philosophers suppose that there are mental events. They need some additional aid that only philosophy can provide. Here it would be useful to look back at the lists that Davidson offers in his explication of "mental event". I have already noticed that in forming these lists, Davidson favors gerunds. I think he does so, because it permits him to move from "Chomondeley sees the *Bismarck*" to "perceivings". That is, he can get away from a person who perceives, remembers, hopes, and so on, and get to such noun forms as "perceivings", "rememberings", and "hopings", with their implication that what they name could exist separately and independently. This is the way grammar helps the seeker for mental events.

But additional, and I suspect even more sustaining aid comes from logic. The logician is accustomed to thinking of the separability of subject terms and predicate terms, of taking one combination and detaching its terms, and then attaching the disconnected bits in new combinations. So for the logician, what a person does is regarded as expressible as a predicate, and consequently separable from the person. Hence a subtle wedge is driven between Chomondeley and Chomondeley's doings, between Chomondeley and his perceivings, and so on; and the philosopher is supplied with mental events, discrete and self-contained, having their lives in causal chains that can easily be thought of quite apart from Chomondeley and what it means for him to be a person.

It is an easy step to talking of mental event's causing physical events, and to concluding that events that are mental must also have a head size that will take a physical hat, so they will not escape the nomological net of physical science. We come again to the explanatory supremacy of physics, which has just been saved by providing a bit of Chomondeley for the system. All of this follows, when we fall under the spell that grammar permits, logic encourages, and our philosophical inclination makes obsessive.

So are there Davidsonian mental events? I am afraid not.

We might stop here, or we might go on to say that there is an alternative to the passionate search for a single all-encompassing explanatory frame. One can recognize that there is more than one form of discourse; and no matter how developed one of these forms is, we need not think that it should swallow up all the others. Nor need we expect one form of discourse to be the essential underpinning for all other forms. To get down to cases, physics is all very well for physicists, when they are doing physics. But doing physics is by no means the sole or ultimate human preoccupation.

My discourse as a person and my discourse about persons differ from the discourse of physics in a way that it is relevant to point out here. When we do physics, we are interested not in individual physical objects, but in kinds. Hence our most interesting conclusions are generalizations that are unvarying and that we take to hold for all instances of that kind of thing. But when it comes to persons, provided we have been properly brought up, we are on a considerably different footing. Among persons, we are interested in individuals; and the engrossing information is individual histories. A knowledge of cultures, a knowledge of political and economic institutions, a knowledge of psychoanalytic theory — all provide rules of thumb for understanding persons. But our understanding of a given person is always subject to the correction, the illumination, that only the individual can provide. In short, in the realm of persons, the most important thing is the individual and not generalizations about kinds. But this is not to say that we cannot understand the threads of our own lives and lives of others. We are not systematically incomprehensible to ourselves. Nor are others, no matter how often we may be puzzled or deceived, systematically incomprehensible to us. So the remark that persons are anomalous would be out of place. But that is not to say that they are nomalous either.

I have touched briefly on these obvious differences between talking physics and talking about persons, because I see philosophy, for example what Davidson has to say about mental events, as a recommendation of a way of talking. The antidote for a philosophically recommended way of talking is to remind ourselves of the forms of discourse already available to us.

Notes to the Text

This paper was written for presentation at a Conference on Ontology and Language, in memory of Professor Neil Wilson, sponsored by the Guelph McMaster Doctoral Programme in Philosophy, University of Guelph, Guelph, Ontario, Canada. I thank the sponsors of the Conference for their invitation. I thank my Brooklyn College colleagues for their comments on a draft of this paper in our departmental seminar. Malcolm Brown and Eric Steinberg saved me from some inaccuracies; and I am grateful for the rescue. I also thank Lowell Kleiman for his comments on an early version of Part II.

Notes

1. Published by Oxford University Press in the series, the Home University of Modern Knowledge, 1912, and subsequent reprints. Parenthetical page references appear in the text.

2. Reprinted in *Essays on Actions and Events*, Clarendon Press, Oxford, 1980, reprinted with corrections 1982, pp 207-225. Parenthetical page references are to this publication of "Mental Events".

Rationality and Realism

Michael Stack

Many different roles have been assigned to philosophy — harbinger of new science, clarifier of language, analyst of ontological angst, among others. But perhaps the oldest task claimed for philosophy was to give us some knowledge of the nature of reality. It is difficult to imagine Plato or Aristotle or Descartes or Berkeley or Kant as being unconcerned, as philosophers, with the existence and nature of God and the physical world and the mind and anything else that there might be.

The realistic attitude towards philosophy, this view that philosophy tells us something about the nature of reality, has been out of favor in this century, at least among Anglo-American analytic philosophers. Perhaps we remember that Hegel, as a philosopher, proved that our solar system only contained seven planets. In general, we are rightly impressed by the success of science, which can plausibly claim to be dealing with the nature of reality: nuclear weapons and cures for polio and trips to the moon are obviously real. Also, common sense, which often conflicts with philosophy, has had many supporters among this century's philosophers. So it is not surprising that non-realistic interpretations of philosophy should flourish. Recently there have been moves back in the direction of realism, but that is only to be expected given the argumentative nature of philosophy. Ethics has become to a considerable extent applied ethics and various philosophers tell us what we should do, which is a form of realism. Kripke tells us that the mind cannot be the brain. But generally philosophers are still somewhat hesitant to tell us what the nature of reality is, whether it is physical reality or ethical or aesthetic or religious.

Neil Wilson was never hesitant. He was clearly a philosopher in the realist tradition of Plato and Kant. He thought philosophy had something to say about the nature of reality, something worth saying, and something which could easily clash with both science and common sense. A few examples: for Wilson, the world is made up of propositions, the most basic form of causation may well be belief-desire causation, our world exists necessarily, empirical linguistics does less justice to the nature of language than does philosophical linguistics, consciousness is real and is completely unamenable to scientific explanation. All of these views fit poorly with science or with common sense or with both. Wilson sees them as solidly supported philosophically, and as therefore far more likely to be true, to indicate the nature of reality. This is philosophical realism with a passion, and it is admirable.

But to be a passion and to be admirable are not sufficient. We are entitled to ask if there is anything legitimate behind the passion, any reason to think that philosophy should have such pretensions, should claim the right to dictate to us what reality is like. Not surprisingly, there is at least something behind the passion. Philosophy as you and I do it is committed to rationality. Pure rational thinking can perhaps provide us with some insight into the nature of reality. Perhaps not too much insight. Perhaps it cannot supply specific information such as the number of planets or whether or not there are electrons. Some specific information may be supplied by reason, such as that we have minds or that we are free. Or even this information may be conditional: given that something else is true, then we are free. Then there are very general features of reality, such as that there are causes. Perhaps rational thought tells us at least this; presumably that is what Einstein had in mind when he rejected the idea of God playing dice in a quantum universe. And then there is the possibility of reason outlining Kantian categories, placing restrictions on the possible nature of reality without attempting to fill in the details.

Obviously then philosophical realism or rational realism, which I take to be the same thing, can take many different forms and can suffer from different degrees of pretentiousness, but they do share a basic characteristic: they all claim that philosophy has at least *something* to say about what the world is like. There can be disagreements about what sorts of things philosophy can reveal and about how to handle matters when philosophy disagrees with other sources of information, but a passionate philosophical realist is going to claim that there are quite a few significant features of reality for reason to explore and is going to be inclined, when there is disagreement, to give more weight to reason than to perception or experimental science or religion or mysticism or common sense or whatever. Or at least will be so inclined when it is good philosophy, when the reasoning is being done right.

I hope the view that I have been attempting to explain does not seem so preposterous as to be a mere straw man. I hope that it has at least some plausibility even if you are not inclined to be a realist with regard to philosophy. Perhaps these hopes would be better grounded if I were to be clearer about what I mean by "rationality". I have nothing novel or special to offer by way of definition, but I think my understanding of the concept is fairly standard. Rational thinking, as we attempt to teach it, involves several elements, which perhaps have an underlying unity or perhaps do not:

(1) Consistency is a rational virtue. Whatever else your beliefs are, they should at least be free of contradiction. They then at least have a chance of being true.

(2) Clarity and precision are good things. As much as possible beliefs should be clear, so that we will know what we are really wondering about when we wonder whether or not those beliefs are true. Definitions will often be the means of achieving this clarity.

(3) Rationalists have a horror of arbitrary choices or distinctions or decisions. Slopes become logically slippery when, having taken one step, we have no grounds for refusing to take another. Parity of reasoning requires that we treat relevantly similar cases in the same way. "Where do you draw the line?" is the rallying question for those who are concerned with euthanasia, personal identity through time, the amount of evidence required for knowledge, and all the belief situations that threaten us with infinite regresses.

(4) Rationalists are concerned with evidence and truth. Truth is our ultimate goal, although we presumably want important truths rather than just any old truths. Good evidence provides us with at least some reason to think that a belief is *true*. Which is why we spend so much time telling students about fallacies. Whatever else they may or may not have in common, fallacies are all arguments which provide no reason for thinking that their conclusions are true.

No doubt there are other features of rational thinking. And probably this list could be reduced to more basic elements, perhaps even only one, such as believe only what you have good reason for thinking to be the truth. Probably this view of rationality could even be modified, without destroying it utterly, to take account of James and the will to believe, and the desirability of taking epistemic risks, and even the importance of letting the passions play a role in belief formation. I may be wrong about this flexibility and in any case I do not wish to argue the point now. What I do wish to claim is that the account of rationality above is fairly standard and non-controversial and at least reasonably clear. Rational realism then is the view that thinking done in accordance with those ideas will indicate at least something of the nature of reality, and is a source of information at times as good as, or even better than, other sources.

I wish to reject rational realism completely and to support scientific realism. But you may not think that there is any such distinction. Reacting against Feyerabend, you may think that science is or should be a rational activity as defined above, especially if the above list is extended by saying something about theories and experimentation. I could rely on Feyerabend, but there is a less controversial way of establishing the distinction.

In practice philosophers and scientists have often disagreed. So it is nice to be able to report of cases where they clearly agree. One such case, apparently, is the question of the reality of secondary qualities. In the seventeenth century, with some earlier instances, philosophy and science agreed that secondary qualities were not part of the external physical world and that ontological room had to be found for them in the minds of the observer. The philosophical argument and the scientific arguments were distinct, even if there are cases of the same person being moved by both.

The philosophical argument is due to Locke and Berkeley. Assume that secondary qualities exist in the world whether or not there are any perceivers. Trouble arises from the fact that one and the same object can appear to have different colours, for instance, to different observers at the same time and to the same observer at different times, without the object undergoing any change. The object cannot really have all those qualities. There would still be no problem if there were some way of deciding which of the apparent qualities were real and which merely apparent. But there is no non-arbitrary way. We then have a choice. We can either be mystics, claiming that some of the qualities are real even though we will never know which. Or we can decide that none is really out there in the world, all are equally only in the mind. It is of course the second option that Locke and Berkeley go for, which is only to be expected given their philosophical horror of non-motivated, arbitrary choices.

The scientific argument against secondary qualities is quite different. Science is our best indicator of the nature of reality. In particular, the laws of physics are our best indicator. Newton's laws of motion make no reference to secondary qualities. Therefore secondary qualities are not part of the physical world.

Both the philosophical and the scientific argument could be expanded to include other elements of a similar nature. The above philosophical argument is found in more detail in Berkeley than in Locke, although Locke uses it as well. Locke spends more time on that other favourite philosophical enterprise, finding the elements necessary to a concept: primary qualities are essential to our very concept of a physical object, secondary qualities are not. The scientific argument could be extended to include Robert Boyle's version of the corpuscular hypothesis, but the same point would remain: science is telling us what is real.

Thus we apparently have two independent sources of information as to the nature of reality. Pure reason requires us to impose certain standards on reality: reality cannot require us to make arbitrary decisions. The scientific enterprise attempts to explain and predict and control. It might seem that the two, reason and science, are really one or at least are connected, in that both are in some sense attempting a cohesive unified view of reality. That this is not the case I hope now to make clear.

The sensible scientific realist is aware of the fact of scientific change. The nature of this change and its significance can be understood in a number of ways, all compatible with my purposes. You may believe, with Kuhn and Feyerabend, in something like incommensurability, and therefore believe that new theories or new paradigms have nothing to do with old ones. You may believe with Peirce that science ideally progresses towards the truth. You may even believe that science right now has some share of the truth, so long as you do not exaggerate that share. What you cannot do is believe that current science is literally The Truth, or even close to that.

Perhaps you think that if you interpret science in these ways you should not be a scientific realist, at least not in the sense of interpreting current science realistically. I will return to that point shortly. For the moment let us continue to be scientific realists and reject secondary qualities, as did Galileo and Newton and Boyle. The point is that we cannot rationally do that and also accept the philosophical realist argument against secondary qualities. We can say with Newton that *current* science tells us to reject secondary qualities, to exclude them from the physical world. But who knows if later science will do the same? Indeed, some people would claim that the Land theory of colour perception reinstates colour into the physical world. I am not sure that is true, but it is a conclusion that I would be happy to accept. In any case, the far-seeing student of science knows that science changes. And this very naturally gives rise to the question, which ontology should he take seriously? The ontology of time t or the ontology of time t+n or t-n? One does not have to deny scientific progress, or even progress towards the truth, to claim that such a choice is arbitrary. Let us concede that the theory at a later time is closer to the truth than earlier theories. That still leaves unchallenged the claim that the ontology of the current theory is likely to be replaced, I would prefer to say is inevitably to be replaced, by the ontology of later sciences. Which ontology should we take seriously? Which apparent colour is real?

My claim is that both questions call for equally arbitrary answers. If you do not mind arbitrary choices, at least some of the time, you can be a scientific realist and reject secondary qualities. If you do mind arbitrary choices you can be a rational realist and reject secondary qualities. If you try to do both you will have to give up another element of rational realism. You can give up consistency, engage in doublethink. If your heart is really set on rejecting secondary qualities, if for instance you think that a really cohesive understanding of reality can thereby be achieved, you can mount a really powerful attack by alternately embracing and rejecting arbitrariness. Of course your rational realist will not allow this, but the scientific realist should have no objection.

A point in passing. I have just stated a willingness to give up consistency, which was the first of the rational virtues earlier mentioned. I do not wish to make the case for inconsistency here and now, but there is one point which ties in particularly with the distinction between rational and scientific realism. Traditionally, the mark of a rational person was the willingness to follow an idea through to its logical consequences. You may at that point wish to give up the idea from which you started, or you may, happily or unhappily, accept whatever conclusions proper reason has led us to. As we all know, in standard logics a contradiction implies every proposition. I am certainly not arguing that we should believe every proposition. So there is a problem.

There is more than one way around the problem. Given my predilection for arbitrary choices I could just arbitrarily choose which of the conclusions I wish to accept and reject the rest. Or one can develop a non-standard logic. But there is an easier and more plausible answer. What is true is the following: if a proposition is true then its logical consequences are true; if "p&-p" is true then "q" is true. It does not *immediately* follow that I should believe the logical consequences of everything that I believe. I do not believe that my beliefs are true. Truth is at best a distant goal and is more likely to be an illusion. I do not accept my beliefs because I take them to be true, but because I take them to be epistemically useful, a notion which I would prefer to leave undefined for today. Whatever exactly it means, p can be worthy of belief, -p can be worthy of belief, but it is unlikely that an arbitrary q will be worthy of belief, unlikely that it will contribute to coherence or explanatory excellence. If it does have some value for your belief set then fine, accept it, but otherwise forget it.

A similar point can be made about that other horror of rationalists, infinite regresses. I take it that the standard view is that to be on an infinite regress is to make no progress at all. For instance, in Hume's *Dialogue* Cleanthes wishes to believe in a designer God in order to make sense out of the coherence of the world. Philo attacks this desire on a number of excellent grounds, but he also has one bad argument. Philo argues that if we believe in God to explain order in the world we will have to believe in a higher order God to explain order in God, and so on, down the slippery infinite regress. But the "have to" in Philo's claim is very dubious. Our immediate concern is to understand this world. If believing in God contributes understanding, then we have good reasons to believe in God. For instance, one might claim that belief in God helps make sense of the scientific enterprise; the world was created by a mind, so it makes sense to think that the world is ultimately intelligible, ultimately knowable by a mind. That is not an argument I would care to defend, but if you are moved by it, don't worry about infinite regresses. Your problem is to understand the world, not to understand God.

Secondary qualities and gods are important enough in their own right, I suppose, but they are not all that important. What is important is the world, and it is directly to that that I now wish to turn. No doubt it is possible for someone to disagree with my brief characterization of science, scientific change, scientific progress, and the relationship between science and truth. But if you happened to agree, you might then be inclined to reject any kind of scientific realism, any idea that science is really an indicator of the nature of reality. If the ontology of science is really here today and gone tomorrow, then why take that ontology seriously? Why not instead move towards some view that science is, at best, useful?

This view depends upon being restricted by the standards of rational realism. Scientific realism is a difficult concept to define precisely, which is itself a bad thing in the eyes of rationalists. Recall the absurd claim that there was something wrong with Kuhn's idea of a paradigm because there were at least fifteen or twenty different meanings that could be assigned to the word and it was not clear which Kuhn meant. Of course it was not clear, even to Kuhn. What else would you expect when we attempt to understand a complex world?

Even if we set aside this problem of unclarity, new problems emerge for the rational realist. Surely, the rationalist thinks, there must be a close connection between realism and truth, and as van Fraassen makes clear at the beginning of *The Scientific Image,* it is difficult to make clear just what this connection could be. Surely the scientific realist is not so naive as to think that science literally is true right now. Partially true or approximately true are more plausible but they are also unclear. Truth is the ultimate goal — that is a more plausible view but it suggests that one should not be a realist about current science, since it is a long way from ultimate science. Van Fraassen then defines the position, implausibly, as the claim that the aim of science is truth (how could that be the aim given the problem just mentioned?) and the claim that to accept a theory is to believe it to be true (how, for the same reasons, could anyone be so foolish?).

As if this point was not bad enough, things get worse. It seems plausible to think that ultimately the world is the way it is independently of our thinking and our theories. Therefore, to be a realist about one's theories is to claim that our theories are made true by a theory-independent reality and that our theories tell us what this reality is really like in itself, not merely as it is reflected or distorted in our thinking. Unfortunately many scientific realists think that our thinking is always theory-laden, that we always perceive reality through a theory, that different theories would always be available to give us different views of reality. Of course one can still claim that all these different theories are made true by a theory-independent reality, but there is not much comfort in that. It is reminiscent of the mystical position that was possible with respect to secondary qualities. Some colours are real, as Guildenstern said to Rosencratz, but we will never know which. There is a reality, but we will never have an idea what it is like. Or rather, but it comes to the same thing, we will have too many ideas what it is like.

It is at this point that easeful instrumentalism starts to look good to a rational realist, at least if one can accept some kind of useful theory-observation distinction. Suppose we are happy with our knowledge of middle-size physical objects. We know them through perception and they seem to meet the standards of rational realism: I rarely want to affirm both that this desk exists and that it does not, and if Aristotle were here he would also affirm that it exists, at least if I taught him the word. This seems to be a nice safe secure kind of knowledge. Matters become far less secure when we try to move on. It is when we enter the realm of theories we suddenly seem to be in quicksand: insecurity, changing ideas, less certainty, less clarity. So stop. Don't extend your beliefs into those areas. This does not of course mean that you have to reject science altogether. Instead you come up with a view that scientific ideas are not meant to be true or false but are simply useful. We can have our cake and eat it too.

But of course this will not do. If there is no epistemically significant theory-observation distinction, then there is no place for easeful rest. There simply is no knowledge of the kind that the rational realist wants. Nor is this any reason to adopt scepticism. In trying to understand a complex world, we are in a constant process of theory formation and testing. The data by which we test theories are not hard facts but simply outgrowths of earlier theories. Which means, of course, as Quine pointed out long ago, that all our beliefs are up for grabs, nothing is sacrosanct. In such circumstances it is virtually impossible that our current theories and beliefs should fit reality really well. That is why the demand for clarity and precision is mistaken. We are almost certainly going to be pulled in different directions by our doxastic environment. That is why the demand for consistency is mistaken. To give in to these demands would be to reject the information that the environment is trying to give us. But again none of this means that we should be sceptics. We simply form the best beliefs we can in the circumstances. Science provides us with such beliefs. That is why we should be scientific realists. Scientific realism means that the best (and it is quite good) indicator that we have of the nature of reality is science. That is why science should provide us with our ontology. Rationality does not help, it hinders.

You may think, among other things, that I have been operating with too narrow a view of philosophy and rationality. There are those like Quine who think of philosophy and science as continuous, both concerned with seeking the best explanation. This might, ideally, be true. But it is not true of philosophy and rationality as you and I are doing them.

Index

PROBLEMS IN CONTEMPORARY PHILOSOPHY